Ideologies of Welfare

Ideologies of Welfare:
From Dreams to Disillusion

John Clarke, Allan Cochrane and Carol Smart

Hutchinson

London Melbourne Sydney Auckland Johannesburg

Hutchinson Education

An imprint of Century Hutchinson Ltd

62–65 Chandos Place, London WC2N 4NW

Century Hutchinson Australia Pty Ltd
PO Box 496, 16–22 Church Street, Hawthorn,
Victoria 3122, Australia

Century Hutchinson New Zealand Ltd
PO Box 40–086, Glenfield, Auckland 10,
New Zealand

Century Hutchinson South Africa (Pty) Ltd
PO Box 337, Berglvei 2012, South Africa

First published 1987

Phototypeset in Linotron Garamond 10/11 pt
by Input Typesetting Ltd, London

Printed and bound in Great Britain by
Richard Clay Ltd, Bungay, Suffolk

ISBN 0 09 164651 0

Contents

The State of Welfare:
Editor's preface

Over the past decade the post-war consensus on the welfare state has been undermined by economic recession and political controversy. In all western countries public debate has focused on the burden of public spending on private enterprise and the measures necessary to reduce it. Austerity policies have squeezed welfare provision under governments of the right in Britain, Germany and the USA and under socialist governments in Sweden, France and Spain. In Britain all sides are dissatisfied with the old system of welfare: the new right denounces the profligacy of public services and the traditional left questions their paternalistic and bureaucratic character. Welfare provision has entered a new phase.

In practice the attempts of governments in Britain and abroad to restructure welfare services have encountered great difficulties. Only the USA has succeeded in making significant cuts in welfare spending at the expense of the unemployed, black people and the poor. Parallel measures in Sweden provoked a trade union revolt in 1986 and Norman Fowler's proposed radical reorganization of social security in Britain was scaled down to a minor administrative reform to avoid political conflict. In 1987 electoral considerations forced Tory Environment Minister Nicholas Ridley to drop proposals for the extension of privatization in local government.

The uneven success of government attempts to restructure welfare has provoked considerable debate. Some consider that capitalist counter-crisis strategies will necessitate a major rationalization of welfare and that the appeal of authoritarian populism can create a new consensus of support for such a policy. Others argue that the economic and political consequences of dismantling the welfare state infrastructure would be too much for any western government to face.

The attack on welfare and its uneven impact provide the context for a new series of books, designed for students of welfare and also for workers in the various welfare services. 'The State of Welfare' will include books on different aspects of the welfare state, analysing new and emerging trends in the organization and delivery of services and the economic and political determinants of welfare policy. They will also examine alternatives to current welfare services. The first book – *Ideologies of Welfare: From Dreams to Disillusion*, by John Clarke, Allan Cochrane and Carol Smart – surveys the changing ideologies of welfare that have influenced the emergence of the present system and will no doubt influence its future evolution.

Mary Langan

Acknowledgements

We originally developed the approach to ideologies of welfare presented in this book while working on the Open University course *Social Policy and Social Welfare*, and we are very grateful to the other members of that course team for the advice and support which they gave us. We would also like to thank David Doughan of the Fawcett Library, and Alan Clarke for their assistance in our researches. Our series editor, Mary Langan, and Claire L'Enfant of Hutchinson have been constant sources of advice and encouragement.

The editors and publisher would like to thank the copyright holders below for their kind permission to reproduce the following material.

Allen & Unwin for pp. 32–4, by C. S. Loch, reproduced from *A Great Ideal and its Champion*, 1923; for pp. 94–6, by W. A. Robson (ed.), *Social Security*, 1943; for pp. 95–6, by J. S. Clark, 'The Staff Problem', in Robson, W. A. (ed.), *Social Security*, 1943; and for pp. 178–81, by R. Hadley and S. Hatch, *Social Welfare and the Failure of the State*, 1981.

Mrs Helen Blackstone for pp. 69–70, by A. Maude Royden, reproduced from *National Endowment of Motherhood*, no publisher, 1918 (extracts from pp. 4–15).

Lord Briggs for pp. 75–6, by W. Morris (1893), *Communism*, Fabian Tract 113, reproduced from A. Briggs, *William Morris: Selected Writings and Designs*, 1962, published by Penguin Books Ltd.

Jonathan Cape for pp. 176–7, by Dr D. Owen, reproduced from *Face the Future*, 1981, published by the Oxford University Press.

Constable Publishers for pp. 59–61, by G. Lansbury, reproduced from *My Life*, 1928.

8 · Aknowledgements

Critical Social Policy for pp. 146–7, by M. McIntosh, reproduced from 'Feminism and Social Policy', *Critical Social Policy*, 1981, vol. 1, no. 1.

The Fabian Society for pp. 164–6, by D. Blunkett and G. Green, reproduced from *Building from the Bottom: the Sheffield Experience*, 1983, Fabian Tract 491; and for pp. 173–6, by P. Townsend, reproduced from *Why are the many Poor?*, 1984.

The Falling Wall Press for pp. 150–1, by S. Fleming, reproduced from *The Family Allowance under Attack*, 1973.

The Gower Publishing Group for pp. 170–2, by A. Webb, reproduced from 'The Personal Social Services', in N. Bosanquet and P. Townsend (eds), *Labour and Equality*, 1980, published by Heinemann; and for pp. 182–4, by N. Deakin, reproduced from 'Planning social priorities – locally', in H. Glennerster (ed.), *The Future of the Welfare State: Remaking Social Policy*, 1983, published by Heinemann.

Her Majesty's Stationery Office, for pp. 76–8, reproduced from the Royal Commission on the Poor Law and Relief of Distress, *Appendix to Vol. 3, Minutes of Evidence, 49th–71st Day*, 1909, Cmnd. 4755; for pp. 90–4 and 101, reproduced from W. Beveridge, *Social Insurance and Allied Services*, 1942, Cmnd. 6404; and for pp. 139–40, reproduced with the permission of the Controller of the Her Majesty's Stationery Office, from *Oral Hearing into the Review of Benefits for Children and Young People*, 1984.

The Institute of Economic Affairs for pp. 137–8, by A. Seldon, reproduced from Preface to H. Parker, *The Moral Hazard of Social Insurance*, 1982, IEA Research Monograph no. 37.

Michael Joseph for pp. 28–9, reproduced from S. Andreski (ed.), *Herbert Spencer: Structure, Function and Evolution*, 1971.

The Longman Group UK Ltd and Churchill Livingstone Publishers for pp. 131–4, by R. Boyson (ed.), reproduced from *Down with the Poor*, 1971.

Marxism Today for pp. 160–4, by A. Walker, 'Why we need a social strategy', *Marxism Today*, September 1982.

New Socialist, for pp. 152–3, by Hilary Land, reproduced from 'Family fables', *New Socialist*, 1983.

The Trustees of the Passfield Estate for pp. 51–3, 55 and 67, by S. Webb and B. Webb, reproduced from *English Poor Law Policy*, 1910, published and reprinted by permission of Frank Cass & Co Ltd, Gainsborough House, 11 Gainsborough Road, London E11 1RS.

Pluto Press for pp. 156–7, by A. Friend and A. Metcalf, reproduced from *Slump City*, 1981; for pp. 158–9, by B. Deacon, reproduced from *Social Policy and Socialism. The Struggle for Socialist Relations of Welfare*, 1983; for pp. 166–8, by J. Seabrook, reproduced from *The Idea of Neighbourhood. What Socialist Politics should be about*, 1984.

Routledge & Kegan Paul plc for pp. 118–22, by F. Von Hayek, reproduced from *The Road to Serfdom*, 1944; and for pp. 135–6 by Sir Keith Joseph, reproduced from *Monetarism is Not Enough*, 1977.

The Socialist Party of Great Britain for pp. 111–13, reproduced from pamphlet entitled 'Family Allowances – A Socialist Analysis', published in November 1943.

Tribune, for pp. 114–15, reproduced from Editorial, 4.12.42 (reprinted in D. Hill, *Tribune 40*, 1977, published by Quartet).

Virago, for pp. 56–8, by Mrs Pember Reeves, reproduced from *Round About a Pound a Week*, 1979 (first published by Bell & Sons, 1913).

All reasonable efforts have been made to contact the copyright holders for the following extracts, but where no reply has been received, we have presumed that their permission would not be withheld.

For pp. 36–7 reproduced from D. G. Ritchie, *The Principles of State Interference* (S. Sonnescheim and Co., 1891).

For pp. 41–6 reproduced from J. A. Hobson, 'The social philosophy of charity organisation', *The Contemporary Review*, vol. 70, 1896, pp. 710–27.

For pp. 65–6 reproduced from F. Pethick Lawrence, 'Will the Insurance Bill be withdrawn?', *Votes for Women*, 15 September 1911, p. 794.

For pp. 97–9, reproduced from J. Griffiths, *Pages from Memory* (Dent, 1969).

For pp. 105–6, 106–8, from E. Abbott and K. Bompas, *The Woman Citizen and Social Security*, Mrs Bompas 1943, pp. 3–4, 5–7, 9, 20.

Introduction: ideologies of welfare

Since the mid 1970s, the welfare state has become one of the central areas of political conflict in British society. A variety of voices has been heard, expressing disenchantment with the ways in which the Beveridge inspired welfare state has developed, and offering alternative views of the welfare services which ought to exist; how they ought to be organized, and, in particular, what role the state should play in the provision of welfare. In simplified terms, this outbreak of political and ideological conflict over the nature of welfare marks the breakup of the post-war 'consensus' about the welfare state, in which a basic 'commitment to welfare' was sustained by all the major political parties.

While the precise character of the post-war consensus on welfare, and the reasons for its collapse, are also the subject of widely divergent interpretations, some crucial economic and political processes recur in the different accounts which have been offered about the current 'crisis of the welfare state'. First, the post-war welfare state was constructed on the assumption that the state was able to manage the British economy and specifically to maintain the conditions for full employment. The recession of the 1970s and 1980s had the effects of reviving mass unemployment and of undermining the belief in Keynesian techniques of economic management by the state. Second, and closely linked with the recession, governments since the early 1970s have been highly preoccupied with state expenditure and the 'problem' of how to reduce it. Although this has been most visible in the pronouncements and policies of the Conservative governments of 1979 and 1983, it was also a running theme in the policies of the preceding Labour and Conservative governments. The economic basis of the welfare state was being eroded for a substantial period before the monetarist attack on public spending was announced by the 1979 Thatcher government. Third, the 'failures' of the welfare state were being explored from a variety of viewpoints during the 1970s, with the post-1945 welfare state increasingly appearing less as the centre-piece of political consensus than as an unhappy compromise to which few owed any continuing allegiance. Ramesh Mishra has recently argued that it is this diversity of attacks on the welfare state which is central to the current politics of welfare:

The state's ability to manage the mixed economy, of which the social welfare sector is an integral part, is in serious doubt. In many ways it is this loss of confidence that is at the heart of the crisis. . . .

This is an entirely new situation since the inception of the post-war welfare state. For, despite differences among social scientists and others on the question of social welfare, the success of the welfare state used to be widely recognised. Grudgingly or otherwise, it was acknowledged as a system that had successfully combined private enterprise and economic growth with social protection and political stability. Few people thought seriously in terms of an alternative path of development for the West. This is no longer the case. The legitimacy of the welfare state is in serious doubt (1984, pp. xiii–xiv).*

It is this 'crisis of confidence' which has underpinned the revival of ideological conflict about the nature of welfare and the role of the state since the mid 1970s. From a number of different political directions, the Fabian assumptions which underpinned the post-war consensus about welfare have come under fierce criticism. This book is, in one sense, a product of that ideological conflict. Its aim is to trace some of the central strands in that conflict – the revival of laissez-faire individualism in the ideology of the New Right; the arguments from socialists about welfare and state; the responses of Fabianism to the crisis in welfare; and the contributions of feminism about the state, welfare and gender divisions.

We have also had a second aim in mind in preparing this book. The ideological conflict which currently surrounds the welfare state in Britain is not new. The historical development of state welfare has, since the end of the nineteenth century, involved recurrent political and ideological conflict over the causes of social problems to which welfare is a response and over the 'proper role' of the state in welfare. The four ideologies on which this book focuses have continually been at the centre of those conflicts. We intend that this book contributes to seeing those ideologies and conflicts as part of the way in which welfare has developed in Britain. In many ways, it is not the contemporary pattern of political conflict over the future of welfare which is unusual. Rather, the period of 'consensus' is the historical aberration, since at other points the development of welfare has been enmeshed in fierce ideological argument.

The main impetus of this book comes from the contemporary politics of welfare. The attacks on the welfare state – most dramatically in the 'monetarism' of the New Right – have revitalized ideological and political conflict over the future of welfare. But at

---

* Full references quoted in text appear in the Bibliography on pp. 197–201.

the same time, these attacks and arguments are not merely the inventions of the 1970s and 1980s; they both draw on, and rework, traditions of thought and criticism which have persistently surrounded the development of welfare. What is different in the contemporary politics of welfare is that we are confronting a position in which welfare has been *re*-politicized. One effect of the post-war consensus was to marginalize political and ideological conflict over welfare. For the most part, welfare was de-politicized and treated as the technical subject matter of social administration, to be viewed as a rational process of matching needs and resources via the most efficient delivery systems. In the hands of neutral (apolitical) experts, welfare was secure.

At the same time that political conflict over welfare was re-emerging, so social administration as an academic discipline dealing with the study of welfare policy was itself becoming politicized. Assumptions of neutral, social-scientific research and analysis were challenged by a rediscovery of the links between welfare, politics and ideologies. One of the major steps in this rediscovery was made by George and Wilding in their *Ideology and Social Welfare*, originally published in 1976. The first chapter of their book began:

Most discussion of the nature of social policy has tended to take place in a theoretical vacuum. Social policy is analysed as if it were an autonomous set of social institutions unconnected with the social and political system in which it is set and which it serves (1976, p. 1).

Ten years later, it is clear that this is no longer the case. The analysis of social policy is now actively engaged with wider theoretical, political and ideological issues and conflicts. The ideological dimensions of welfare have been the subject of a number of analyses (for a critical overview, see Lee and Raban, 1983). Precisely because the study of ideologies of welfare is now so firmly established, one of our tasks in this introduction is to justify making a further contribution to the extensive range of books and articles on this subject by identifying what we believe is distinctive about this book.

Perhaps the most significant feature of this book is that it is intended as both an analysis of ideologies of welfare and as a 'source' book. We have constructed it around extensive extracts from books, articles, pamphlets and newspapers in which positions about welfare are being argued. Our role has been to provide introductions to and commentaries on these 'ideological sources'. Our reason for approaching the study of ideologies of welfare in this way is based on a reluctance to 'pre-digest' such source material and to tidy it into a neat and coherent package.

The way in which we have constructed this book does, of course, involve some simplification. The selection of four key ideologies means that some arguments around welfare and the state which do not easily belong to these positions have been ignored, and, in addition, our 'labelling' of the different positions means that we offer what is perhaps an 'over-unified' view of each of these positions. We have tried, within each of them, to maintain an awareness of the internal tensions and differences which go on. There is no single 'pure' representative of laissez-faire or feminism, socialism or Fabianism, but a range of more or less consistent arguments which we have grouped under those headings. Similarly – because such ideologies are not pure abstractions of principles – there are overlaps at different points between some of the ideologies which we present. As such positions are shaped and changed in the process of conflict over welfare, so there are sometimes alliances made, lessons learnt, ideas borrowed – or rejected. But we do believe that by working around original materials some of this richness and complexity of ideological conflicts over welfare has been maintained.

In preparing this book, we have tried to identify four main strands of political ideology of welfare. Our selection of these four strands does not precisely match any of the other schemes or typologies for the study of ideologies of welfare which other writers in the field have used. In addition in the first period, we have identified a fifth – the New Liberals – whose contribution also sets up later echoes. Our selection differs because most of these other typologies have been drawn up to distinguish such ideologies along one or two main 'principles' (e.g. provision by the state vs. provision through the market). While it is true that such oppositions do play an important role in the ideologies of welfare, they also oversimplify the political arguments involved. For example, the principle of state 'collectivism' is one which is shared by a variety of ideological positions which nevertheless differ radically from one another in many ways. Our selection of ideologies is not, therefore, an attempt to construct a tidy typology of easily distinguishable positions, but to chart the development of the major positions which have taken part in the conflicts over the development of welfare in Britain.

The four main ideologies on which we have chosen to focus attention in this book are laissez-faire individualism, feminism, Fabianism and socialism. They can be crudely distinguished in a number of ways. Laissez-faire views of welfare rest on the foundations of classical political economy, with a hostility to state intervention based on the view that the 'invisible hand' of the market is the best regulator of social affairs and the guarantor of individual freedoms. By Fabianism, we mean a view of the state as the means of improvement for its citizens – the machinery of progress guided by careful analysis of social problems and the construction of solutions through professional expertise. The dividing line between socialism and Fabianism has always been an uneasy one, not least because of the powerful influence of Fabian ideology within the 'broad church' of the British Labour Party. But while Fabianism may have influenced British socialism, it is by no means identical to it. There are other powerful currents at play within socialism; in particular, a recurrent suspicion of the limits of 'reform' within the framework of a capitalist society. We have included feminism within the ideologies which are at work in the political conflicts over welfare. Although feminism's relationship to the public and political conflicts over welfare has been more uneven than the other three ideologies which we have identified, its views of the relation between welfare, the state and gender divisions have recurrently raised problems about the nature and functions of state provision. Too many of the studies of welfare ideology have, in our view, had the effect of reproducing the invisibility of the relation between women and welfare in social policy by omitting the historical and contemporary contributions of feminism to the politics of welfare. (Wilson, 1983, provides a valuable summary of these arguments.)

• Our reason for choosing 'ideologies of welfare' as our focus for this book is that these ideologies provide a significant and continuing link between the most abstract 'philosophical' judgements and analyses of welfare – those which deal with the concepts of need, justice, equality and freedom – and the more particular institutional politics of welfare – the creation and implementation of party political programmes and welfare. In this field of ideologies – viewed as relatively systematic theories of the relationship between needs, welfare, the state and policy – arguments are developed and presented which link the issues of welfare policy with more general questions about welfare needs and the proper role of the state. These systematic patterns of argument, in our view, provide the main organizing positions or frameworks for the public and political conflicts over the welfare state which have taken place in British society over the last century.

We need to distinguish the nature of the ideologies with which we are dealing here from a number of other ways in which welfare has been treated as 'ideological'. We can identify a number of different meanings of ideology in relation to welfare. First, there is the most abstract level of 'philosophical' ideologies to which we have already referred. The philosophical investigation and system-atization of concepts such as 'need', 'freedom' and 'equality' in relation to welfare and the role of the state have become a subject of increasing attention in recent years, not least because of the New Right's use of the philosophical vocabulary of freedom and individual rights, and its attack on state policies based on principles of 'equalization of opportunity'. While our discussion does relate to such issues and is informed by 'philosophical' debates, we are not trying to contribute to them directly. Our focus is broader.

We are interested in the constantly changing relationships between these more abstract questions and the process of policy formation.

Second, we would want to distinguish our interest in political ideologies of welfare from what we might term 'party' political ideologies. We see them as political in the sense that they represent distinctive traditions of thought and intervention in the politics of welfare. More explicitly, 'party' political ideologies would include those ideas expressed in the manifestos, statements, programmes and policy initiatives of particular political parties. We need to discriminate between these two types because, although there are, at particular times, clear overlaps and connections between political ideologies and those expressed by specific political parties, the relationship is a complex one. For example, the Labour Party, in its approach to welfare, has drawn on more than one of the political ideologies which we present in this book. Fabianism, feminism and socialism have been contributors to Labour Party welfare politics. In a different way, the ideology of 'laissez-faire' (or free market individualism) has found different party political homes during the last century. For most of the nineteenth century its 'natural' political home was in the Liberal Party, while from the mid 1970s its influence has been felt through the Conservative Party.

For these reasons, we have chosen to focus in this book on these broader political ideologies, rather than on the more detailed twists and turns of party politics and welfare policy. Each of these ideologies has developed and fought for distinctive visions of what the relationship between the state and welfare ought to be. Within these ideologies, there is movement between the most abstract issues of philosophical and conceptual analysis and the most concrete issues of policy formation, assessment, and criticism. At different times, and in different ways, these ideologies have been drawn on and their concepts and arguments used in party political arguments about the welfare state and welfare policy. For our purposes, they have the twin advantage of being relatively continuous and systematic sets of thinking about welfare and the state (which party political ideologies are not), and deeply involved and engaged in conflicts over particular welfare policies in the historical periods on which we have focused attention (in a way that more abstract 'philosophies' of welfare are not). In that sense, these ideologies provide organizing and linking systems of thought, connecting general principles and particular issues.

At this point, we need to add a few words about what this book does *not* intend to cover. It is not a detailed analysis of welfare policy or the historical development of the welfare state. There is rarely any direct correspondence between the positions presented in these political ideologies and the policy of welfare developed in the state, and, indeed, to look for such direct correspondences would be a mistake. Policies as enacted by the state are the outcomes of complex political processes in which these ideologies play only a partial role. The tracing of policy creation requires detailed attention to the political struggles which go on around welfare, and an examination of how different interests are organized and represented in such struggles. It also requires analysis of the political processes inside the state – as well as those outside it. The ways in which political programmes and initiatives become policy involve the administrative as well as the political structures of government, along with the different interests (professional bodies, for example) affected by such policies. Such analyses are beyond the scope of this book, and our purpose is an altogether more modest one: to trace the development of key arguments about welfare which have played a role in those political conflicts.

Finally, this book has a historical structure. Our aim is to reveal how deeply these ideological patterns are embedded in the politics of the British welfare state. The contemporary arguments around the future of welfare in Britain draw on a legacy of well-established positions and arguments about welfare and the state. But it is not the case that what this history reveals is simply the recurrence of certain basic positions – unchanged and unchanging. There is not, in that sense, an essential feminism or socialism which we can discover here in the 1980s speaking the same things as they did at the turn of the century. For us, part of the significance of this study of ideologies is also to explore the ways in which those ideologies have changed during the last hundred years. They have changed under the impact of new political and economic conditions in British society, they have changed in response to the shape of the conflict over welfare in which they are engaged, and they have changed as the nature and operation of the welfare state itself has been reconstructed.

We have not, however, provided a continuous, narrative history of the development of these ideologies over the past hundred years. We have been selective in one further way, by focusing on three significant periods of conflict over the future of welfare in Britain. Each of these moments involved extensive public and political debate over the future relationship between welfare and the state. The first (Part One) is the period at the turn of the century, when the dominance of laissez-faire individualism and its embodiment in the Poor Law was coming under increasing attack from a variety of demands for a more active and interventionist state. The second is the moment of the Beveridge Report, which was to dominate the post-war development of the welfare state in Britain, and the political consensus on welfare which supported that development. Our final period is that of the 1970s and 1980s, when ideological conflict over the welfare state returned to the centre of the political stage. The Conservative Party, under the leadership of Margaret Thatcher, has played a major role in reviving that conflict. Indeed, in a speech to the United Nations in 1975, Mrs Thatcher announced the nature of the conflict to come:

> Most outside observers have not noticed that amidst our well-publicised difficulties a vital new debate is beginning, or perhaps an old debate is being renewed, about the proper role of government, the Welfare State and the attitudes on which it rests. Many of the issues at stake have been debated on countless occasions in the last century or two. Some are as old as philosophy itself. The Welfare State in Britain is now at least thirty years old. So after a long period in which it was unquestioningly accepted by the whole of society, we can now do more than discuss is strengths and weaknesses in the hackneyed abstract language of moral and political principles. We can see how it has operated in practice in the light of a substantial body of evidence (Thatcher, 1977, pp. 3–4).

This book is both a product of, and a contribution to, the revival of that old debate. As we said earlier, it was the renewal of ideological conflict which focused our minds on this exercise of reconstructing the debate over welfare. In doing so, one of our aims has been to bring to light some of the voices in that debate which the New Right would perhaps rather not have remembered. At least, we hope that this book provides a reminder that the debate has never been an argument solely between defenders of the welfare state and its free market critics.

The structure of the book: a reader's guide

The book is divided into three main parts, each of which examines the ideological conflict over welfare in a particular period. Each part begins with a brief historical introduction to the period, assessing the major political developments and the place of conflicts over welfare within them. The introduction is followed by essays on each of the major ideologies, in which our commentary is intended to link the extracts from original sources. The book ends with a postscript on the relationship between ideology and welfare politics in contemporary Britain, through an examination of the Fowler Review of Social Security (1985).

Part One

The Birth of the Welfare State
(1900–14)

Introduction to Part One

Beginning in the 1880s, British society experienced a profound, complex and long drawn out political crisis, whose resolution involved the creation of a new relationship between the state and society. One element of this crisis was the growth of extensive ideological conflict concerning social problems, social welfare and the role of the state. Throughout the nineteenth century, the dominant voice which pronounced on these issues had been that of laissez-faire individualism. The laissez-faire orthodoxy – about the need for a minimal or non-interventionist state, coupled with the responsibility of individuals for ensuring their own economic well-being – was embodied in the major institutions of welfare which had developed in the nineteenth century. On the one hand, it provided a motive force in the Poor Law's punitive treatment of paupers, to ensure that their 'relief' from poverty did not undermine the incentive to work. On the other hand, it linked the Poor Law to the extensive networks of philanthropy and charity which aimed to 'improve' the 'deserving poor' (those of good character who were not feckless, work-shy or idle).

The dominance of this laissez-faire orthodoxy had been somewhat eroded in practice in a number of ways, such as the creation of municipal powers in public health and housing, and in the beginnings of state education. Nevertheless, it had persisted as the dominant political ideology about the social and economic role of the state in nineteenth-century Britain. But from the 1880s onwards, this ideological dominance began to encounter increasingly sharp challenges from a wide range of conflicting political ideologies which sought to prescribe a different – and more actively interventionist – role for the British state.

Before considering these attacks – and their implications for social welfare – in more detail, it is worth sketching some of the major features of the broader political crisis within which these conflicts about the role of the state took place. The first, and perhaps most significant, feature is the changing position of the working class in Britain. The period is shaped by the increasing unionization of the working class, especially in the growth of the new 'general unions', which extended the principles and practices of trade union organization beyond the limited circle of skilled and craft workers into the wider arena of semi- and unskilled sectors of the working class. The new unions made their presence felt both in extended disputes with employers over pay and conditions (most famously in the Dock Strike of 1889) and in a wider articulation of working-class demands, especially in a period of economic decline. This more assertive organization of working-class interests provided a crucial basis for campaigns against unemployment, and for the right to work, at the end of the century.

These changing patterns of trade union organization overlapped in a variety of ways with the new developments in working-class political organization, most particularly in the development of socialist parties who addressed themselves to the questions of the independent political representation of working-class interests. The Trades Union Congress established its Labour Representation Committee in 1899, which was to play a significant role in the development of the Labour Party. In addition, by the end of the century a variety of other socialist parties, such as the Social Democratic Federation (established in 1883), and the Independent Labour Party (started in 1894) were actively organizing in the working class.

The development of such parties coincided with growing pressure to enlarge the franchise, and the combined effect of these two processes was to throw the existing parliamentary parties (Conservative and Liberal) into disarray. The threat of independent working-class political representation meant the established parties went through a protracted period of internal conflict about how to cope with this threat, and how they could ensure the political support of the working class in the face of new alternatives. The consequences of these changes were most visible in the Liberal Party, where the impact of labour and socialist parties on working-class politics looked likely to have the greatest impact. Liberalism split in complex ways over how to face this challenge; on the one hand looking to electoral alliances with Labour, and on the other, exploring new programmes, policies and political directions aimed at the working-class vote (see Dangerfield, 1984).

Third, it is important to register the significant role played by the growth of feminist politics in this period, and the contribution this development made to the sense of deepening political crisis. Again, one of the central features is the campaigns around suffrage. The best known aspect of the struggles to widen the franchise to women is the suffragette movement, thanks to its upper- and middle-class composition and its dramatic public tactics. But there were also a variety of other suffrage movements active during this period, many of which addressed and involved working-class women more directly. This was particularly the case in Lancashire, where suffrage campaigns intersected with strong patterns of women's active involvement in trade unionism. Nevertheless, while such campaigns for the vote form the most public aspect of feminist politics in this period, feminism was also very active in other areas of political life. Many feminists – both individually and collectively – opened up public debate about the 'private' areas of the family. In particular, they raised questions about the relationship between poverty, the family and the state.

Fourth, the deepening economic recession of the late nineteenth century combined with the growing economic and imperialist competition from other countries. The challenge from Germany, in particular, gave rise to a widespread concern over Britain's 'fitness' to compete – both economically and militarily. One very clear focus of this concern was on the health of the working class, and was expressed in the idea of 'national efficiency'. This idea lay behind a number of initiatives aimed at improving the 'quality of the race', prompting demands for better medical services, housing and the care of children. As well as generating pressure to improve the environmental conditions of the working classes, it also provided a powerful impetus to the ideas of the eugenics movement. Eugenics aimed to be the science of improving the 'British race's breeding stock'. The feeble-minded, feeble-bodied, and otherwise defective sections of the race, it was argued, needed to be restrained from breeding lest they contaminated the wider population. The 'scientific' appeal of eugenics led to its being taken up by representatives of an otherwise widely diverse set of ideological positions. References to the need for 'eugenic measures' appeared in Fabian, socialist, liberal and feminist literature and speeches which, in other respects, were intent on arguing for quite distinct approaches to political change. Together these four strands made up the political crisis of the turn of the century. All of them fed into and found a clear expression in the conflicts which developed around the issues of the state's role in welfare at that time.

The established orthodoxy of economic individualism and the laissez-faire view of the state was challenged by a diverse variety of 'collectivisms' – political positions committed to an expanded and more interventionist role for the state. Not all of the different views of collectivism sat comfortably together – there were both overlaps and tensions between the view of the state offered by the Fabians, by the New Liberals and by socialists. At points, the attack on the laissez-faire orthodoxy formed a sort of common ground, at others their divergent views of how progress was to be achieved, and of what sort of progress should be sought, pulled them in different directions. The distinctions between these different views of 'collectivism' mattered comparatively little to the defenders of laissez-faire, who tended to lump them together under the single label of 'collectivizers' or – more abruptly – 'socialists' (see Langan and Schwarz, eds, 1985).

The arguments between the defenders of individualism and its diverse critics were focused around two welfare issues in particular.

The first was the Royal Commission on the Poor Law, established in 1905, which reported in 1909. This commission was a major battleground for the contending ideologies. The existing Poor Law – and its intersection with charitable organizations – was seen by the defenders of laissez-faire as the acceptable limit of state intervention in the problem of poverty. Precisely for this reason the commission was used by opponents of laissez-faire – both as members of the commission itself and in giving evidence to it – as a setting in which not merely the Poor Law itself, but also the ideology which it embodied, could be subjected to a severe assault.

The second focal point for arguments about welfare and the state was the series of welfare measures introduced by the Liberal government between 1906 and 1914 (see Hay, 1975). These measures, ranging from the introduction of school medical inspections, through the creation of labour exchanges to the provision of state old age pensions, represented a major shift in the principles of the state's involvement of welfare – a growth of one form of 'collectivism'. As such, they were also a focus of heated political debate – not merely from the defenders of individualism, but from other political directions too. These two areas of conflict form the basis for most of the ideological conflicts discussed in the sections which follow.

1 · *Laissez-faire*

Perhaps the most significant feature about laissez-faire in this period is the change from the self-confident assumption that it represented the natural and obvious theory of British society. It had developed during the eighteenth century as an attack on the 'old corruption' of British society – proclaiming the need for individual freedom against aristocratic trade monopolies, patronage and the corrupt use of state power. In its attack on corruption and privilege it had provided an ideological voice for the rising class of industrial entrepreneurs in their efforts to clear away the economic and political 'blockages' that stood in the way of unfettered capitalism in Britain.

By the mid nineteenth century, laissez-faire had assumed a double status, proclaiming itself as a *description* of the way society worked and as the model of the way society *should* work – since the combination of the free individual, the free market, and the minimal or 'night watchman' state represented the highest stage of human development. The role of the state was to guarantee the conditions within which individuals could freely pursue their own interests. Consequently, the state was necessary first, to provide national security through its military forces, second, to preserve the rights of individuals to enjoy the benefits of their efforts – the rights of private property, and third, to regulate the exchanges between individuals so as to prevent corrupt dealing – the rights and duties of contract. Beyond this, the primary obligation of the state was to allow individuals the greatest possible freedom.

So far as welfare was concerned, laissez-faire ideology identified three different ways in which the welfare of the individual should be preserved. First, and most importantly, was the philosophy of *self-help*. The central tenet of laissez-faire's approach was that individuals should and would strive to protect and improve their own interests. By such efforts, by thrift and industriousness, individuals could secure their own welfare. Family and friends also provided a 'natural' social network who would strive to provide mutual assistance in times of stress. Thus, laissez-faire ideologists looked with favour on the efforts of the working class to organize themselves in societies of mutual insurance and support, such as the Friendly Societies – though, of course, such principles of collective combination when applied to the workplace in the form of trades unions received considerably less favour, as limiting the freedom of the individual (or at least the freedom of the employer).

Where self-help failed, the welfare of the individual might be safeguarded by the voluntary efforts of others – through the charitable relief of 'distress'. Charity, however, needed to be organized along strict principles to avoid encouraging the work-shy to become dependent upon it. The aim of charity needed to be the restoration of the principle of self-help – to enable individuals to take charge of their own situation once again. The trade depressions of the mid nineteenth century created a considerable upsurge in charities for the poor, and this unregulated growth of charity threatened to undermine the 'discipline' which charity should impose. This fear led to the creation of the Charity Organisation Society (COS) in 1869, dedicated to the co-ordination of charitable relief, and its distribution according to strict principles. As you will see in the COS guidelines reprinted on p. 34 below, these principles emphasized that charity should only be given to the 'deserving' poor: those who were the victims of circumstances and whose moral character indicated that they were able to use charitable assistance to restore themselves to a state of self-help. The assessment of moral character (whether the applicant showed the desirable habits of thrift, sobriety, industriousness and decency) became a central issue in the distribution of charity.

Finally, if all other means failed (or the applicant for charity was deemed 'undeserving'), the state provided one means of poor relief – under the Poor Law. On a local basis the Poor Law Guardians were empowered to levy rates in order to support the destitute. Even so, relief through the Poor Law was constrained by strict conditions which emphasized the principle of 'less eligibility'. The Poor Law dependant had his/her civil rights removed, and the 'relief' given had to be below the level of existing wage rates to ensure that no incentive was given which threatened the will to work. The Poor Law was intended to be as much a deterrent to poverty as a provision of relief from it. The most important agency of deterrence was the workhouse, where relief was conditional on the performance of labour. Poor Law Guardians were regularly discouraged by national governments from providing 'outdoor relief', i.e. without making those applying for relief undergo the 'workhouse test'.

These three elements – self-help, charity and the Poor Law – were developed as a systematic set of principles at the height of nineteenth-century laissez-faire. However, by the end of the century, laissez-faire could no longer adopt the self-confident position of being the obvious prescription for state action. It was in the position of having to justify itself against new enemies. The enemy was no longer aristocratic power, privilege and patronage, but a new threat arising from the proponents of social reform and revolution. As we can see elsewhere, there are important distinctions between those who attacked laissez-faire capitalism in the names of reform and revolution; but to the defenders of laissez-faire, these distinctions were of small significance; they all belonged to the 'collectivist' threat which aimed to overturn individualism. All of them were 'radical' in their challenges to the principles of laissez-faire. George Jacob Holyoake provided an early warning of the radical threat – and a fairly characteristic rebuttal of it.

The better sort of 'Saviours' have invented seductive phrases which have heretofore beguiled me into expressions of admiration, until more discernment taught me to distrust their tendency. One was that 'Property has its duties as well as its rights'. Property, honestly come by, is for security, pleasure, and power. It has no obligations save those dictated by its interests. All men have a right to an equitable chance of property for the ends of protection and enjoyment; and in a justly organized society there ought not to exist either the necessity or duty of parting with it, when rightly obtained. When something is required to be done for those who have no means of doing it for themselves, the richer people are now expected to assist in providing what is wanted. What is this but a humanitarian confiscation of the property of those from whom such help is exacted? What is this but industrial mendicancy on the part of those who receive it? Why should workmen stoop to this? Why should they not possess the means to provide themselves with what they need? A municipality of independence, desiring some improvement, does not beg; it assesses itself for the expenses. In the same manner, the working class anywhere needing an institution, or an advantage, should do the same – pass a levy upon themselves – not pass round the hat to their richer neighbours. Property has no intrinsic duties of charity. It is the poor who have duties, not the rich and it is the first duty of the industrious poor not to be poor (Holyoake, 1879).

The voices of these new 'saviours' were to become louder and more insistent by the end of the century, and the defenders of individualism rallied to protect the principles of laissez-faire against socialists, radicals and collectivists. By the end of the century, a whole range of organizations had been created to fight off the collectivist threat and preserve individualism. Their various titles are resonant not only of what they wished to defend, but of whom they identified as the 'enemy'. Their origins lay in the 1880s with bodies such as the State Resistance Society and its successor, the Liberty and Property Defence League. These were followed by many others – the British Constitution Association; the London Municipal Society (to counter the growth of 'municipal socialism'); the Industrial Freedom League; the Middle Classes Defence League; and the National Free Labour Association (whose aim was to protect workers from 'socialist' trades union leaders). Many of these groups were affiliated to the Anti-Socialist Union, created in 1905 as a body to co-ordinate the fight against socialism (Brown, ed., 1974).

One of the most active campaigners in this fight against socialism was W. H. Mallock, an energetic author, pamphleteer and speaker, who constantly warned of the dangers posed by socialist theories, as in this extract from his book, *A Critical Examination of Socialism*.

Of the individual demands or proposals put forward by socialists many point to objects which are individually desirable and are within limits practicable; but what hinders, more than anything else, any successful attempt to realise them is the fact that they are placed in a false setting. They resemble a demand for candles on the part of visitors at an hotel who would have, if they did not get them, to go to bed in the dark – a demand which would be contested by nobody if it were not that those who made it demanded the candles only as a means of setting fire to the bed curtains. The demands for old age pensions, and for government action on behalf of the unemployed for example as put forward in Great Britain by labour members who identify the interests of labour with socialism, are demands of this precise kind. The care of the aged, the care of the unwillingly and the discipline of the willingly idle, are among the most important objects to which social statesmanship can address itself; but the doctrines of socialism hinder instead of facilitate the accomplishment of them, because they identify the cure of certain diseased parts of the social organism with a treatment that would be ruinous to the health and ultimately to the life of the whole (1909, pp. 292–3).

Our next extract is taken from the writings of Herbert Spencer, a sociologist and political philosopher, who across the broad range of his work constantly addressed the question of the relationship between the individual, society and the state – and equally consistently argued against the dangers of socialism – the 'coming slavery'. In this extract he deals in characteristic fashion with the relationship between state power and individual freedom:

The individual versus the state

Hence, to be rightly drawn, our conclusions about impending social changes must be guided by observing whether the movement is towards ownership of each man by others or towards ownership of each man by himself, and towards the corresponding emotions and thoughts. Practically it matters little what is the character of the ownership by others – whether it is ownership by a monarch, by an oligarchy, by a democratic majority, or by a communistic organization. The question for each is how far he is prevented from using his faculties for his own advantage and compelled to use them for others' advantages, not what is the power which prevents him or compels him. And the evidence now to be contemplated shows that submission to ownership by others increases or decreases according to the conditions, no matter whether the embodiment of such others is political, social, or industrial.

This general drift towards a form of society in which private activities of every kind, guided by individual wills, are to be replaced by public activities guided by governmental will, must inevitably be made more rapid by recent organic changes, which further increase the powers of those who gain by public administrations and decrease the powers of those who lose by them. Already national and municipal franchises, so framed as to dissociate the giving of votes from the bearing of burdens, have resulted, as was long ago pointed out they must do, in multiplied meddlings and lavish expenditure. And now the extension of similar franchises to the parish will augment such effects. With a fatuity almost passing belief, legislators have concluded that things will go well when the many say to the few: 'We will decide what shall be done and you shall pay for it'. Table conversations show that even by many people called educated, Government is regarded as having unlimited powers joined with unlimited resources; and political speeches make the rustic think of it as an earthly providence which can do anything for him if interested men will let it. Naturally it happens that, as a socialist lecturer writes: 'To get listeners to socialist arguments is to get converts', for the listener is not shown that the benefits to be conferred on each, will be benefits derived from the labours of all, carried on under compulsion. He does not see that he can have the mess of pottage only by surrendering his birthright. He is not told that if he is to be fed he must also be driven (Spencer, 1868, quoted in Andreski, 1971, pp. 184–5).

Where Spencer and others focused on the social consequences of state intervention, defenders of laissez-faire views of the state were also concerned with the economic effects of greater state 'interference'. The following discussion of the economic implications of state activity echoes many of the themes of the contemporary debate about public spending and its impact on the 'wealth-producing' sector.

State and economy

The increase of expenditure of the State is the one invariable element in the Budget. . . . No one runs any danger of being proved wrong if he assumes that next year the total expenditure will be larger than that of the year before.

If we analyse this growth of expenditure, we shall find that it is largely due to the growth of Government action in the various departments of civil life. . . . Little by little, and year by year, the fabric of State expenditure and State responsibility is built up like a coral island, cell by cell. Every year, half-a-dozen Acts of Parliament are passed which give the State new powers and new functions, and enact that new departments and new inspectors shall supervise, and new officials carry out these powers and functions. But new departments, new inspectors, and new officials mean the expenditure of more money, and often on a most lavish scale. . . . They are in effect orders to engage and pay so many more clerks, to print so many more pages, and to use up so much more foolscap and red-tape. Practically you cannot spend more money without raising more taxes. Hence the creating of new duties for the State and the development of new means of interfering with individual action are in essence the imposition of new burdens on the taxpayer. The fact may not be superficially apparent, but it is nonetheless true.

So much for what we may call the direct economic objections to the increase of State interference. The indirect injury done to the community considered in its economic aspect – that is, as a wealth producing and wealth accumulating entity is hardly less serious. No unprejudiced observer can fail to have noticed that two things always accompany interference with the freedom of individual action in matters of trade and commerce – waste and inefficiency. The trade which flourishes most is the trade which is most let alone – most free to develop itself in its own way. Directly you put the pressure of State interference on an industry it begins to suffer a certain loss of vigour. In extreme cases, indeed, the industry actually shrivels and withers. And even where the interference is most scientifically employed, there is a certain injury inflicted. And this withering, or tendency towards withering, cannot but inflict an economic loss, great or small in proportion to the nature and amount of the interference which takes place. Hence the interference of the State in matters of trade and industry not only inflicts a burden on the nation, but makes the nation less able to bear the burden. . . . However, it is looked at economically, State interference in the dominion of civil life and with the machinery of production is an evil (*The Economist*, 1895).

Welfare and individual responsibility

One of the sharpest areas of conflict between laissez-faire ideologists and the variety of 'collectivist' arguments for greater state intervention was around the question of how to respond to poverty, in which the role of the Poor Law and the provision of 'relief' was central. Among the principal defenders of the Poor Law at the turn of the century was Thomas Mackay, author of a range of books and articles on poverty, a Poor Law Guardian and a member of the Charity Organisation Society. Mackay constantly insisted on the need to rationalize the relief given to the poor to ensure that it did not undermine the responsibility of individuals to take care of their own welfare. For Mackay, the ideal situation was:

that there should be no system of Public Relief at all, and that the relief of the unfortunate should be attained by a more perfect development of the natural benevolence which is inherent in family, social and industrial relationships. With an abolition of public systems of relief, the burden to fall on this private benevolence would be much lightened by the more rapid development of the self-regarding virtue of thrift, mainly, in all probability by the expedient of insurance in many forms. It may seem a bold assertion to make, but this consummation is not, perhaps, so far out of our reach as we generally suppose (Mackay, 1901, p. 182).

However in the absence of this ideal state, Mackay continued to be a powerful advocate of a rationalized Poor Law, coupled with systematic charitable assistance, as the best approach to the problem of the poor. It was in this vein that he appeared as an expert witness before the Royal Commission on the Poor Law (1909).

The following brief extracts provide an illustration of the sort of rationalization that he hoped to see in the administration of the Poor Law. To begin with he was hostile to the granting of 'outdoor relief', arguing that Poor Law benefits should, for the most part, be dependent on the admission to the workhouse:

I will not conceal my opinion that except in cases of emergency . . . the best thing to do would be to abolish it altogether. . . . If you lay it down in a parish that every widow with so many children shall get so many shillings a week, then it becomes a regular thing for them to have it, if it is certain. I think that is not a desirable result for the parish. . . . You say, you are an orphan, and you get so much. If you are a widow you get so much. It would be a sort of permanent endowment of people to neglect to provide for those risks of life (Royal Commission, 1909, pp. 228–34).

Mackay was also concerned about the political control exercised over the Poor Law by locally elected Boards of Guardians. The election of labour and socialist politicians to Boards of Guardians was seen by laissez-faire ideologists as resulting in the payment of over-generous and over-certain outdoor relief in some parishes. Such 'generosity' was thought to undermine the spirit of independence which needed to be fostered in the poor, and in his evidence Mackay turned to the fallibility of democracy as a means of ensuring a rational system of Poor Law administration:

It is, I submit, no disrespect to popular local government to say that in the multiplicity of local bodies, such things as an apathetic election, an irrelevant election, an imperfectly informed election, are possible occurrences. . . . An ideal administration, it may be admitted, would result from a local electorate which had made a competent study of the subject, and which, having arrived at a right principle, appointed representatives to carry it out. . . . Nothing but confusion and miscarriage can result from confiding administrative duties to bodies which may be unsympathetic and ill-informed as to the wishes of Parliament . . . especially when such bodies have full power to set the decision of Parliament at Defiance (Royal Commission, 1909, p. 228).

Although the Majority Report of the Royal Commission was to echo the concerns of Mackay and others like him in calling for a more disciplined administration of poor relief, it was to some extent outflanked by the welfare measures introduced by the Liberal government between 1906 and 1914. These measures shifted the focal point of arguments about the state and welfare away from the Poor Law. Predictably, the introduction of state benefits and interventions in sickness, old age and unemployment were greeted with alarm by the guardians of laissez-faire principles. The following extract is taken from Charles Loch, one of the founders of, and a central influence in, the Charity Organisation Society. Here Loch outlines the case for voluntary rather than state responses to such social problems:

The value of charity

In Charity Organisation, then, what is the field for enterprise? The position of the moment is peculiar, and affects all social enterprise alike. The entrepreneur of the day is not the responsible volunteer, who, if he fails, is thrown to the lions of criticism and forgotten, but the ultra-responsible Government, which, if its measures fail, is nevertheless armoured against criticism and has the financial machinery and the credit of the State behind it. The larger the field its enterprise covers, the more does it reduce the enterprise of social workers to that of assisting the Government. Voluntaryism becomes an authorised sub-service. This is the tendency of the moment, though, no doubt, besides the scope which the State affords for supplementation, there are parts of the field still unenclosed by it.

I would set out the chief Social Acts since 1900 – the Enclosure Acts of the last seven years. They are these:

> The Unemployed Workmen Act, 1905
> Workmen's Compensation Act, 1906
> Education (Provision of Meals) Act, 1906
> Education (Administrative Provisions) Act, 1907: Medical Inspection of School Children
> Old Age Pensions Act, 1908 and 1911
> Children Act, 1908
> Children's School Care Committees reorganised in London, 1909
> The Labour Exchanges Act, 1909
> Juvenile (Labour) Advisory Committee, 1910
> National Insurance Act, 1911

The Poor Law remains untouched at present, but it is already being affected by the growth of State enterprise round and about it. For the rest, this list shows, all must admit, an astonishing revolution, and indicates very clearly that the spirit of enterprise in social matters has passed from the people to the State, and the people's enterprise, as must naturally follow, becomes, as I have said, the enterprise of a sub-service. What the Government has established, be it rightly or wrongly, assumes such large proportions and involves so many interests that the people, or those interested in any branch of relevant work, have, by a kind of social compulsion, to arrive at the conclusion that they must make an effort to back the Government venture and do their best to make it work well. I notice, too, with some interest, that the most recent proposals for charitable progress are, in the main, proposals to link charity or social work locally to municipal bodies and generally to Government Departments. Thus the enterpreneurs of charity are running to shelter, like creatures out in a storm. The status of a Government alliance gives them protection and a certain sense of dignity.

We make numerous and almost encyclopaedic laws, and then we fail to enforce them. Can it be wondered that social conditions alter but a little among the very poor, while we press ever for more and more legislation? State authorities are wary prosecutors. They can hardly face failure. Your volunteer is a free-lance. If he fails in a good endeavour, little harm is done. He has no prestige to lose. But when it is a State affair the very amplitude of our machinery and our responsibilities, and the very largeness of the numbers with which we have to deal, may prevent our doing even simple things that require prompt attention and firmness.

These things we have noted. State philanthropy brings large numbers of the population to its ministrations. The poor, as Mr. Mackay used to say, are not usually importunate or aggressive in the case of charitable relief. Their expectations are limited. But where there is a State fund, it is to them as the income of many multi-millionaires, and there is not the same reluctance to turn it to account. A very large number of applicants necessitates alike wide supervision and a close attention to an immense amount of detail. This again necessitates a large staff and a large extension of methods of routine; and the outcome is likely to be a large and increasing bureaucracy and a popular desire to obtain Government situations such as afflicts the people of some foreign countries. Further, as this tendency prevails, the individual with his need of special help and personal attention, is apt to become one in a queue of claimants, to get a turn of help and then pass quickly out of sight. Many seek because much is offered. There is a displacement of the general will. What was left to the general public before now comes within the duty of the State as caterer-in-chief for its citizens. Thus the individual in distress and his family may find less help and consolation where they found it before, while at the same time the offers which are made to them in the new regime of State intervention may fail to meet their real wants.

What, then, is our enterprise? If it be possible, to humanise the action of the State, to keep alive, in spite of it, the initiative of the people, their spontaneity of character, and their independence. To humanise, as I understand it, is to keep alive and make effectual in social life that humanity or feeling of personal kindness which preserves the common sense of a race and recognise its characteristics. It is the enemy of hasty sympathy that would be good by short cuts and forced marches. It vows to be thorough in its work, because the want of thoroughness is inhumane. For the same reason, it would not act without knowledge or without anxious scrutiny of the bye-results of action. It would be adequate in its aid, because inadequate aid is but a kind of neglect. It would face the worst conditions and would not turn aside, but make a gallant and persistent effort to alter them by direct or indirect means. The humanity that would do less is a humanity dashed with fear or faithlessness. It would hand a good tradition on, for tradition lives in the safest place, the hearts and wills of good people. It would prevent pauperism, the unsettlement, listlessness, and discontent of the pauper mind, which always creep in as responsibility is diminished and independence decreases. It would prevent institutions from crushing individuality. It would apply close tests to all schemes and mark sharply what good they produce, or what weaknesses they breed. It would let no department evade this testing. It would have a measuring-rod of results, as for so many years we used the Poor Law returns, as a test of the fall or rise of dependence. State action and legislation, tested and proven to be of an injurious nature, it would oppose whole-heartedly and, if possible, criticise out of existence, whether the people were in favour of it or not. It would be inventive to meet the hundred and one difficulties of different cases, and would use all the means of suggestion and persuasion and legal constraint that are available that it may better the conditions that are found in these cases. And it would be brave (Loch, 1913, p. 209–14).

As a final note on the welfare implications of laissez-faire ideology, we have reproduced the notice which the Charity Organisation Society issued to those who applied for assistance. Its conditions and warnings are a firm expression of the moral imperatives behind the Society's view of the poor:

Charity Organization Society: Notice to persons applying for assistance

1. The Society desires to help those persons who are doing all they can to help themselves, and to whom temporary assistance is likely to prove a lasting benefit.
2. No assistance should be looked for without full information being given in order that the Committee may be able to judge:
    (1) Whether the applicant ought to be helped by charity
    (2) What is the best way of helping them. . . .
3. Persons wishing to be assisted by Loans must find satisfactory security, such as that of respectable householders. . . . Loans have to be paid back by regular instalments.
4. Persons who have thrown themselves out of employment through their own fault ought not to count upon being helped by charity.
5. Persons of drunken, immoral or idle habits can not expect to be assisted unless they can satisfy the Committee that they are really trying to reform.
6. The Society does not, unless under exceptional circumstances, give or obtain help for the payment of back rent or of funeral expenses. But when help of this sort is asked for, there may be other and better ways of assisting.
7. Assistance will not, as a rule, be given in addition to a Parish Allowance.

By Order,
C.O.S.
.... Committee

(COS Form No. 28, reproduced in Woodroofe, 1962, p. 41)

2 · *The New Liberalism*

This term is rather confusingly applied to both the Liberal government's programme of social reform and welfare measures introduced between 1906 and 1914, and to the work of a group of liberal intellectuals who, from the 1880s, sought to redefine the political tasks of British Liberalism with an emphasis on the need for social reform (Weiler, 1982). As we shall see, these two different aspects of the New Liberalism are not identical, but what they have in common is the construction of a political ideology which is sharply distinguished from 'old' liberalism, particularly in its view of the state and welfare.

'Old' liberalism had been the central political expression of laissez-faire ideology, propounding free trade against Tory economic protectionism; free enterprise against 'corrupt' economic monopolies and patronage; and the freedom of the individual against the 'impositions' of state power. As such, liberalism had insisted on the role of the state being a 'minimal' one, primarily devoted to the maintenance of freedom through law, but making no further encroachment on the workings of the market.

From the 1880s, a group of liberals – the New Liberals – began the task of redefining liberalism in response to changing economic, political and social circumstances. Two things in particular concentrated their minds. One was a series of electoral defeats which threatened their loss of political power in a way which mirrored the decline of other European liberal parties, who were being supplanted by socialist or social democratic parties. These political dangers, which included the threat of losing working-class political support to the emerging labour and socialist parties, created a political crisis of liberalism. British liberalism was split into a number of fragments, each of which became engaged in the attempt to redefine and reconstruct liberalism's political future. We shall not be attempting to follow the fortunes of all of these different segments of liberalism, preferring instead to concentrate on the New Liberals because their efforts to redefine the relationship between the state and the individual were to have a substantial impact on British political culture, and on ideologies of welfare in particular.

The second major factor in the development of New Liberalism was the growing body of evidence of poverty, destitution and human misery within British society. In particular, studies such as Henry George's *Progress and Poverty* (1881) and Charles Booth's *The Life and Labour of the People of London* (1889) raised new questions about the relationship between poverty and the economic organization of British society. Most significantly, the evidence and arguments of such studies challenged the central presumption of laissez-faire views of poverty: that individuals were personally responsible for their own misfortunes.

While the New Liberals maintained something of the traditional liberal emphasis on individual freedom, they also identified economic circumstances as a potential inhibition on people's ability to achieve and make use of the benefits of freedom. They began to develop a conception of equality of opportunity which would ensure that all members of society had a base from which they could benefit from individual freedoms. Enforced poverty – just as much as unreasonable state interference – could be the cause of people being unable to live freely.

From this starting point, they drew out a very different view of the relationship between the individual and the state from that offered in laissez-faire ideology. Where laissez-faire saw a direct opposition between the interests of the individual and those of the state, the New Liberals argued for a more 'organic' view of the relationship. The state, they argued, was not an alien power set against the 'free individual', but was the 'collective will' of the society, and should promote the best interests of the whole society and its members. This view of the 'organic' state is reflected in the following extract from the philosopher D. G. Ritchie. Here Ritchie argues against the individualist view of the state:

Individual as part of the state

Underlying all these traditions and prejudices there is a particular metaphysical theory – a metaphysical theory which takes hold of those persons especially who are fondest of abjuring all metaphysics; and the disease is in their case the more dangerous since they do not know when they have it. The chief symptom of this metaphysical complaint is the belief in the abstract individual. The individual is thought of, at least spoken of, as if he had a meaning and significance apart from his surroundings and apart from his relations to the community of which he is a member. It may be quite true that the significance of the individual is not exhausted by his relations to any given set of surroundings; but apart from all these he is a mere abstraction – a local ghost, a metaphysical spectre, which haunts the habitations of those who have derided metaphysics. The individual, apart from all relations to a community, is a negation. You can say nothing about him, or rather it, except that it is not any other individual. Now, along with this negative and abstract view of the individual there goes, as counterpart, the way of looking at the State as an opposing element to the individual. The individual and the State are put over against one another.

Their relation is regarded as one merely of antithesis. Of course, this is a point of view which we can take, and quite rightly for certain purposes; but it is only one point of view. It expresses only a partial truth; and a partial truth, if accepted as the whole truth, is always a falsehood. Such a conception is, in any case, quite inadequate as a basis for any profitable discussion of the duties of Government.

It is this theory of the individual which underlies Mill's famous book on *Liberty*. Mill, and all those who take up his attitude towards the State, seem to assume that all power gained by the State is so much taken from the individual; and conversely, that all power gained by the individual is gained at the expense of the State. Now this is to treat the two elements, power of the State and power (or liberty) of the individual, as if they formed the debit and credit sides of an account book; it is to make them like two heaps of a fixed number of stones, to neither of which you can add without taking from the other. It is to apply a mere quantitative conception in politics, as if that were an adequate 'category' in such matters. The same thing is done when society is spoken of as merely 'an aggregate of individuals'. The citizen of a State, the member of a society of any sort, even an artificial or temporary association does not stand in the same relation to the whole that one number does to a series of numbers, or that one stone does to a heap of stones. Even ordinary language shows us this. We feel it to be a more adequate expression to say that the citizen is a member of the body politic, than to call him merely a unit in a political aggregate. . . .

Thirdly, and lastly, be it observed that the arguments used against 'government' action, where the government is entirely or mainly in the hands of a ruling class or caste, exercising wisely or unwisely a paternal or 'grandmotherly' authority – such arguments lose their force just in proportion as government becomes more and more genuinely the government of the people by the people themselves. The explicit recognition of popular sovereignty tends to abolish the antithesis between 'the Man' and 'the State'. The State becomes, not 'I' indeed, but 'we'. The main reason for desiring more State action is in order to give the individual a greater chance of developing all his activities in a healthy way. The State and the individual are not sides of an antithesis between which we must choose; and it is possible, though, like all great things, difficult for a democracy to construct a strong and vigorous State, and thereby to foster a strong and vigorous individuality, not selfish nor isolated, but finding its truest welfare in the welfare of the community (Ritchie, 1891, p. 11–12).

In part, this changing view of the state was influenced by changes in the British political structure. The defence of the individual against state power in laissez-faire ideology had been constructed in response to a political system which was dominated by aristocratic interests, and whose 'corruption' (in voting and in civil service employment) embodied aristocratic patronage. But the nineteenth century saw gradual victory for the traditional programme of liberalism, with the decline of aristocratic power and the growth of a professional state bureaucracy. The electoral franchise was extended and the state was increasingly open to pressures from non-aristocratic social groups, particularly Britain's commercial and industrial bourgeoisie and the new middle classes. Consequently, it was easier for the New Liberals to view the state as the expression of a social will, rather than as a threatening power.

From this changing view of the state, it was possible for the New Liberals to argue that the state could – and should – be used as a vehicle for social reform, to improve the condition of the weakest and the poorest to allow them to participate in the life of society. Collective provision could be made to safeguard against the risks of disaster – whether those disasters were 'natural' (sickness) or social (unemployment). It was also potentially a means of defusing some of the more fundamental threats which might be posed by the growing links between the increasing demands of organized labour and socialist ideas.

The New Liberals did not develop specific programmes of social reform. Rather, their efforts were primarily devoted to producing an intellectual and political rationale for the Liberal Party and its 'friends' to take up the issue of social reform and become a 'progressive' party. Central to this rationale were the arguments about 'opportunity' and the theme of 'citizenship', in which the state was seen as having the role of safeguarding the interests of all its citizens, and guaranteeing the rights (e.g. to a degree of economic security) which would become the baseline for their individual development. By the 1890s, this commitment to reform had extended to the idea of a 'guaranteed minimum' income funded through progressive taxation, so as to promote income redistribution from rich to poor.

This New Liberalism evolved out of a complex series of political alliances and conflicts. Within the Liberal Party itself, they fought a constant battle against the old liberalism, trying to 'modernize' the party. During the 1880s and early 1890s, they formed close contacts with the early Fabian Society around the criticism of laissez-faire economics, the attack on the principles of the Poor Law, and the development of a collectivist view of the state and social reform. This alliance broke down in 1893, when the Fabians withdrew from contact with the Liberal Party over the failure of the Liberal government to implement a programme of social reform. Subsequently, the New Liberals were to be critical of what they saw as the Fabians' increasingly mechanical and bureaucratic conception of state social reform.

Throughout this period, the New Liberals were emphatic in their view that the Liberal Party must address itself to the interests of labour. There were a number of different aspects to this 'alliance' with the organized working class. First, New Liberalism was profoundly influenced by the sense of 'mission' forged in the University Settlement Movement (most famously in Toynbee Hall in the East End), which had called upon the young middle class to live and work among the poor of Britain's cities. Second, their attack on laissez-faire economics led them to a view of the legitimate interests of labour in wage bargaining, trade union organization, and protection against the 'malorganization' of the economic system. Throughout the years between 1880 and 1920, they actively campaigned in defence of trade union rights, and supported working-class organizations in conflicts with employers. One of the leading members, L. T. Hobhouse, took an active role in trying to organize agricultural workers while at Cambridge. Third, they recognized that, with the extension of the franchise, the 'working-class vote' was increasingly significant to the political survival of the Liberal Party. They argued that the Liberal Party had to take account of working-class interests, both in its own programmes, and through political alliances with Labour MPs on the basis of 'progressive policies'. This 'progressive alliance' found its clearest expression within the Progressive Party which contested LCC (London County Council) elections during this period, combining both Liberal and Labour representatives.

There were, however, limits to their support for 'working-class interests'. They identified their role as promoting a Liberal Party which would provide a middle way between the excesses of laissez-faire individualism on the one hand, and the extremism of socialism on the other. The Liberal Party should offer a means through which the working class could see their interests being protected, thus preventing them from resorting to the revolutionary doctrines of socialism. When the Labour Party introduced a bill for the provision of work at standard wages for the unemployed, the New Liberal journal the *Nation* was quick to draw the boundaries between acceptable reforms and unacceptable demands:

Now it is essential to sound unemployed policy that it shall be regarded as a species of social palliative for a specific industrial disease, not as part of an organic attempt to reconstruct society. This requires that while the conditions of public relief works must be such as shall not impair the economic efficiency of the worker and his family they must not be such as to tempt him to remain in public employment a single day longer than the state of the outside labour market warrants (*Nation*, 1908, p. 863).

This quotation gives some indication of the complexities of the ground on which the New Liberalism attempted to take its stand. It was virulently critical of the individualist ideology of laissez-faire, but tried to construct a politics of reform which did not err too far in the direction of socialism. As if the problems of these 'external' alliances and conflicts were not sufficient, the New Liberals were also at war with influential sections of their own party about foreign policy. Attitudes to the Boer War were the touchstone of these arguments. 'Liberal Imperialists' supported the war against the Boers in Africa, and more generally defended imperial expansion. By contrast, the New Liberals opposed military aggrandisement, and argued that civilized nations had a moral obligation to follow civilized standards in their foreign policy dealings.

Ironically, both the New Liberals and the Liberal Imperialists came to support the welfare measures of the 1906 Liberal government – though from rather different view points. For the Liberal Imperialists, welfare reforms were rational measures aimed at improving 'national efficiency' – the level of functioning of the whole population. Concern over national efficiency had arisen at the start of the Boer War when medical inspections of recruits had indicated that around a third were unfit for service. With growth concern about competition and conflict between the imperial powers, welfare reform was one means of improving the 'fitness' of the British race to conduct the defence and expansion of its interests.

For the New Liberals, welfare reforms were identified as steps on the way to creating a 'minimum standard' and promoted the organic relationship which they sought between the state and its citizens. The reforms provided protection for the most 'vulnerable' citizens – the young, through school meals and school medical inspections; the elderly poor, through a limited scheme of old age pensions; the unemployed, through unemployment benefit and labour exchanges; and the sick, through national insurance. Each of the reforms was limited to those who could demonstrate that they were 'deserving', either through their good personal history (pensions) or through their having built up a contributions record for the insurance-based unemployment and sickness benefits.

The New Liberals also supported the reforms because of the proposals worked out by Lloyd George, Asquith and Churchill for their financing. New Liberals, like J. A. Hobson, had long discussed the reforming merit of progressive income tax – particularly a tax on 'unearned income' from land and shares. The 'People's Budget' introduced in 1909 by Lloyd George contained just such a progressive income tax.

The New Liberals did not 'deliver' a programme of welfare reform, though the 1906 Liberal government did. What they did provide was a new political ideology which challenged laissez-faire individualism, and provided a political language about the state and its citizens which justified an expanded role for the state in collective welfare provision. They marked out an ideology of state welfare which provided a 'middle way' between individualism and socialism. Churchill – before defecting to the Conservatives – summed it up as follows:

Something more is needed if we are to get forward. There lies the function of the Liberal Party. Liberalism at once supplies the higher impulse and the practicable path; it appeals to persons by sentiments of generosity and humanity; it proceeds by course of moderation. By gradual steps, by steady effort from day to day, from year to year, Liberalism enlists hundreds of thousands on the side of progress and popular democratic reform whom militant socialism would drive into violent Tory reaction (Churchill, 1906).

Our final extract in this section on the New Liberalism is a lengthy one, chosen to demonstrate the depth of opposition between the traditional individualism of laissez-faire views of poverty and that of the New Liberals. In this extract the economist J. A. Hobson, one of the most radical of the New Liberals, dissects the economic, moral and political views of the Charity Organisation Society's approach to poverty. His extensive criticisms show just how far the New Liberals had gone in developing a radically new alternative to the ideology of laissez-faire.

Individuals are not to blame

In setting itself to discover and to stamp out pernicious forms of alms-giving, to order, direct, and economise the charitable energy which comes from the moneyed classes in gifts or endowments to unknown recipients, the Charity Organisation Society performs a service of great and easily recognised value.

The chief work they have essayed is, by establishing a class of expert middlemen, to provide a substitute for the broken personal nexus between donor and recipient. In the course of such work, and the study it involves, it is only natural that certain rules of general application to classes of cases should emerge. But of late it has become apparent that some of the most active organisers, especially in the Metropolis, are indulging more ambitious claims. *From the narrow empirical rules they ascend to principles, or perhaps it would be more true to say, they interpret their rules in the light of superimposed and externally derived principles. Those familiar with the tone and method of their recent criticism of the new social movements are now aware that this group of influential leaders in charity organisation work lay claim to an exclusive possession of the right principles of social reform in relation to all problems of the poor.* What exactly were these principles it was not, until lately, easy to ascertain, though their broader tenor was unmistakable. But we have now a book* which from the conjunction of its authorship and its avowed object, may be taken as an authoritative revelation of this charity organisation philosophy. Covering, more or less, the whole field of social study, from the minutae of Poor-law administration to the vague vastness of 'the general will', it brings theory and practice into contact in a most instructive way. We are now able for the first time to test the logic and the 'scientific' character of charity organisation. *The book may therefore be regarded as an authoritative statement of the opposition of the propertied classes to schemes of old age pensions, feeding of school-children at the public expense, public*

---

* *Aspects of the Social Problem*, by various writers, Mr Bosanquet, Mr C. S. Loch, Mrs McCallum, Miss Dendy.

provision of work for the unemployed, and other proposals of public aid for the poor and needy.

Such schemes are one and all condemned with the same condemnation that is meted out to indiscriminate charity and wasteful doles. *They sap the sense of responsibility in the individual, weaken his incentive to effective work, and break up the solidarity and unity of family life.* With the practical assumptions which underlie this criticism – *i.e.* that every willing worker can get work sufficiently regular and well-paid to enable him to provide for himself and his family all that is necessary for a decent life, to set by enough to keep him in old age, and to secure him against all the contingent misfortunes and burdens of a working life – we shall deal later on. It is more convenient to approach the position of this social philosophy by turning to that theory of the 'dole' which has arisen most naturally from charity organisation work, and by seeking to understand this theory in relation to the wider principle of property which is laid down as the basis of the social philosophy of this school of thinkers.

It is now commonly recognised that a dole is injurious in its direct effect upon the recipient, and in its indirect effect upon others. It acts as a 'demand for idleness' and thus weakens character. But why is a dole injurious to the recipient and to society? Why does it degrade character? The real answer is a simple one. *It is an irrational mode of transfer of property.* Let Mr. Bosanquet explain.

> 'The point of private property is that things should not come miraculously and be unaffected by your dealings with them, but that you should be in contact with something which in the external world is the definite material representation of yourself.'

It is true this passage occurs in an essay defending the institution of private property, but it casts so clear a light upon the theory of doles that I quote it here. A dole is condemnable because it comes 'miraculously' to the recipient and not as the natural result of personal effort; it is not a 'definite material representation' of himself. *These charitable 'windfalls' violate the rational order of life, lead weakly human nature to detach the idea of enjoyment from related effort, to expect an effect without a cause.* Thus false notions are engendered which break the back of honest regular effort.

Nothing can be more convincing than this condemnation of the dole, derived from the theory of private property. But why stop at doles? Are there no other forms of private property which should stand in the dock with 'doles' to the poor? *How about gifts and bequests to the rich?* Do they too not come 'miraculously'? Are they 'affected by your dealings with them'? Are they 'definite material embodiments' of their owners? Here no question arises as to the just limit of the right of the donor or legator over his property. Mr. Bosanquet in his theory of private property has chosen to take his stand by 'origin'; his test of valid property is the way it comes into the possession of its holder. Why do the Charity Organisation Society and their philosophers constantly denounce small gifts to the poor, and hold their peace about large gifts to the rich? We might press the application of this admirable rule of private property a little further and ask whether the economic rent of land and certain elements in the profits of invested capital, do not come under the same category of the 'miraculous', or, whether they are the natural results, the 'material presentation', of the productive efforts of the receivers. *Can anything be more miraculous than that I should wake up to-morrow and find certain shares which to-day are worth £100 are then risen to £105?* These gains which grow 'while men sleep', are they sound forms of private property according to Mr. Bosanquet? The positive defence of private property rests, according to Mr. Bosanquet, upon the need which every one has for possessing 'a permanent nucleus in the material world' wherewith to help to plan out his life as a rational whole. I here suggest that his view of private property passes a twofold condemnation upon economic rents and other unearned elements of income. Firstly, by enabling a man to reap where he has not sown, by divorcing satisfaction from previous effort, they crush the sense of independence in the recipient and derationalise his life. Secondly, since all 'unearned' elements of income are truly the earnings of the work of some one else, or of society, such individual or such society, by losing the natural reward of its effort, is disabled from realising itself. The ground landlord who 'realises himself' in the rents he draws from his slum property is preventing the docker and the seamstress from realising themselves, and is destroying for them the possibility of rationally organising life. Do the Charity Organisation thinkers apply their solicitude for the maintenance of moral responsibility in these directions? No! Their logic makes a dead halt on the other side of this just economic application. They are all fear lest the poor should suffer from the degradation and the ignominy of receiving something they have not earned. Yet they never lift their voice to say the characters of the well-to-do which are constantly assailed by these same demoralising forces. . . .

One phrase of positive enlightenment his argument contains. Property is bad when it does not form *'the basis of a social vocation'*. This brings us close to the root fallacy of his reasoning. Private property he justifies solely by the use to which it is put. If an owner uses his ground rents or his monopoly-profits as 'the basis of a vocation', returning to society by his voluntary effort what he chooses to regard as a *quid pro quo*, he is blameless. So 'unearned incomes' are treated as a social 'trust', a 'charge'. To use Mr. Bosanquet's own ingenuous words, 'if one has enough to live on, that is a charge – something to work with, to organise, to direct'. Mark what has taken place in passing from the application of the theory of property in the case of 'doles' to the case of 'unearned' incomes. *Doles were shown to be pernicious by reason of their origin, i.e. as windfalls; unearned incomes are to be tested not by origin but by use.* If they are put to a good use, we are to keep silent about their origin, and about the injury which their payment inflicts upon those whose work they represent and who need them for self-realisation. The ground rents of London are a trust, a 'charge' socially bestowed upon the Dukes of Westminster, Bedford, Portland, & c.; society has designed them so as to give these noblemen 'something to work with', an opportunity to serve London and to be a glory and adornment of our social life; if they faithfully execute this 'trust', fill their high 'vocation', they have earned their ground rents, if not – well for this not very improbable contingency Mr. Bosanquet and his friends make no provision! *What are they prepared to do when the 'trust' is plainly violated?* Will they provide means for deposing the fraudulent trustee? Of this we have no word. Possibly Mr. Loch will bring the matter under the notice of the Liberty and Property Defence League, with the view of ascertaining how far they are prepared to go to enforce the conditions of the 'trust'. Speaking candidly this talk about a 'charge', a 'trust', is a wanton abuse of language, applied as it is to describe elements of income which pass to the owners from exercise of sheer economic might. . . .

This language indeed emerges in the philanthropic cant of all ages. When we are dealing with the poor, we are to brace their character and to remove everything then enervates and induces to idleness; when we are dealing with the rich, we must encourage them to make a good use of the means which, in their origin, are helping to maintain poverty. We must simply remember 'if one has enough to live on, that is a charge'. We need not investigate too curiously how 'one' comes to 'have enough to live on'! 'No, we are not economists,' say these gentlemen, when they are invited to trace back 'unearned incomes' to economic rents and the superior bargaining power of the rich as compared with the poor. *The answer is: 'You are economists when it suits your purpose; your condemnation of the effects of indiscriminate almsgiving, or the operations of the poor law, is based on "economic" reasoning, but your "economics" are selective and partial in their application.'*

What it all comes to is this: *that the poor can provide for themselves, and need not be poor if they choose to exert themselves.*

The argument from personal experience is vitiated by two fallacies. First, the ancient fallacy of 'any and all'. In American schools it is not unusual to encourage the boys by reminding them that, by industry and perseverance, any one of them may rise to the position of President of the United States; but to say that all of them could attain the position would be plainly false. Yet the individualist argument by which our Charity Organisation thinkers seek to show that because A, or B, or C in a degraded class is able, by means of superior character or capacity, to rise out of that class, no one need remain there, contains the same fallacy. It assumes what is required to prove – viz., that there are no economic or other social forces which limit the number of successful rises. It assumes that every workman can secure regularity of employment and good wages; that the quantity of 'savings' which can find safe and profitable investment is unlimited; and that all can equally secure for themselves a comfortable and solid economic position by the wise exertion of their individual powers. *Now if there exist any economic forces, independent in their operation of individual control,* which at any given time limit the demand for labour in the industrial field and limit the scope of remunerative investment, these forces, by exercising a selective influence, preclude the possibility of universal success in the field of competitive industry. All economists agree in asserting the existence of these forces, though they differ widely in assigning causes for them; all economists affirm the operation of great tidal movements in trade which for long periods limit the demand for labour and thus oblige a certain large quantity of unemployment. The Charity Organisation Society's investigator naturally finds that the individuals thrown out of work in these periods of depression are mostly below the level of their fellows in industrial or in moral character, and attributes to this 'individual' fact the explanation of the unemployment; he wrongly concludes that if these unemployed were upon the same industrial and moral level as their comrades who are at work, there would be work for all. He does not reason to this judgment, but, with infantile simplicity, assumes it. This arises from a curious limitation which the Charity Organisation Society places upon the meaning of 'fact'. *Professing to be devoted lovers of 'facts', and to be exclusive possessors of the facts relevant to the study of poverty, they confine themselves wholly to facts in their bearing on individual cases, ignoring those facts which consist in the relation of individual to individual, or, in other words, 'social' facts.*

The Charity Organisation philosophy, crystallised in the single phrase *'in social reform, then, character is the condition of conditions'*, represents a mischievous half-truth, the other half of which rests in the possession of the less thoughtful section of the Social Democrats and forms the basis of the cruder socialism. Neither individual character nor environment is 'the condition of conditions'. The true principle which should replace these half-falsehoods is a recognition of the interdependence and interaction of individual character and social character as expressed in social environment. . . . The principle that individual 'character is the condition of conditions' is much worse than a half-truth in its application. *For it is used to block the work of practical reformers upon political and economic planes, by an insistence that the moral elevation of the masses must precede in point of time all successful reforms of environment.* Plenty of people are only too willing to listen to insidious advice which takes the form; why disturb valuable vested interests, why trouble about ground values, why stir a general spirit of discontent in the masses, why suggest 'heroic' remedies for unemployment, when all that is needed just now is a quiet, careful, organised endeavour to induce habits of sobriety and cleanliness in the homes of the poor, to teach them how to expend their money more advantageously, to practise saving habits, and gradually, by gentle persistent endeavour, to build up individual character? To most who have not studied the industrial structure of society it sounds reasonable to suggest that such moral reforms should come first. In reality it is a falsehood. In the education of a class as of an individual child the historic priority of attention must be to the *corpus sanum*, the material physical environment, in order that the historic conditions of the *mens sana* may exist. *Though moral reform may be prior in 'the nature of things' economic reform is prior in time.* Better late than never our religious and temperance missionaries are coming to recognise that intimate dependence of drunkenness, gambling, and other personal vices upon the economic conditions of industrial life. Take the signal *example of prostitution.* Does any experienced person really believe that moral influences directed to the inculcation of personal chastity will have any considerable effect, so long as the economic conditions which favour and induce prostitution remain untouched? *Here is the case of a trade dependent both in volume and in character upon supply and demand.* So long as the ill-paid, precarious and degrading conditions which attach to the wage-work and home-life of many women present prostitution as a superficially attractive alternative, or a necessary supplement, to wage-work or wifedom, supply will be maintained. So long as large numbers of men own money not earned by hard regular work, and not needed for the purchase of legitimate satisfactions, and leisure in excess of the wholesome demands of a natural life, while others are deterred by the economic constitution of society from the establishment of normal family relations, the demand for prostitution will continue. This analysis does not deny the operation of definitely personal vicious forces, not closely connected with the economic factors; but it affirms the latter as larger determinants. *The refusal of the 'purity' party to face definitely and fearlessly the economic supports of impurity has rightly brought upon them the imputation of shallowness, or even insincerity, for shallowness always implied imperfect sincerity. . . .*

Those engineers who seek to lift the moral nature of the masses by means of a force which they think will emanate from their correct conduct and elevated tastes are apt to be hoist with their own petard. Be sure your 'illogic' will find you out. These persons are not wrong in saying that poverty and the social problem have a moral cause, and that the force which shall solve the problem may be regarded as a moral force; but they are wrong in the place where they seek the moral cause. *It will be found ultimately to reside not in the corrupt nature of the poor, worker or idler, but in the moral cowardice and selfishness of the superior person, which prevent him from searching and learning the economic supports of his superiority, and which drive him to subtle theorising upon 'the condition of conditions' in order to avoid the discovery that his 'superiority' is conditioned by facts which at the same time condition the 'inferiority' of the very persons whom he hopes to assist.* The work of gradually placing 'property' upon a natural or rational basis, offering that equality of opportunity which shall rightly adjust effort to satisfaction, is a moral task of supreme importance.

Only upon the supposition that environment affords equal opportunities for all can we possess a test of personal fitness. Then only should we be justified, after due allowance for accidental causes, in attributing the evil plight of the poor or the unemployed to personal defects of character; then only would the scientific treatment consist wholly or chiefly, in the moral training of the individual. As matters actually stand, the philosophy which finds the only momentum for social reform in the moral energy of the individual members of the masses is just that smart sophistry which the secret self-interest of the comfortable classes has always been weaving in order to avoid impertinent and inconvenient searching into the foundations of social inequality. This, of course, involves no vulgar imputation of hypocrisy. Many of the men and women who hold these views are genuinely convinced of their accuracy. But they have permitted the subtle, unconscious bias of class interests and class points of view to limit their survey of the facts of the social question, to warp their intelligence in the interpretation of the facts, and to establish false theories of the operations of moral and economic forces, so as to yield an intellectual basis of obstruction to all proposals of practical reform in the structure of political and industrial institutions. Their fault is not that they are too hard-hearted, but that they are not sufficiently hard-headed: it is not a lack of feeling, but a lack of logic. They are simply not the scientific people that they claim to be, for they have not learned to think straight against the pressure of class interests and class prejudices (Hobson, 1896, pp. 710–27).

Hobson's criticisms of the COS highlight some of the central arguments of the New Liberalism. The challenge to individualist assumptions about the causes of, and solutions to, problems of poverty, and the insistence on connecting poverty with an analysis of the distribution of wealth and economic opportunity were recurrent themes of the New Liberalism. It was the combination of economic radicalism with a new view of the state's responsibilities to its citizens which were to be the lasting core of New Liberalism's contribution to the political development of welfare in Britain. Ironically, though, its main political impact was not to be made through the Liberal Party, which underwent a severe political decline after the First World War, but through the new political vehicle of the Labour Party.

New Liberalism's ideas of social reform through a more interventionist state, and of 'citizenship' involving a complex of rights and obligations between the individual and the state, found a natural affinity with the emerging ideology of Fabianism. As the Labour Party developed as a political force, it drew heavily on the ideologies of both Fabianism and New Liberalism in its thinking about welfare, social reform and state intervention. 'Citizenship' was adopted and adapted into one of the central themes of Labourist politics. The culmination of these political and ideological alliances was, as we shall see, to be found in the 1945 Labour government's adoption and implementation of the Beveridge Report.

3 · *Fabianism*

In retrospect, it is difficult not to see the early years of the twentieth century as the period which marks the start of Fabianism's apparently inexorable rise as the orthodox theology of welfarism. Yet at the time it was the New Liberals who carried the standard of collectivism in the crucial debates over social reform, while the Fabian Society looked like a slightly eccentric group of middle-class intellectuals dabbling uncertainly in the sea of socialism. In the years up to 1914 the society was riven by major splits over policy matters, as first H. G. Wells and later G. D. H. Cole, William Mellor and Clifford Allen challenged its leadership.

The initial strategy adopted by the society's leading figures, particularly Sidney and Beatrice Webb, was one of permeationism. They sought to influence key individuals within the state (such as leading politicians and state officials) by encouraging them to recognize the need to accept collectivist solutions to social and economic problems. They had little success in achieving these ends despite extensive personal contact, dinner parties and the preparation of detailed and carefully argued research reports. At the time the very commitment of the society to the fledgling Labour Representation Committee was seen as confirmation of its marginal importance. And within the labour movement, too, the Fabians were frequently distrusted because of their intellectual snobbery and cursory dismissal of labour organizations and their leaders (see, for example, Cole 1961, p. 94).

Yet it was in this period that many of the key features of what we have called Fabianism began to crystallize, both within the society itself and more widely within the politics of Labour. The Fabians came to symbolize those groups of radical intellectuals, sympathetic to Labour, who would be prepared, on the basis of research and technical expertise, to develop practical policies of social reform utilizing the existing structures of the state. And as the New Liberals faded into history the Fabians also began to take on their mantle as the true defenders of social welfare.

The Fabianism of the early Fabian Society was strictly an ideology of socialism – the end result of Fabian policies was to be a socialized economy based on the historically inevitable triumph of collectivism organized through the state. Much Fabian writing was intended to show the logical necessity of collectivist development and the illogicality of any other. And this emphasis, which achieved full dominance within the society at this time, despite the misgivings and active resistance of some members, continued to be a central one in the broader tradition of Fabian welfarism.

A second central characteristic following from these arguments was a fundamental commitment to 'gradualism' stemming from the conviction that Fabian collectivism was moving with the grain of history. A third was a great belief in the importance of professional expertise, usually channelled through the state. This would allow for welfare to be provided in an efficient rather than a wasteful way and, more important perhaps, would define welfare provision as a means of imposing order on an otherwise chaotic society. The professionals were to be the carriers of a new concept of public service which challenged the normal 'morality' of capitalism.

The strength of Fabianism as an ideology of welfare lay in its ability to reflect a much wider constituency than its initial base in a small group of socialist intellectuals might suggest. It offered a ready-made ideology for the new political representatives of labour on various bodies, from boards of guardians to school boards, claiming that all their separate and apparently unconnected decisions on individual cases were in fact part of the inexorable development of a new society within the body of the old. The local and national leaders of the growing Labour Party tended to define themselves in terms of the party's class (and trade union) base rather than any socialist political programme. In so far as they had one, it was rooted in a moral belief in socialism as a utopian project. Clearly such a belief was unlikely to provide much guidance in terms of day-to-day political practice. Fabianism helped to provide the bridge between the two in a way that the New Liberalism could not, even if many of its ideas continued to feed into the politics of labour, through Fabianism.

If the 'socialist' element of the Fabian package was important for its acceptance within Labour politics, it could also easily be detached by others who did not share socialist aims, even for the distant future. Much Fabian writing was based on detailed analysis of existing state institutions and careful proposals for practical reforms which made it easier for those institutions to achieve their stated ends. Even the Fabian Society's own pamphlets and reports did not always stress the socialist conclusion of their arguments, except in terms which emphasized that this was the direction being taken by society in any case. They stressed the importance of state provision of welfare services, within a framework of rational administration based on expert professional support and supervision by democratically elected representative bodies.

The Minority Report

It is in this period before the First World War that the first clear statements of the Fabian approach to welfare appear. The Webbs had already turned their attention to the trade unions, retail co-operatives, the London County Council and industrial democracy: now it was the turn of the Poor Law. Beatrice Webb was appointed a member of the Royal Commission on the Poor Law set up in 1905 by the Balfour government. Her inclusion on the commission was probably the greatest success of Fabian permeation and the result of her personal friendship with Balfour. With the help of her husband Sidney, she used her position mercilessly to harrass witnesses committed to the 1834 Poor Law system, and eventually to prepare a detailed report of her own which became the Report of the Minority on the Commission (it was also signed by Francis Chandler, George Lansbury and the Reverend Prebendary H. Russell Wakefield, later Bishop of Birmingham).

The Majority Report also called for an end to the 1834 system (above all the workhouse system), but it was the Minority Report which dominated the debate which followed publication in 1909. It was used as the basis for a political campaign (organized through the National Committee to Promote the Break-up of the Poor Law), which, although not then successful, helped to provide the model for reform in the future.

Some of the key factors in the Webbs' approach which still have a resonance today can be identified in the lengthy extracts from the Minority Report which follow, although, of course, the explicitly socialist strand is underplayed. The very tone of the report reflects the extent to which the authors saw themselves as part of a wider policy community within which, if arguments and evidence were persuasive enough, rational debate could take place and appropriate conclusions be drawn. It is assumed that there is a shared concern to deal with the problem of destitution and that a solution can be found through the application of systematic, rigorous and 'scientific' analysis. There is thus no suggestion that any of the problems identified might result from the perfectly rational decisions of some groups, which leave others in permanently disadvantaged positions.

The Minority Report stresses the importance of expert state professionals in identifying potential social problems and then *preventing* them from becoming reality. This approach encapsulates one of the features of the post-war welfare state which has come under increasingly heavy attack but which has historically been a central part of the Fabian projects. Professionals are expected to seek out individuals likely to have problems and, where possible, to cure those individuals so that they no longer also pull down the families of which they are a part. Officials, generally under the control of a specialist local authority, would be expected methodically to identify social, educational and medical problem cases and to intervene to protect or cure the individual involved before destitution occurred, thus saving and disciplining the family into the bargain. In this model the family with a male breadwinner is still the fundamental building block of society and the role of the state is to act in place of the parent, where the parent, for whatever reason, cannot cope. Prevention under the aegis of trained officers is the key to success.

The principle of prevention

Now the inherent vice of the vast expenditure at present incurred by our Poor Law Authorities is, to the economist, not its amount, nor its indiscriminateness, but the absence of this Principle of Prevention. Except with regard to the small minority of 'indoor' or 'boarded-out' children, and a small proportion of the sick, it cannot be said that the Poor Law Authorities make any attempt to prevent the occurrence of destitution. It is, indeed, not their business to do so. Unlike the Local Health Authorities, the Destitution Authorities cannot reach out to prevent the neglect of children which will, in time, produce 'unemployables'. The whole of the action and the whole of the expenditure of the existing Boards of Guardians, and equally that of the new Public Assistance Authorities proposed in the Majority Report, must, in law, be confined to the relief of a destitution which has already occurred.

If we wish to prevent the very occurrence of destitution, and effectively cure it when it occurs, we must look to its causes. Now, deferring for the moment any question of human fallibility, or the 'double dose of original sin', which most of us are apt to ascribe to those who succumb in the struggle, the investigations of the Royal Commission reveal three broad roads along one or other of which practically all paupers come to destitution, namely: (a) sickness and feeble-mindedness, howsoever caused; (b) neglected infancy and childhood, whosoever may be in fault; and (c) unemployment (including 'under-employment'), by whatsoever occasioned. If we could prevent sickness and feeble-mindedness, howsoever caused, or effectually treat it when it occurs; if we could ensure that no child, whatever its parentage, went without what we may call the National Minimum of nurture and training; and if we could provide that no able-bodied person was left to suffer from long-continued or chronic unemployment, we should prevent at least nine-tenths of the destitution that now costs the Poor Law Authorities of the United Kingdom nearly twenty millions per annum. The proposal of the Minority Report to break up the Poor Law, and to transfer its several services to the Local Education, Health, Lunacy, and Pension Authorities, and to a National Authority for able-bodied, is to hand over the task of treating curatively the several sections of the destitute to *Authorities charged with the prevention of the several causes of destitution* from which those sections are suffering. This means a systematic attempt to arrest each of the principal causes of eventual destitution at the very outset, in the most incipient stage of its attack, which is always an attack of an individual human being, not of the family as a whole. . . . Hence it is vital that the Local Health Authority should be empowered and required to search out and ensure proper treatment for the incipient stages of all diseases. It is vital that the Lunacy Authority should be empowered and required to search out and ensure proper care and control for all persons certifiable as mentally defective, long before the family to which they belong is reduced to destitution. It is vital that the Lunacy Authority should be empowered and required to search out and ensure, quite irrespective of the family's destitution, whatever Parliament may prescribe as the National Minimum of nurture and training for all children, the neglect of which will otherwise bring these children, when they grow up, themselves to a state of destitution. It is becoming no less clear that some Authority – the Minority Commissioners say a National Authority – must register and deal with the man who is unemployed, long before extended unemployment has demoralised him and reduced his family to destitution. It is important to put the issue quite clearly before the public. The systematic campaign for the prevention of the occurrence of destitution, that the Minority Commissioners propose that the community should undertake by grappling with its principal causes at the incipient stages, *when they are just beginning to affect one or other members of a family only*, long before the family as a whole has sunk into the morass of destitution, involves treating the individual member who is affected, in respect of the cause of his complaint, even before he is 'disabled' or in pecuniary distress. It means a systematic searching out of incipient cases, just as the Medical Officer of Health searches out infectious disease, or the School Attendance Officer searches out children who are not on the school roll, even before application is made. . . .

Prevention is not only better, but also much cheaper, than cure. What the Minority Report asserts – and the assertion cannot fairly be judged except by reading the elaborate survey of the facts and the whole careful argument, that it has now become possible, with the application of this Principle of Prevention by the various Public Authorities already at work, for destitution, as we now know it, to be abolished and extirpated from our midst, to the extent, at least, that plague and cholera and typhus and illiteracy and the labour of little children in cotton factories have already been abolished. If this confident assertion is only partially borne out by experience, it is clear that, far from involving any increase of aggregate cost to the community, the abolition of the Poor Law and of the Poor Law Authority will have been a most economical measure.

The 'moral factor' in the problem of destitution

There are those who see in this proposal to 'break up' the Poor Law . . . an ignoring of what they call the 'moral factor'. To speak of the prevention of destitution is to such critics, equivalent to implying that all destitution is due to causes over which the individual has no control – thus putting aside the contributory causes of idleness, extravagance, drunkenness, gambling, and all sorts of irregularity of life. But this is to misconceive the position taken up by the Minority Commissioners, and to fail in appreciation of their proposals. They do not deny – indeed, what observer could possibly deny or minimise? – the extent to which the destitution of whole families is caused or aggravated by personal defects and short-comings in one or other of their members, and most frequently in the husband and father upon whom the family maintenance normally depends.

The Minority Commissioners certainly do not ignore the fact that what has to be aimed at is not this or that improvement in material circumstances or physical comfort, but an improvement in personal character.

Two considerations may make the position clear. However large may be the part in producing destitution that we may choose to ascribe to the 'moral factor' – to defects or shortcomings in the character of the unfortunate victims themselves – the fact that the investigations of the Royal Commission indicate that at least nine-tenths of all the paupers arrive at pauperism *along one or other of three roads* – the Road of Neglected Childhood, the Road of Sickness and Feeble-mindedness, and the Road of Unemployment (including 'Under-employment'), must give us pause. If it can be said that it is to some defect of moral character or personal shortcoming that the sinking into destitution at the bottom of the road is, in a final analysis, more correctly to be ascribed – though on this point which among us is qualified to be a judge? – it is abundantly clear that the assumed defect or shortcoming manifests itself in, or at least is accompanied by, either child-neglect, sickness, feeble-mindedness, or unemployment. These are the roads by which the future pauper travels. Moreover, if these outward and visible signs of the inward and spiritual shortcomings are sometimes caused by these latter, it is at least equally true that the defects of character are aggravated and confirmed by their evil accompaniments.

It is by dealing with the individual through these manifestations or accompaniments of this inward defect, that we can most successfully bring to bear our curative and restorative influences (Webb and Webb, 1910, pp. 299–307).

Even at this stage clear differences can be drawn with other approaches discussed in this book. Despite the importance of Beatrice Webb as theorist and campaigner, unlike the feminists the Fabians paid little attention to the special position of women in the provision of welfare (except in a rather patronizing fashion), yet the role of women in sustaining families is implicit throughout the report and the extract above. And, despite the Fabians' position withinn a broad socialist tradition, this approach had little to do with the fundamental critiques of capitalism being launched by others. Indeed the Fabian approach was criticized by some, such as Morris and Quelch, for making it more difficult to challenge the poverty and inequality which was the inevitable product of capitalism.

The Webbs' arguments were principally directed against the laissez-faire ideology which still dominated at the time. And in that context their arguments are telling. They undermine the view that contemporary policies were cost effective and instead indict them for wastefulness. And they challenge the notion of morality which underlay the laissez-faire view of poverty. The moral factor is all very well, they suggest, but unless other factors are taken into account the possibility of moral choice or moral behaviour among the poor is negligible.

The position of Fabianism as part of a wider socialist tradition has already been noted, but it is also important to note its links to the British philosophical tradition of utilitarianism. It shares this heritage with many of the ideologists of laissez-faire, which helps to explain the strength of the argument between them as they fight over the souls of John Stuart Mill and Jeremy Bentham. Laissez-faire thinkers would normally expect to have a greater claim to the tradition since its conclusions are basically liberal. They suggest that state interference must inevitably run counter to the best interests of individuals in economic and social life. Yet even Mill, towards the end of his life, argued for some form of socialism. Utilitarianism left powerful critical weapons in the hands of the Fabians (as well as the New Liberals) since it allowed them mercilessly to flay existing institutions asking, like Bentham, whether they had a greater tendency to 'augment the happiness of the community' or to diminish it (Bentham, 1789, p. 33). If the answer was negative, new arrangements had to be made and if necessary the state had to be reconstructed on a more rational basis. This was the task the Fabians set themselves.

This helps to explain the focus on state institutions in the Webbs' arguments. The argument for the abolition of the Poor Law was predicated on the transfer of responsibilities to already existing local authorities (with specialist responsibilities for education, asylums, and health, for example) and the creation of a new national body responsible for the unemployed. The growth of these authorities was intended to remove an illogical area of government (the Poor Law Boards of Guardians) which existed to police spending on public dole and was, therefore, unable to prevent the develop-ment of social problems in the first place. The latter task, they argued, could best be performed by other authorities – that is, multi-purpose local authorities with specialist departments covering the areas referred to above. They were committed both to an expansion of municipal activity (see also, for example, Shaw, 1912) and the creation of a national authority to oversee local authorities and deal with national problems, such as unemployment.

As we have indicated earlier, the Webbs and other leading Fabians saw poverty as a structural feature of capitalism. Unem-ployment, in particular, was explained as a consequence of the anarchy of capitalist markets, to be dealt with through public works, rural labour colonies and labour exchanges. But both in this report and in other research – such as that summarized in the extract from Pember Reeves below (pp. 56–8) – the detailed analyses of Fabianism stressed the problems faced by individuals within families. Solutions, too, therefore tended to be developed at that level. The issue was how to rescue individuals and families from the constraints which they faced. A central element in the Fabian case was that the intervention of the state should also make it easier for individuals and households to take increased responsibility for their own actions. But the state would always be there to assist and advise as well as supervise. The state was often referred to as a guardian. This was particularly true of their attitude to the care of children. Here a key aim was to increase parental responsibility (implicitly and sometimes explicitly maternal responsibility, in particular). And, as the following extract indicates, if support did not do the trick, then coercion would be used.

State as guardian

The working-class woman is as devoted to her children as any other mother. But it is one of the dire results of the poverty of the poor, manifested in overwork and wages insufficient for family requirements, especially in the conditions of overcrowding and dirt imposed by residence in the slums of great cities, that the standard of cleanliness, of clothing and generally of the watchful care required for healthy childhood, almost inevitably declines. In the ignorance and listlessness and absence of standards, which characterise whole sections of slum-dwelling families, there was in the past, and but for the influence of the elementary school there would be again to-day the very minimum of fulfilment of parental responsibility. It is the watchful influence by inspection and visitation, advice and instruction, brought to bear on the mother of the children from infancy to school-leaving age that evokes the sense of responsibility, guides and assists its fulfilment, imposes continually the higher obligations of rising standards, and has, in fact, already resulted, as all evidence proves, in the working-class mothers of the present day devoting much more time and personal labour to cleansing, clothing and generally caring for their offspring than was given, in literally hundreds of thousands of cases, by the working-class mothers of the English industrial towns and the slum quarters of the Metropolis a century ago. . . .

The community cannot permanently continue to allow tens of thousands of its children to be . . . physically and mentally damaged, whether the immediate cause be poverty or cruelty, many of them inevitably graduating into crime and its accompanying dissoluteness and destitution – even if the necessary Framework of Prevention proves to be a more drastic application of the law requiring the removal of children from parents who show themselves incapable of giving to children what is understood by parental care . . . (Webb and Webb, 1910, pp. 613–14).

Clearly this has little in common with feminist approaches, but Fabians did succeed in exposing some of the difficulties faced by poor mothers in trying to reach the high 'moral' standards set by the charities and their visitors. In a report on conditions in South London, published by the Fabian Women's Group in 1913, the position was presented in a rather more sensitive way, stressing the need for support rather than control – even if in retrospect the possibility of an effective divorce between the two in welfare provision may seem a little naïve. As well as the call for a national Public Guardian – a typical Fabian demand – it hints too at some of the issues which feminists were beginning to raise, even if it studiously avoids suggesting that problems may arise from relations between men and women within the family, and continues to stress a paternalistic role for the state.

Support for parents

What is needed is the true fulfilment of human parenthood which is a natural unforced and unforceable relation of the spirit as well as of the flesh. Money, and the efficient, skilled service it procures, can be provided from any source. But that close, personal affection and watchfulness essential to children which no other guardianship can replace can only be given by parents. Yet even parents can be thwarted and embittered by crushing toil and slavish drudgery until their natural affection is destroyed. The nation needs the active and free co-operation of fathers and mothers in the upbringing of its children, and it must enable them to do their share of the work.

At the present moment the nation, as super-guardian of its children, acts, in the case of the children of the poor, in a manner so baffling, so harassing, so contradictory, that the only feelings it induces in the minds of parents whose lives are passed in incessant toil and incessant want are exasperation, fear, and resentment. . . .

Suppose the State, as co-guardian of the child, stripped off, when dealing with parents, the uniform of a police-constable with a warrant in his pocket. Suppose it approached them in some such spirit as that displayed by the Public Trustee when dealing with testators and executors. He offers advice, security, a free hand in carrying out any legal purpose, and he acts with or without other executors, as the case may require. Why should not the nation place all the information, all the security, all the help at its command at the service of its co-guardians, the fathers and mothers? Why should it not act frankly with them in the national interest, and help them to see that the needs of the child are supplied?

The final responsibility for the child's welfare, the paramount authority in securing it, belong to the State. Why not recognise the national responsibility by the definite appointment of a public Guardian who would enter upon the relation of co-guardian with the parents of every child at the registration of its birth?

Even now fundamental parental obligations are supposed to be the same in all classes, but the well-to-do can fulfil them after a fashion without the assistance of the State, though often with much insecurity and strain. Were there a department of Public Guardianship upon which every parent might rely for counsel and effective help, very many whose difficulty is not the actual housing and feeding of their children would be only too glad to take advantage of its advice. And even amongst the well-to-do, fathers and mothers die or lose their faculties, or are unfit, and the nation's children are the sufferers.

The appointment of a Public Guardian to cooperate with parents in all ranks of society is the only effective method, not only of preventing the national disgrace of 'waste children' but of doing away with the hardships, the distrusts, the fears and the resentments caused amongst the workers by the present harsh and ill-defined exercise of national Guardianship.

It is to the collective interest of a nation that its children should flourish. They are the future nation. To them the State will be entrusted. To them the work, the duty, the scheme of things will be handed on. Suppose children were recognised to be more important than wealth – suppose they were really put first – what machinery have we which already deals with their lives, their health, and their comfort? We have a national system of education which we propose to extend and elaborate, and to which we have recently attached medical inspection, and we have the time-honoured machinery of the home. The children of the poor pass their lives within the limits of these two institutions, and behind both stands the State, which entirely regulates one and is constantly modifying the other.

To equip the home for the vital responsibility committed to its care, the new administrative agency must have the power to go further than the offering of advice and information to its fellow-guardians, the parents. It must endow every child who needs it with a grant sufficient to secure it a minimum of health and comfort. Maintenance grants from the State are no new thing. Inadequate grants are now made to the parents of free scholars in secondary schools. What is wanted is the extension and development of the idea. Based on the need of the child and limited thereby, the grant would not become a weapon to keep down wages. Men and women whose children are secure are free to combine, to strike and take risks. Men and women who have the burden of a family on their shoulders are not free to do so.

A guarantee of the necessaries of life to every child could be fulfilled through various channels – some of them, as the feeding of schoolchildren, already in existence. This is no suggestion for class differentiation. The scholars on the foundation of many of the great public schools, such as Eton and Winchester, are fed, as well as housed and educated, from the funds of old endowments. National school feeding, endowed from national wealth, would be an enlargement and amalgamation of systems already in being. There should be no such thing as an underfed school child: an underfed child is a disgrace and a danger to the State.

The medical inspection of school-children, extended to children of all classes, should lead to a universal system of school clinics, where the children would not only be examined, but treated. Baby clinics should be within the reach of every mother, and should be centres where doctors and nurses, at intervals to be dictated by them, would weigh and examine every child born within their district. At this moment any weighing centre, school for mothers, or baby clinic which does exist is fighting the results of bad housing, insufficient food, and miserable clothing – evils which no medical treatment can cure. Such evils would be put an end to by the State grant.

Nor would an intolerable system of inspection be necessary in order to see that the co-trustees of the State – the parents – should faithfully perform their part of the great work they are undertaking. At every baby clinic the compulsory attendances of a well-dressed, well-nourished, well-cared-for child would be marked as satisfactory. No inspection needed. An unsatisfactory child would perhaps be obliged to attend more often, or its condition might require the help and guidance of a health visitor in the home. In this way a merely less efficient home would easily be distinguished from one which was impossible. The somewhat inefficient home might be helped, improved, and kept together, while if the home conditions were hopelessly bad, the public guardian would in the last resort exercise its power of making fresh provision for the ward of the nation in some better home.

As things are now, we have machinery by which the State in its capacity of co-guardian coerces the parents and urges on them duties which, unaided, they cannot perform. Parents are to feed, clothe, and house their children decently, or they can be dealt with by law. But when, as a matter of fact, it is publicly demonstrated that millions of parents cannot do this, and that the children are neither fed, clothed, or housed decently, the State, which is guardian-in-chief, finds it convenient to look the other way, shirking its own responsibility, but falling foul, in special instances of parents who have failed to comply with the law.

The law which is supposed to exist for the purpose of protecting children, seems to exist for the purpose of punishing parents, while doing nothing, or next to nothing, for the children. The idea still prevails among some care committees and school authorities that a 'bad' parent must not be 'encouraged' by feeding his children at school, and cases are known to exist where, in order to punish the parent, a hungry child is not fed. The one mistake an authority which considered the children first would not make would be that of punishing the child to spite the parent. Between Boards of Guardians, Care Committees, School Authorities, and Police, parents who are poor are baffled and puzzled and disheartened. It would be well for them to have a central authority whose first thought was the real welfare of the children of the State, and who blamed and punished parents only when it was clear that they deserved blame and punishment. That would be real, not false, 'relief' of the poor (Pember Reeves, 1979, pp. 223–4 and 226–31, first published 1913).

One of the problems with Fabian approaches is hinted at in this extract. The Public Guardian – the state – is expected to act for the 'real welfare' of children and the poor. In practice it has been far more difficult to disentangle policing and welfare activities, at least from the point of view of those on the receiving end of welfare. Welfare justifications for detailed intervention may be just as irksome as more legalistic ones.

Local struggles over welfare

The Fabian Society, or at any rate some of its members, developed an increasingly consistent position on welfare in this period, but it would be misleading to focus solely on this. Fabianism became a more widely accepted ideology of welfare through its developing relationship with the growing numbers of labour representatives on government institutions, such as boards of guardians, mainly at local level. These representatives were in practice wedded to a process of compromise and pressure within the state: whatever the May Day rhetoric of some of them, they were increasingly committed to a path of gradualism, proceeding piecemeal towards socialism. In a sense this was Fabianism in practice and helps to explain the extent to which the Fabians themselves were increasingly adopted as intellectual advisers within the Labour Party. They seemed to be articulating in a more coherent way the lessons of practical experience; providing a justification for the detailed committee work and battles over apparently minor concessions which were being undertaken locally. Hobhouse sums this up as follows 'the Fabian Society brought Socialism down from heaven and established a contact with practical politics and municipal government' (Hobhouse, 1964, p. 112, quoted in Sutton, 1985, p. 65).

The following extract from George Lansbury's autobiography reflects the attitudes of many labour representatives on boards of guardians. Lansbury was a leading municipal socialist of the period and probably better known for his brief imprisonment in 1921 as one of the Poplar guardians who refused to pay the London County Council rate precept, as a protest against the way in which poor boroughs like Poplar had to raise high local rates to maintain their poor, while wealthy outer boroughs had far lower costs. They wanted the burden to be shared more equally and, in fact, won major concessions on the issue. In the early 1930s, following MacDonald's defection to form a National government, Lansbury also became leader of the Labour Party.

In the period before 1914, however, he and his colleagues were searching for ways of turning socialism into a practical creed at local level. As elected guardians they did their best to reflect the interests of their communities, operating the Poor Law in a more sympathetic manner. But Lansbury highlights some of the limitations of this approach, which meant that the guardians could do little more than offer financial palliatives to the poor. Fabianism seemed to offer a way out of this trap, suggesting that a social policy could be developed at local level which might begin to solve more fundamental problems. As a member of the Royal Commission on the Poor Law, Lansbury signed the Minority Report.

Lansbury and Poplar

A great part of my life has been given to the work of a Guardian of the Poor and local Town and Borough Councillor. I was first elected in 1892, when I was thirty three years of age. . . . From the first moment I determined to fight for one policy only, and that was decent treatment for the poor outside the workhouse, and hang the rates! This sort of saying brings censure on me and on the movement: it cannot be helped. My view of life places money, property, and privilege on a much lower scale than human life. I am quite aware some people are bad and deceitful. I know this because I know myself. I know people drink, gamble, and are often lazy. I also know that taken in the mass the poor are as decent as any other class, and so when I stood as a Guardian I took as my policy that no widow or orphan, no sick, infirm, or aged person should lack proper provision of the needs of life, and able-bodied people should get work or maintenance. To-day everybody agrees with this policy. I also determined to humanize Poor Law administration: I never could see any difference between outdoor relief and a state pension, or between the pension of a widowed queen and outdoor relief for the wife or mother of a worker. The nonsense about the disgrace of the Poor Law I fought against till at least in London we killed it for good and all. . . .

My first visit to the workhouse was a memorable one. Going down the narrow lane, ringing the bell, waiting while an official with a not too pleasant face looked through a grating to see who was there, and hearing his unpleasant voice – of course, he did not know me – made it easy for me to understand why the poor dreaded and hated these places, and made me in a flash realize how all these prison or bastille sort of surroundings were organized for the purpose of making self-respecting, decent people endure any suffering rather than enter. It was not necessary to write up the words 'Abandon hope all ye who enter here.' Officials, receiving ward, hard forms, whitewashed walls, keys dangling at the waist of those who spoke to you, huge books for name, history, etc., searching and then being stripped and bathed in a communal tub, and the final crowning indignity of being dressed in clothes which had been worn by lots of other people, hideous to look at, illfitting and coarse – everything possible was done to inflict mental and moral degradation.

During my period as a Poor Law Guardian I was appointed a member of the Royal Commission on the Poor Laws and Relief of Distress. This was in December 1905. I received this appointment without any influence being used on my behalf, either by myself or anyone else. It came as a bolt from the blue when I received the letter from Mr. Walter Long asking if I would serve. . . .

This Commission published its report in 1909; there was a majority and a minority report. The minority report was the work of Beatrice and Sidney Webb, and was signed by myself, Mrs. Webb, Mr. Chandler, and Bishop Wakefield. I have never pretended to agree with every detail contained in the minority report, but broadly speaking all of us who signed agreed with its main principles. We were unanimous that the present system had outgrown whatever usefulness it had ever possessed, and that the overlapping between the Poor Law and Public Health services should be got rid of, and so we plumped straight for the abolition of Boards of Guardians, workhouses, and all such institutions. We desired that the work of Boards of Guardians should be undertaken by town, county, and urban authorities doing similar work – that is, children of school age should be under the control of education authorities, all sick persons suffering from any sickness should be cared for by the public health authority, able-bodied unemployed men and women by a national authority. There were, of course, many other details, but these were the broad principles, laying stress, of course, on the word 'prevention' rather than 'curative'.

The years spent on this Commission were amongst the best I have spent so far as local government is concerned, because almost every moment was one spent in gathering information and knowledge concerning administration. . . . But at the end, although I still remained a Guardian and local government worker, and in a way retained my faith in parliamentary action, I came from the Commission a more convinced Socialist than when I started. My conviction grows stronger as the years pass that everything we do on palliative lines leaves some evil behind it, and that there is no remedy for poverty and destitution except the total and complete abolition of the causes which produce these evils, and that in the main, though there are many individual exceptions, these evils are social and not personal; that drunkenness and other crimes of that sort are incidental, and not of themselves the primary causes which bring about destitution most people deplore . . . (Lansbury, 1928, pp. 129, 133, 135–6, 138–9, 142–3, 145, 146–7, 152–4, 169).

The tone of Lansbury's argument is different from that of the Webbs. He and the other Labour guardians were still less sympathetic to a focus on the individual as the source of problems, but in practice accepted it as necessary for practical intervention. Lansbury's concluding rhetoric would also have had little place in the more measured context of Fabian influenced reports, but it was the intersection of this local reformism (by the 1920s also strongly reflected in national Labour politics) and the arguments of the Fabians which was to provide a solid base for Fabianism in welfare in later years.

4 · *Feminism*

As our introduction to this section on the birth of the welfare state has indicated, feminism had become an increasingly important part of the political forum in the early twentieth century (Durham, 1985). Women's organizations had been active in the fields of health, education and employment since the mid 1800s (Strachey, 1978) and many feminists working independently or through the existing political party structures were intensely concerned with the question of welfare and the poverty of women and children.

Although feminism still had much to achieve (including the vote) it had become a visible element in the politics of the times. Yet the contribution of feminists and the existence of a feminist dimension to the debates on welfare have been largely overlooked in histories of welfare. Indeed, even some feminists at the time were dismissive of campaigns against government proposals to introduce welfare provisions which discriminated against women. For example Sylvia Pankhurst wrote,

During the truce to Suffragette militancy the National Insurance Act was passing through Parliament. The suffrage movement on the whole opposed it, if for no other reason than on the grounds that all social legislation required the women's point of view. . . . I could not content myself with destructive criticism of this far-reaching legislation, but worked in conjunction with Kier Hardie, preparing amendments to increase proposed benefits (Pankhurst, 1977, p. 353–4).

It is, therefore, important to relocate feminism in the gradual development of the welfare state and to identify themes which were central to feminist ideology at the time, but notably absent in the mainstream, dominant, competing ideologies of laissez-faire, liberalism and Fabianism.

The most important element of the feminist position in the early twentieth century was the assertion that the poverty and (ill) health of women required a different explanation to that put forward to explain the poverty of men or the family as a whole. The early feminists, in looking at the family, identified a structure of power and an unequal distribution of resources therein. Although child health and infant mortality had become matters of wide concern, the feminists identified the role of mothers as another vital factor for consideration. This period was marked by an extensive concern for children, whether deriving from eugenic or from socialist principles, which placed mothers in a key position regarding the care of children, and frequently condemned them for their failure. By contrast, the feminists focused on the general material position of women in the family, and looked for structural explanations for their as well as their children's poverty.

Feminists recognized that not all poverty and associated ill health and suffering derived solely from low wages or such factors as idleness or fecklessness. For women and children there was an intervening factor, namely marriage. This legal institution, they argued, subordinated the rights and needs of women to those of men, placing women in a particularly vulnerable economic position. At the same time marriage meant repeated pregnancies for women whose health and welfare could suffer dramatically as a consequence (Llewellyn Davies, 1978). Although the 'popular' view of marriage was that it was a form of protection for women, feminists argued that women needed protection inside marriage, both from poverty and from their husbands. This position is stated most clearly in the following extract from *The Mother and Social Reform* by Anna Martin (1913) who worked with working-class women in the docklands of East London.

The mother and social reform

Now, the rearing of the child crop is, confessedly, the most vital to the nation of all its industries, being that which alone gives to other industries a meaning or importance; but though its quality is occasioning grave concern, no attempt has been made to apply the above principles to those on whose care and devotion it necessarily depends. Theoretically, no one would deny that the mother is the main influence in the life of the child and its moral and physical development is closely conditioned by hers. Practically, there has been no grasp of the significance of the fact that it is precisely in that portion of the community where the dysgenic effects of alcoholism and of syphilis are rifest, and where the young are constantly thrown on the public for support, that the married women are still little removed from a state of domestic slavery, dependent solely on the goodwill of their husbands for any chance of a decent life. 'Begin with the child' was a popular cry; 'Begin with the mother' would have been a sounder principle.

The wealth of a country does not consist of its gold and silver, but of the vast complicated production and exchange of goods and services whereby the wants of the community are supplied. Unfortunately, the fact that these goods and services are usually measured against each other by means of money tends to an ignoring of goods and services not so appraised; but this does not alter their real nature. The woman's work in the home is cooking, washing, cleaning, nursing, managing and is every whit as essential to society as her husband's work in bricklaying, hawking, or driving a motor-bus, and often demands greater brain power. That she should be forced into accepting degrading terms of labour, injurious to a healthy, self-respecting life, is just as detrimental to the body politic as if men were the sufferers. That the wife is in the disadvantageous position of being tied to only one possible employer should have been the most powerful of reasons for safeguarding her interests, for protecting the weaker party to the bargain.

Inquiry, however, into the actual facts of the daily life of the humbler classes, as distinguished from legal fictions and conventional beliefs, reveals the truth that, as compared with the male worker, the wife suffers from two fundamental disabilities: firstly, the law does not enforce contract for her as against her employer–husband; secondly, it does not, save in the feeblest and most inefficient way, protect her from his personal violence.

Misled by the fact that in one small section of the community the husband bestows on the wife much greater economic advantage than he derives from her, Mr Harold Owen and other distinguished anti-suffragists attempt to justify the political subordination and other disabilities of women as a natural corollary of their economic dependence. But in nine families out of ten the husband is as fully dependent on his wife's work as she is on his. He may mend tin kettles for the public and with his earnings provide the raw material for a dish of tripe and onions, but unless she cooks the viands neither he nor his children will be fed. His wages may buy sheets and underclothing, but unless she keeps them washed the family will speedily come under the notice of the sanitary inspector.

From one point of view marriage is merely the most important of all civil contracts. Countless unions confessedly exist where the great natural forces of love of man for woman, and of woman for man, render any idea of a hard-and-fast bargain between the parties unthinkable; where the joy of each is found in the happiness of the other, and where both willingly sacrifice themselves for their children. Nor are such unions found only among the well-to-do. But the fact that marriage in most cases has an emotional and spiritual side seems an inadequate reason for permitting the relationship in a large number of others to sink below the every-day level of business honesty and fair play. The woman takes permanent service under her husband–employer, who in return, is supposed to bind himself to support her and the children she may bear, and this must be taken as meaning to support adequately. But, contrary to the general belief, the law affords her no effective redress for her employer's default (Martin, 1913, pp. 1063–5).

The feminists of the early twentieth century were therefore critical of the idea that marriage and the family were the only form of welfare that women needed. They argued that direct assistance had to be provided to women and mothers. This took the form of demands for more equal treatment under the 1911 National Insurance Act, demands for a cash maternity benefit payable to mothers under the same act, and demands for an 'endowment of motherhood' (family allowances). Yet the supporters of these varied campaigns differed significantly from one another. For example, Anna Martin thoroughly disagreed with the idea of an endowment of motherhood; Eleanor Rathbone, who proposed the endowment scheme, was not in favour of extending it to support all mothers.

In addition, she was opposed to equal pay, which was the corner-stone of the beliefs of the feminists pushing for more equal treatment under the Insurance Act. These differences are vital in as much as they reveal that the feminism of the period was not a unitary ideology. There were two main axes of disagreement. One axis was on a continuum from paternalism to independence, the other was on a continuum from collectivism to individualism.

Broadly speaking the paternalist stance attempted to do good to women, often for ulterior reasons. For example, the provision of an endowment of motherhood was proposed on the grounds that it would keep women at home and improve the 'child supply' for the nation. Those emphasizing independence, however, required that policies should be framed to give women freedom of choice as well as security. The continuum of collectivism to individualism highlighted rather different factors. The collectivist tendency in some feminist approaches demanded nurseries for child-care and ways of enabling women to join the labour market, trades unions etc. The individualist emphasis preferred measures to require individual men to provide more adequately for individual women inside the private sphere. Where particular feminists were located on these axes varied over time, but some of the following extracts clearly reveal these differences. The uniting factor among feminists, however, was their central concern with the poverty and welfare of women and children.

These differences between the feminists did not overshadow their main arguments for adequate provision for women under a new system of welfare. However they do make it extremely difficult to locate feminism on the traditional left/right political spectrum. In many ways this conventional way of identifying a political tendency was quite inadequate where feminist politics were concerned. The following passages provide examples of the debates within feminism. The first comes from *Votes For Women*, which was the paper of the Women's Social and Political Union (WSPU). In this article Frederick Pethick Lawrence (1911) points both to the failings of Lloyd George's National Insurance Bill, and to the need to give women the franchise.

Will the Insurance Bill be withdrawn?

[I wish] to direct attention to the new discrimination against [women] which will be set up if the Insurance Bill now before Parliament is allowed to become law. . . .

When the Insurance Bill was first introduced, I, in common with many others, hoped that it might really be the means of securing to men and women of the working classes release from the haunting spectre of destitution consequent upon sickness, which is today never wholly absent from their minds. We believed that the hiatuses in the Bill could be filled and that the differentiation in treatment between men and women could be obliterated. A closer study has, however, failed to justify this optimistic forecast. We have learned to our disappointment that the most serious defects are not accidental but inherent.

The fundamental principle of the Bill is not national insurance of the working class, but insurance of the wage-earner, and in consequence one half of the women of the country are omitted from its provisions. This applies not merely to benefit money paid during sickness but to medical attention, which will accordingly be withheld from a vast number of women. The result is to penalise the valuable work which women are doing in the home without wages, whether as wives or as daughters or sisters. Moreover, it is not only that they are excluded from benefit while so engaged, but for every year that they have given up their lives to the care of others they are penalised by having a lower benefit when they enter upon remunerative employment.

The woman who from the time she has left school has kept house for her father, or for her brother, or for some other relative, will find when she subsequently goes out to work that she cannot join the scheme at the same rate of contributions as her brother who began to earn wages directly he left school: unless she can pay down a lump sum of money she will have to be content till the end of her life to get for the same premium a reduced benefit, dependent on the number of years she has devoted to her family: if she marries and is subsequently left a widow all the years of her unmarried life devoted to her parent's home and all the years of her married life will be reckoned against her. The only exception to this rule is that of the woman who after devoting her unmarried life to wage earning employment marries and is subsequently left a widow, in which case she is allowed to re-enter at the normal premium and obtain the normal benefit; but even this case is not really a concession to women, for the whole burden of the arrangement falls on the women's side of the fund and is therefore chargeable upon the unmarried working women, who in consequence get a lower rate of benefit than working men (*Votes For Women*, 15 September 1911, p. 794).

The WSPU was not the only feminist organization to make these points. The Women's Cooperative Guild was also extremely active in its campaigning against the bill and was able to call on very wide grass roots support. On 2 June 1911, a letter from the Guild was published in *Votes For Women* outlining their objections to the bill. The significance of this lies in the fact that the Guild claimed to represent 27,000 working-class women. Hence the campaign against the bill was not a purely middle-class one.

Other feminist papers such as *The Vote* and *Common Cause*, also carried articles critical of the bill and suggestions for amendments. Most of the arguments which were raised focused on women's role as non wage-earning carers, on how this role excluded them from the provisions of the bill, and on how special provision was necessary. At the same time the WSPU pushed home points on the problem of discrimination and the need for equal treatment for women. These potentially conflicting lines of argument were, interestingly, not present at all in the arguments about the clause in the bill on maternity benefits. Here the focus was not just on the adequacy of the benefit level, but on the extremely patronizing assumptions behind the idea that benefit should be payable on behalf of mothers to pay for medical attendance at birth. This kind of paternalism was rife even in the Fabians' view of working-class family life. For example the following passage from the Webbs, previously quoted at greater length in Chapter 3, reveals how different to the feminists was their position on women and mothers.

In the ignorance and listlessness, and absence of standards, which characterise whole sections of slum-dwelling families, there was . . . the very minimum of fulfilment of parental responsibility. It is the watchful influence by inspection and visitation, advice and instruction, brought to bear on the mother . . . that evokes the sense of responsibility, guides and assists its fulfilment, imposes the higher obligations of rising standards . . . in the working class mother of the present day (Webb and Webb, 1910, p. 613).

It was this view of working-class mothers which particularly angered Anna Martin and fuelled her campaign against the bill, as well as her longer term work with slum dwelling mothers. The following extract from *Common Cause* reveals her dislike of paternalism.

The Maternity Benefit

In the extract quoted last week from Mr Lloyd George's Birmingham speech, he intimated that the reason he had determined that the maternity benefit should be spent for and not by the mother, was his desire 'to put an end to the disgraceful infantile mortality we have in this country'. By which remark the Chancellor showed he had not mastered the elements of the problem. He errs, indeed, in good company.

Lord Crowther last Spring, in an Anti-Suffrage speech, charged the working class women of England with being responsible for the high death rate among their babies. On April 11th Dr Addison, the member for Hoxton, on introducing a Bill into the House of Commons to secure the instruction of girls in infant hygiene, declared that 150,000 children under the age of five died every year in this country, and that in at least 50,000 cases death was due to parental ignorance. Nay, more. Sir George Newman, now Chief Medical Officer of the Board of Education, whose own book on 'Infant Mortality' ought to have taught him better, quotes on p. 262 with approval, the dictum of the Medical Officer of Health for Burnley that 'death in infancy is probably more due to ignorance and negligence than to any other cause'. All such statements seem to show that men do not possess and, apparently, cannot acquire the specialised knowledge necessary to interpret statistical tables dealing with the family. This is not surprising, of course. Women would probably make just as sorry an exhibition over – say – the shipping returns. The mischief is that men, in their genuine desire to improve social conditions, keep on trying to legislate about questions of which they have this inadequate comprehension. . . .

If a baby is to survive, Harley Street tells us, it must have plenty of air and space, abundant mother's milk or satisfactory substitute, regular hours for food and sleep, and exercise. All these the typical Hampstead baby has, none of these are available for the average Bermondsey one. It shares two or three small, dark, low rooms, perhaps up a court, with the rest of its family; its overdriven, under-nourished mother, knowing she cannot afford the expense of artificial feeding, suckles it to the last possible moment, but her milk often lacks all nourishing qualities, and to still the baby's hunger it has to be given bits from the family table. If the natural supply fails altogether, the baby is perforce fed on boiled bread and tinned milk. So far from being solely the child's nurse, the woman has to attend to the wants of the entire household, and the infant must take its sleep, food, and exercise as happens to be convenient to its father and other relations. The fact that the infantile death-rate in places like Bermondsey and Shoreditch (the two worst in London) differs so little from those of Hampstead and Lewisham (the two best) is, in truth, a magnificent tribute to the skill, devotion, and self-sacrifice of the average working-class mother. The trained nurse who presides over a local Babies' Institute exclaimed lately to the writer, 'Not with all my training and experience could I do half as well with their babies in their circumstances as they do!' And yet these women, who against such odds wage such a successful fight for their children's lives, are not considered fit by the Chancellor of the Exchequer to be trusted with the spending of their own maternity benefit! When will our legislators learn that the only way to improve the condition of the masses is to raise the status of the mother? They will not do this by treating her as if she were a child or an idiot. But Mr Lloyd George had probably other ideas in his mind. Do not drunken and bad husbands exist, and might not such conceivably appropriate the money to their own uses? The intemperate husband is no new phenomenon in English society, nor his luckless wife a new apparition in our police courts. English Law has left her to struggle on all these centuries as best she could, giving no right to release, no legal claim to any proportion of her husband's earnings, yet practically holding her responsible for the condition of the children. She has had nothing to aid her in her unequal contest but her own moral force, and the remnants of good left in her husband's character, and the public opinion of her street. Yet the worst drunkard knows that if he means to drink his wages he must visit the public house before he reaches home. Once the money gets into his wife's hands, he realizes he has little chance of seeing it again. Let the maternity benefit be paid to the wife, and she will not fail to hold it in nine hundred and ninety-nine cases out of a thousand. At least this is the opinion of working-class women themselves, and no one is more likely to know (*Common Cause*, 6 July 1911, 11, p. 224).

The campaign to make maternity benefits payable in cash to women was only partly successful. Women would only receive the benefit if they were insured themselves, otherwise their insured husbands would receive it. The National Insurance Act did, however, include a clause making it an imprisonable offence for a husband to fail to provide for his wife's confinement. The maternity benefit was set at thirty shillings and was to be paid in cash rather than in services. However, under certain circumstances, the cost of medical treatment could be deducted from the benefit. In this respect the act marked an important, if small, shift in welfare policy away from oppressive benevolence, but the policy of paying maternity benefit (maternity grant in today's terms) to all women rather than their insured husbands took much longer to achieve.

The campaign for the endowment of motherhood was a parallel attempt to provide benefits for women, payable to women. In 1917 Eleanor Rathbone, with Mary Stocks and A. Maude Royden, established the Family Endowment Society. The aim of this society was to create benefits payable to mothers as a recognition of their vital work in raising children, and also as a means to prevent child and maternal poverty. The scheme was based on a recognition of the total inadequacy of the 'family wage' which was paid to all men regardless of whether they had any children, and which did not increase according to family size. Moreover, its proponents were able to rely on evidence arising from the success of Separation Allowances during the First World War which showed that men's wages did not prevent family poverty. These allowances were paid to wives during the war while their husbands were posted abroad. While in receipt of these allowances – as opposed to the usual housekeeping money from their husbands – child health in poor families improved considerably. Hence Eleanor Rathbone and her colleagues were able to argue, on the basis of child health, that these endowment of motherhood allowances should continue to be paid in peacetime. The following passages from A. Maude Royden's pamphlet entitled *National Endowment of Motherhood*, outline some of the main points of the scheme.

National Endowment of Motherhood

What exactly does [the Endowment of Motherhood] mean? It means that the state shall make a grant to every mother of children, plus an allowance for each child up to the age when it goes to school. . . .

In such a scheme there is no taint of pauperism or philanthropy. It is a recognition of the inestimable services rendered to the state by the mother, and so long ignored. It should therefore be given not to 'necessitous' mothers only, as though it were a kind of charity, but to all. . . .

Such women [the working classes], when they become mothers, must toil day and night, and yet their work is never done. . . . She may be an ideal mother, leaving no duty undone, but if her husband loses work she is left without resources. . . . If he is a good husband he gives her all he can spare; but then where is she to look for extra provision for extra children? If he is a bad husband he may give her very little. She has no remedy except, in cases of actual starvation, the Poor Law. What worker, doing her duty to the utmost of her ability, do we threaten first with starvation and afterwards with pauperism? No-one is so treated except those about whom there is the most sentimental talk, the mothers.

Let us admit that the desire to have a little money of one's own, well earned, is not a wicked, but a perfectly legitimate and just one. Let us admit that, if mothers were to be endowed by the state, the money they received would be earned and not lightly earned. In honesty, we must admit the economic value of the mother's work, for if she does not do it someone else must be paid to take her place. . . .

Finally the endowment of motherhood would help to eliminate from the vexed question of wages the eternal dilemma of the under-payment of women. At present this is continually justified on the ground that men have, or will have, families to support, while women have not . . . the different rates paid to men and women are, without doubt, one of the sorest of sore points in the labour market, and, so far as it is created by a different estimate of responsibility of men and women as citizens, the endowment of motherhood would go far to remove it. For the home would become a real partnership. . . .

In another way endowment of motherhood would contribute, not, as some fear, to lower, but to keep up the rate of wages in the industrial world, for it would withdraw from the labour market a very large number of married women who are now compelled to seek paid work outside the home. . . . The endowment of motherhood would withdraw many thousands of such women from the labour market altogether. And in their homes there would be an element of stability which would be of enormous economic value. At present, when wages are in dispute, the sharpest weapon used against the workman is the dread of physical privation – even of starvation – for his wife and children. . . . If therefore the wife and children of the worker are at least secure from actual starvation, the industrial battles of the future will be fought on something like more equal terms than in the past.

The endowment of motherhood seems therefore to have all the qualities of a great constructive reform (A. Maude Royden, 1918, extracts from pp. 4–15).

It was these final points on equal pay and removing married women from the labour market which drew dissent from other feminists. Liddington and Norris (1984) point out that the idea of being paid to stay at home and look after children did not go down well with married women in the cotton towns of Lancashire. In fact the feminist movement was severely strained, if not split, by Rathbone's proposals. Ada Nield Chew, who was an organizer of the National Union of Women's Suffrage Societies (NUWSS), demanded that all enlightened women fight against the proposals. Her preference was for community nurseries to enable more mothers to go out to work, not fewer. In other words some feminists preferred a collective rather than an individualist solution to women's poverty.

There were other criticisms too, based on quite different premises. Anna Martin took the view that the endowment of motherhood would bring with it greater surveillance and inspection of working-class life. She also felt it would undermine men's duty to support their wives and children. This was a duty she wanted law and social policy to enforce, not relax. The following passage expresses her concern.

The father or the state?

All human problems are at bottom ethical, and all legislation must finally be judged by its tendency to produce healthy, industrious, and high-minded citizens, or their contraries. It is therefore on this aspect of State Maintenance for Children that the writer desires to dwell. . . .

The fact that these women hesitate to grasp the greatest bribe ever held out to any section of the electorate, is so remarkable that it may well repay examination.

Their profound conviction is that the removal from the father of pecuniary responsibility for his children would inevitably demoralise him: and they believe that nothing which degrades men, in the long-run benefits their wives and children.

Within the privacy of their homes, furthermore, women speak very plainly on this point. The relief of the father of all pecuniary liability for his offspring would, they declare, tend to destroy whatever continence at present exists within the marriage relation. They insist that the physical demands of men on their wives would, in thousands of cases, be remorselessly increased, and that families of ten or twelve children would become common.

Under a system of child endowment, all forms of self-control would be felt to be unnecessary. Even quite decent men would be conscious of no wrong-doing.

A worse form of evil would, moreover, easily arise. Professor Karl Pearson has recently pointed out that were the endowment extended to illegitimate children, a new profession for a low class of woman would spring up – as indeed, we are told happened under the old Poor Law. A more disastrous result would be the rise of a low class of men whose sole work would be the begetting of legitimate children, each of whom would bring a trickle of hard cash into the home. One contemplates with dismay the provision of such a temptation to sloth, self-indulgence, and sensuality.

True, many optimistic investigators into social conditions see little force in the above forecasts. They argue that, under a system of adequate child endowment, large families would no longer mean squads of ill-nourished and diseased boys and girls, but would be sources of national wealth and strength. Supposing this turned out to be true, it would not save the mothers from the moral and physical wreckage consequent on over-fertility, and, unfortunately, it is too late in the day to deny that they are ends in themselves, just as much as are their husbands.

It is clear that the question of the endowment of children is intimately bound up with another question. How would the system affect the general production of the country? Would not most men work less? Only by the remorseless use of the whip of hunger has animate nature been driven along its upward path, and to most human beings effort is painful. Only a small minority work for love of work, or because they desire to find self expression (Martin, 1922, pp. 308–14).

Martin's anxieties about the effects of the benefit seem to coincide with the laissez-faire assumption that state intervention leads to various forms of social evil. Yet there is clearly a conflict in her work between the wish to protect women and her suspicion about the interventionist state. She continuously emphasized the protection that women needed from their husbands, from sexual exploitation in marriage and from the tyranny of repeated childbirth. Like many feminists at this time she identified men as extremely 'base' creatures requiring the threat of punishment to humanize them. Although she did touch upon the issue of illegitimacy and immoral women, her most sustained criticisms were of men. Hence her criticisms of the endowment scheme were based on her concrete experience of the way in which women were exploited inside marriage. She assessed the endowment to be a means of increasing men's power in the family to the detriment of women.

Anna Martin was not Eleanor Rathbone's only critic. In many circles her proposals were regarded as a socialist ploy to undermine the family; yet at the same time they were condemned by the trades unions and Labour Party as a means to reduce men's wages and as an unwarranted attack on the 'family wage'. Rathbone and the Endowment Society intended neither of these things. Rather they argued that the proposal would strengthen the family by making wives equal partners – and at the same time keeping them out of paid employment to be home makers. In fact Rathbone's commitment to this model of married family life brought her, although not the society, to recommend that the endowment should only be paid to married mothers. In *A Proposal for the National Endowment of Motherhood* (1918) Rathbone puts the following case.

A Proposal for the National Endowment of Motherhood

The case of the ordinary 'chance child' is very different. Undoubtedly if we had merely to consider the interests of already existing children and their mothers, it would be better to include them. But in framing a permanent national scheme, what we have to consider is how to secure the best sort of 'child supply', since it is upon the quality of its citizens – their physical, mental and moral quality – that the well-being of the community must in the long run mainly depend. . . .

Seeing then that the assumption on which the whole scheme is based is that the mother is rendering a service of importance to the state and that the state should secure to her the minimum of material well-being necessary for the proper performance of her task, is it not fundamentally inconsistent with this assumption to admit to the benefits of this scheme those mothers who refuse their part in the implied contract by securing to their children the other minimum conditions of well-being represented by a stable home and an acknowledged father? Into no other branch of service, whether to the community or to the individual, is the servant allowed to thrust himself without complying with the stipulated conditions of enrollment, and then to claim the same recompense as the properly enrolled (Rathbone, 1918, pp. 56–8).

Rathbone's proposals to separate out women according to a moral evaluation did not win support among her colleagues and the issue was dropped. It is none the less important to recognize that moral issues were a vital element of the arguments put forward by many feminists in the first decades of the twentieth century. Much of this moral ideology was of a conservative nature and would probably now be regarded as anti-feminist. However it should not detract from the importance of the economic analysis of poverty at the root of the wide-ranging strategies espoused by different feminists.

This broad analysis identified the special position of women in relation to poverty as deriving from women's role in marriage and in the family. For some feminists this led to proposals for policies which would lessen the effects of women's financial dependence or subordination in the family. Rathbone wished to replace this personal dependence with a dependence on state benefits while securing women's place inside the family. Others, more closely associated with the labour movement, preferred an independence achieved through contact with the labour market and adequate wages. Others, like Anna Martin, attempted to improve the terms and conditions of the existing form of dependency by making men more responsible and giving mothers access to more resources inside marriage. Yet all argued for some form of increased independence for women. Martin wanted independence from state 'paternalism', while Rathbone saw state 'intervention' as the only means of protecting women in their special position as mothers and child-rearers. Neither saw women's entry into the labour market as a primary solution to women's poverty in the family however. It was probably only the feminists more closely aligned with the labour movement who adopted this position.

5 · *Socialism*

The relationship between socialist ideas and debates around welfare has always been an equivocal and ambiguous one. Socialism is a political approach based on a critique of capitalist society which sees many of the social problems supposedly tackled by the welfare state as caused by the fundamental structures of that society. As a result its supporters tend to view the welfare state with a high degree of scepticism. Welfare reforms are welcomed for implicitly challenging the economic priorities of capitalism and for improving the current position of the poor. But the extent to which they can achieve either of these aims is consistently questioned. The socialists fear that the reforms may be used to defuse threats of more fundamental change by offering minor concessions to the poor. Worse, they fear that such reforms may be turned around to act as new sources of oppression and state control over the working class.

In socialist writing on welfare and social policy there is a constant tension between a fundamental critique of capitalism and the development of more immediate policies which can both bring gains today and point towards a socialist future. The attempt to reconcile this tension is central to debates within the socialist tradition and often links them back to the Fabian tradition.

The critique of capitalism

The tension was particularly apparent in the early years of the century when there was sharp debate between and within socialist organizations – such as the Social Democratic Federation (SDF) – about the value of electoral politics and the role of socialists within the Labour Representation Committee and later the Labour Party (see for example, Kendall, 1969, chapters 1–4). However, for the largest party whose members espoused a socialist programme, the Independent Labour Party (ILP), some of these issues had already been settled. It was committed to working through the existing democratic structures of the state, although the different wings of the party viewed the possibilities quite differently. Others, later in the Socialist Labour Party, rejected electoral politics completely, believing instead in a focus on industrial politics, leading ultimately to a revolutionary general strike.

The Fabians set out their own attempts at political and social change in deliberate contrast to both the revolutionary (Marxist) socialists of the Social Democratic Federation and its factions and what they saw as the more woolly minded utopians of the Independent Labour Party. They believed that practical proposals would lead inexorably, if slowly, to socialism and that it was necessary to be systematic in approaching this task without being diverted by the sentimentality to which ILP leaders were sometimes prone.

William Morris, however, in the extract printed below (ironically taken from a Fabian Tract), takes the Fabian approach to task suggesting that, however laudable some might be, their policies would merely support a society based on inequality, instead of challenging it. The symbols of socialism, he suggests, are being mistaken for its full content.

Communism

While I think that the hope of the new-birth of society is certainly growing, and that speedily, I must confess myself puzzled about the means towards that end which are mostly looked after now; and I am doubtful if some of the measures which are pressed, mostly, I think, with all honesty of purpose, and often with much ability, would, if gained, bring us any further on the direct road to a really new-born society, the only society which can be a new birth, a society of practical equality. Not to make any mystery about it, I mean that the great mass of what most non-Socialists at least consider at present to be Socialism, seems to me nothing more than a *machinery* of Socialism. . . . Who can quarrel with the attempts to relieve the sordidness of civilized town life by the public acquirement of parks and other open spaces, planting of trees, establishment of free libraries, and the like? . . . More time might be insisted on for the education of children; and so on, and so on. In all this I freely admit a great gain, and am glad to see schemes tried which would lead to it. But great as the gain would be, the ultimate good of it, the amount of progressive force that might be in such things would, I think, depend on *how* such reforms were done; in what spirit; or rather what else was being done, while these were going on, which would make people long for equality of condition; which would give them faith in the possibility and workableness of Socialism. . . . If the sum of them should become vast and deep reaching enough to give to the useful or working classes intelligence enough to conceive of a life of equality and cooperation; courage enough to accept it and to bring the necessary skill to bear on working it; and power enough to force its acceptance on the stupid and the interested, the war of classes would speedily end in the victory of the useful class, which would then become the new Society of Equality. . . . Here again come in those doubts and the puzzlement I began by talking about. . . . Whether the Society of Inequality might not accept the quasi-Socialist machinery above mentioned, and work it for the purpose of upholding that society in a somewhat shorn condition, maybe, but a safe one. That seems to me possible, and means the other side of the view: instead of the useless classes being swept away by the useful, the useless classes gaining some of the usefulness of the workers, and *so* safeguarding their privilege. The workers better treated, better organized, helping to govern themselves, but with no more pretence to equality with the rich, nor any more hope for it than they have now. But if this be possible, it will only be so on the grounds that the working people have ceased to desire real Socialism and are contented with some outward show of it joined to an increase in prosperity enough to satisfy the cravings of men who do not know what the pleasures of life might be . . . (William Morris, 1893, pp. 154–5).

Practical debates

The uneasy balance between propaganda and a commitment to political administration within capitalism came out clearly in the consideration of particular aspects of social policy. The Social Democratic Federation (then Britain's largest Marxist organization and *not* a distant precursor of today's Social Democratic Party)* presented evidence to the Royal Commission on the Poor Law which revealed just such tensions (part reprinted in the first extract below). On the one hand, their critique is forceful, blaming poverty and destitution on the operation of capitalism, in particular its use of machinery to raise productivity and destroy craft skills. But on the other, they appear to be presenting a set of practical proposals in much the same way as the Fabians. The principal difference, and it is an important one, is that the problems and the proposals which they present are explained solely in terms of the structures of capitalist society. They reject the idea of expert professionals to advise, supervise and control even if in paragraph 18 they stress the need for 'kind-hearted attendants'.

Poverty as a class issue

13. Before coming to our proposals of what should be done on the abolition of the workhouses, we would impress on the members of the Commission the fact that a great deal of poverty arises from causes over which the workers as a class have no control whatever. It is no loose statement to say that over the whole field of industry such changes have taken place since 1834 as practically to revolutionise the entire system of production. The universal introduction of machinery has been a very great factor in throwing the worker out of employment, and thereby rendering him an applicant for Poor Law relief. Even where machinery has been long in use, constant improvements render a less number of human workers necessary. A great deal of machinery is automatic, and, once set going, needs scarcely any looking after. This tendency is rendering the craftsman in many industries a thing of the past; unskilled labourers – mere tenders of machinery – replace the skilled workers. This being the case, it is grim

* At the turn of the century 'social-democratic' was largely synonymous with 'socialist' and perhaps even 'Marxist'.

satire to see apprenticeship and the learning of a trade advocated as a step towards the solution of the unemployed question by those who should and probably do know better. The 'drive' of modern industry, that is, the high pressure at work as now carried on, also ages men more quickly, and, once their early manhood is gone, employers are not anxious to employ them. It is quite clear that this makes it harder for men and women to provide for their old age.

14. The sole object of all employers of labour, be they private individuals, or companies, or corporations of any kind, is of course to make profit. This constant casting aside of the workers, when they cease to be human profitmaking machines of the highest efficiency, is a fruitful source of pauperism. The unemployed worker parts bit by bit with his home, becomes 'unemployable' and inevitably drifts into the workhouse at last. . . .

16. We may divide those coming under the Poor Law broadly into three classes: 1st the children; 2nd, able-bodied men and women capable of earning their living by labour; 3rd, the aged, sick and infirm generally. With regard to the first and third, people of all descriptions are agreed that adequate and proper provision should be made, yet the practice has not followed this humane theory.

17. Dealing first with the children, social-democrats are of this opinion that a far higher standard should be aimed at in the rearing of the children than now obtains. Schools should be built in the pure air of the country districts, the school not being one large barrack-like building, but consisting of a number of residences, each accommodating say thirty children, and each with a house-mother in charge. Meals could be taken either in the dining-room of each house, or a larger number could be grouped together. Swimming, physical exercises, music, etc., should form part of the education, and each boy and girl should be trained to some calling. Their subsequent career we will touch upon presently. The buildings should be of tasteful design and of the best material, and the food, education, and, indeed, everything in connection with the life of the children should be of the best. A sufficient amount of land should be taken in every case to provide plenty of space for playing fields and garden cultivation. The object must be to rear the youth of both sexes in the best possible way in order to produce the best possible results.

18. The aged should receive an adequate sum to live upon if they reside in their own homes or with relatives, the money being regarded as an honourable pension, and not as pauper relief. Those not able or willing so to live are to be provided for in houses situated in rural districts, near enough to towns for the old people to feel that they are still in the living world, yet sufficiently far from the towns to avoid the evils of town life. Each home should accommodate a certain number of the aged, and be under the care of kind-hearted attendants. The sick should be attended at their own homes, or in excellently appointed infirmaries, and as quickly as possible sent to convalescent homes provided by the nation, the object being to restore them to robust health in the quickest and surest way. Special homes for all other infirm (epileptics, mentally deficient, deaf and dumb), should be provided nationally, and the treatment should be of a curative character.

19. The 'able-bodied' are the thorn in the side of the middle-class Poor

Law administrator. Yet we are convinced that inability to find employment is at the bottom of the trouble. If employment at proper remuneration were provided for all able and willing to work, the problem of the 'loafer' and the 'casual' would be solved, and those refusing to work, yet endeavouring to impose on others, could be dealt with. Firstly, there is scope for a large amount of employment in undertakings of national importance, such as afforestation, national main roads, reclamation of foreshores. Secondly, land could be taken over by the nation, and the men could most usefully be trained to agriculture, and to become tenants of the nation, and instead of being herded together should be paid a wage, and enabled to live with their wives and families within easy access of their work until actually becoming tenants.

20.   It will thus be seen that the abolition of the workhouses could easily be brought about, and with the abolition the many evils inevitably connected with them would disappear. Other wasteful and ridiculous phases of Poor Law maladministration, such as settlement and disfranchisement, would be relegated to the limbo of the past.

21.   In conclusion, as social-democrats, we want to make it perfectly clear that the problem of the Poor Law is the problem of poverty, and that poverty will be the portion of large numbers of the working class whilst the land and the wealth of the country are privately owned and industry is carried on for profit. We assert that only when the land is decreed the common property of the nation, when the wealth created by the people shall belong to the people, and when industry is organised and controlled by the people in their collective capacity, will poverty be banished and the Poor Law or its equivalent be unnecessary . . . (Evidence of the *Social Democratic Federation*, Royal Commission, 1909, paras 13–14 and 16–21).

Social and local democratic control

The programme outlined by the SDF to the Royal Commission was rather brief. Little detailed consideration was given to the different elements but the basic lines are clear enough. Some SDF members were, however, at this stage also elected members of boards of guardians dealing with the day-to-day problems of administering the Poor Law and the federation's response to the Minority Report reflected this. They explicitly attacked the Fabians' penchant for new specialist professionals and the argument for a national officer responsible for the unemployed. Local (working-class) democracy should be defended, they argued, so that pressure could be placed on those allocating funds to the destitute. They were sceptical of notions which implied that it was possible to find some objective measure of destitution which would ensure that funds were allocated to those facing special problems. Instead they argued that better provision should be made available to all. They make no reference to professional intervention at the individual level, and would, indeed, have opposed it as an unnecessary increase in public bureaucracy and state control over the working class. If capitalism could not provide the minimum conditions for a reasonable life, free from poverty – and they doubted whether it could – then it should be replaced by a more far-reaching socialism. They refused to accept that poverty, which they saw as a social disease, could ever be explained in individual terms or solved by action which was concentrated on 'preventing' individuals from developing into social problems.

The extract below comes from the minutes of a debate between George Lansbury and Harry Quelch (representing the SDF) over the issues raised in the Minority Report.

Quelch versus Lansbury

H. Quelch, after expressing the very high esteem in which Lansbury was held by himself and the SDF generally, regretted that Lansbury's name should have been appended to the Minority Report. He could quite understand that Lansbury, after his experiences on the Poplar Guardians with the ever-rising tide of poverty all around him, was heartily sick and tired of the whole business, and wanted to sweep it all away. But they did not sweep the thing away by merely changing names. There was scarcely a word that Lansbury had said in denunciation of the administration of the Poor Law with which he did not agree. But what did the Minority of the Commission propose? To abolish the directly-elected Guardians, and constitute in its place an independent bureaucratic authority; to abolish the poor rate, and have instead a parish rate; to abolish outdoor relief, but have 'home aliment'. They had changed the names but had not touched destitution. They could not touch destitution until they were prepared to deal with the root causes of poverty. Destitution was not a thing apart, but only a degree of poverty, which was very difficult sometimes to define. Some of the Minority proposals put forward were good, and such as Social-Democrats could support, but they had nothing to do with the fundamental changes proposed. The main proposals were anti-democratic, anti-Socialist, superficial and fallacious. They were anti-democratic because they proposed to abolish the Boards of Guardians, and every good thing that Lansbury had suggested could be carried out without abolishing them. The Guardians were the most democratically-elected body in the kingdom, and if they had not been so good as they should have been, that was the fault of the people, and their business was to educate the people to elect proper Guardians. But their administration had improved, and could improve still further. It was proposed to hand over the duties of the Guardians to the committees of the various borough councils and county councils.

What they ought to do was not to abolish the Guardians, but to abolish the pauper status. This sentiment of poor people against having recourse to the Poor Law must be broken down. He had tried to get the unemployed all to go into the workhouses, so as to force the hand of the authorities. He remembered in his young days when they had to clem and hunger day after day, week after week, because his parents would rather starve than have recourse to the Poor Law. Why did the poor resent the Poor Law?

Because the bourgeois class had always so administered the law as to make it hateful and deterrent, so that people would rather die than apply for its relief. That spirit must be broken down. He did not mind the children all being under one education authority, but let it be a good education authority elected by the people for that purpose. But under the Health Authority, the mentally defective under the Asylums Committee, the aged under the Pensions Committee, they would still need a destitution authority to deal with destitution, and to see that every person who was entitled to assistance had it. The Minority admitted that, but they wanted 'a god out of the machine' – a Registrar of Public Assistance was to be a permanent, irremovable official; not subject to, but above, all the authorities to whose care the destitute were to be committed. His duties were thus defined:

'(i) Keeping a Public Register of all cases in receipt of public assistance; (ii) Assessing and recovering, according to the law of the land' – it was something to know he was not to be above the law – 'and the evidence as to sufficiency of ability to pay whatever charges Parliament may decide to make for particular kinds of relief or treatment; and (iii) Sanctioning the grants of Home Aliment proposed by the committees concerned with the treatment of the case.'

Thus, in the last resort, it was the irresponsible official and not the local authority who would decide whether relief should or should not be granted. Yet how often, as Lansbury knew, did the relief committee of the Guardians have to override the relieving officer, and give relief against his advice!

The Minority proceeded on the assumption that destitution was an individual and not a social disease. They were merely proposing to apply curative treatment to individuals – to sort them out cheap and cure these individuals of destitution! They were not going to abolish or prevent destitution by any of these proposals. It was the bourgeoisie, the capitalist class, who were responsible for the idea of the stigma of pauperism. Destroy that idea; that was the one thing necessary to do. Whatever the form of public assistance, it was still public assistance. The great mass of the people to-day were in need of public assistance, and if the Registrar of Public Assistance were going to deal with them all he had his work cut out. By these proposals they were not abolishing Bumble, but were putting him in a higher position. It was no part of the business of the Social-Democracy to create a central authority removed from the control of the people in the locality instead of an elected body bound to give an account of its stewardship periodically. . . .

Parliamentary control over local matters and details was not altogether satisfactory, and could not be more democratic than a local body. He objected to the idea that Socialism meant more public officials; it did not mean a universal bureaucracy. Tramway drivers and conductors were not public officers in the useless bureaucratic sense. They must have local democratic control of the relief of destitution by a body directly elected by and responsible to the electors . . . (Anon, 1910, pp. 4–7, 8, 9–12).

At the turn of the century, the socialists were already airing questions which were to become of increasing relevance as the welfare state became fully established. At a fundamental level they were suggesting that most welfare reforms were bolstering up the system they were supposed to be altering, and that the system would continue to generate inequality and poverty. There was a danger that the reforms would undermine the possibility of resistance but achieve little more. More subtly, it was implied that the reforms themselves might be turned against the poor instead of helping them. In terms of positive policies, an attempt was made to point towards a wider system of support which would neither stigmatize nor discipline the recipients of assistance. And, although the Fabians were also enthusiastic proponents of their own form of municipal socialism, the socialists were alone in emphasizing the importance of local democratic control as a means of exerting working-class pressure on the nature of provision.

One gaping hole in the socialist policies being developed at this time should also be clear, however. Despite the particular impact welfare policies (and the lack of them) could be expected to have on women there is little reference to their position. They are assumed to be subordinate to men in or out of employment and this is not challenged in any of the arguments. A solution to the problems of male unemployment is also assumed to solve the problems of women and, more explicitly, children. The socialists, for all the sharpness of their criticism of laissez-faire and Fabian approaches, remained vulnerable to a feminist critique, although they paid little attention to it at the time.

Part Two

The Beveridge 'Revolution'
(1942–8)

Introduction to Part Two

What kind of Britain do we want at home? . . . New Britain should be free, as free as is humanly possible, of the five giant evils, of Want, of Disease, of Ignorance, of Squalor and of Idleness (Beveridge, 1943, p. 81).

Neither the Minority nor the Majority Reports of the Royal Commission on the Poor Law had much immediate effect on its operation. Its foundations were far more fundamentally undermined by the implications of mass unemployment in the interwar period. National insurance soon proved totally inadequate in meeting the needs of the long-term unemployed. And the old Poor Law rules on benefit for the able-bodied poor (the unemployed) made less and less sense, except as a means of keeping spending under control. It was harder and harder to justify an approach based on the idea that reasonable benefit levels might discourage people from seeking work – when there was clearly no work available. The old rules simply could not cope with the changing circumstances.

But there was no comprehensive reform of the system. On the contrary, the period was characterized by *ad hoc* responses to immediate problems which left the impression of an increasingly ramshackle system generally unsympathetic to those it was supposed to support. In 1929, the Poor Law Guardians were abolished and – echoing the proposals of the Minority Report – their functions were transferred to local authority Public Assistance Committees. These committees also began to take on responsibility for functions already transferred to local authorities, such as childcare and support for the long-term sick. In practice the transfer did not have the hoped for consequences – for many of the unemployed, the new committees seemed even worse than the Guardians because they were often more effective in restricting benefit and less sympathetic towards the claims of the unemployed. The 'means test' seemed harsher even if the workhouse test was ended in 1930. Nor did the transfer to local authorities stop the wide divergence between benefit rates and eligibility for benefits between different areas. There were significant variations between regions and even individual local authorities. In London, Poplar remained notorious as an authority which had little regard for official government rules, but by the early 1930s 'Poplarism' had spread to several other

London boroughs and even beyond (see, for example, Macintyre, 1980, and particularly his discussion of the Vale of Leven, pp. 105–6).

In 1934 – again apparently echoing the Webbs – an Unemployment Assistance Board was set up at national level to take on the tasks of the Public Assistance Committees in providing assistance to the unemployed. The intention was to ensure nationally consistent scales of relief and criteria for their distribution. The board began work in 1935, but the government was forced to retreat temporarily, because its benefit rates were lower than those of some local authorities and, until 1937, some PACs continued uneasily alongside the UAB and the unemployed were able to choose between them.

Many of the institutional 'reforms' which took place between the wars were taken further after 1945, but the context was different. The Poor Law had effectively gone and was waiting for the final nails in its coffin. Welfare was beginning to be seen as a right, rather than a grudging concession.

The period between 1942 and 1948 is recognized as a turning point in the history of welfare in Britain. The Beveridge Report (1942) has come to symbolize a break with the past and to represent the threshold of a new consensus on matters of social policy. A number of factors interacted at this time to produce a moment in history which might be called 'revolutionary' in terms of the changes that were ushered in.

First, there was the cessation of hostilities with Germany and Japan, and the return to peacetime. This produced an historical moment in which a break with the past – the Old Britain – became conceivable. Second, there was the pressure for social change which had built up during wartime and which had become irresistible by 1945. Third, there was the effect of 'consensus' government during the war which allowed planning for a better future in a political atmosphere less riven with party divisions than in peacetime. For example, in 1942, William Beveridge was able to say of his blueprint for the introduction of the modern welfare state that, 'the Plan raises no party issues. Social Insurance is not a party preserve' (Beveridge, 1943, p. 76). While this was undoubtedly an instance of rhetorical overstatement, it is none the less indicative of a political climate in which progressive or reformist ideas could be seen as consensual.

The post-war period marked an important change in public opinion on the questions of state provision, unemployment, poverty and social and economic distribution. These shifts had, however, been carefully nurtured during wartime. Social reform in the areas of education, employment, health and welfare became a part of wartime propaganda in as much as they symbolized the hopes of a brighter future for which it was worth fighting. But equally important was the development during the war of policies based on rational social planning, on the production of blueprints for social reform, masterminded by experts outside mainstream political parties but able to influence government (Addison, 1977). These experts, like William Beveridge (with links back to the New Liberals of the earlier period) and John Maynard Keynes, produced integrated proposals apparently based on expertise rather than political dogma or a party line. They were able to provide the necessary building blocks for realizing the aspirations of a population anxious to see the end of gross inequalities, unemployment and poverty.

The blueprint for the welfare state

The Beveridge Report on 'Social Insurance and Allied Services' (1942) was a blueprint for eliminating Want (or in today's terms, poverty). Beveridge saw poverty as the result of a loss of earning power or removal from the labour market. He proposed a system of social insurance which was based on contributions made during times of employment. For those who could not meet the contributions criteria, a safety net – National Assistance – was to be created. Some of the limitations of these proposals will be discussed later in this section of the book, but it is important to point out that, for Beveridge, tackling the giant evil of Want was defined as a relatively easy task – but one which was dependent upon a more substantial package of reforms. This package required reforms to eliminate the other giant evils of Disease (through the introduction of the National Health Service), of Ignorance (through the reform of education), of Squalor (through rational town planning and rebuilding programmes) and of Idleness (through the creation of full employment). Beveridge made it clear that his proposals to tackle Want could not succeed without these other reforms.

The proposals in the report were not in themselves especially radical. The idea of social insurance based on a contributory principle had been established in 1911. Yet the proposals were radical in that Beveridge closely associated them with a means of redistributing income, if not from rich to poor, at least over a life cycle (i.e. horizontal redistribution rather than vertical redistribution). Furthermore they were distinctly utopian in character with the firm promise of a new Jerusalem for all – a Jerusalem built on common endeavour and hard work.

Beveridge's wartime speeches about his 'Plan' evoked a powerful vision of reform which ultimately failed the test of practical politics. Oddly, his rhetoric has sustained the belief that his proposals ushered in a social revolution even in the face of their practical failure to solve the problem of poverty. In this respect the report symbolizes the aspirations of a population rather than a turning point in a capitalist nation divided by class and gender. The following passage is typical of Beveridge's oratorical style.

To win this war will tax all our strength, courage and staying power, and the strength, courage and staying power of our Allies. To solve in advance at the same time as the main problems of the peace, will tax to the utmost our imagination, our intelligence and our good-will. But both things have to be done. Let's do them. There are not easy times ahead in the war or in the peace. Which of you has asked for an easy time?

Beveridge managed to capture the 'public imagination' through his patriotic rhetoric and he created a consensus view of the new way forward at a time when there was a coalition government which had created a climate of political consensus. Indeed this wartime coalition was followed by a period in British political history now referred to as 'Butskellism'. (This was a neologism coined to imply that there was little difference between the main policies pursued by either the Tories or the Labour Party, derived from the names of R. A. Butler and Hugh Gaitskell who were successive Chancellors of the Exchequer of those respective parties).

Yet this ideology of consensus must not be overstated. There were dissenting voices, most notably feminists and socialists who recognized, in their separate ways, that the Beveridge Report would not transform the social order. While these voices could hardly be heard above the clamour of support, their trenchant criticisms later emerged as powerful critiques of the edifice created by Beveridge. The proponents of laissez-faire, on the other hand, were largely silent at this time, although it was the reassertion of individualism and a faith in the minimal state that was eventually to produce the fiercest challenge to the ideals of Beveridge.

6 · *Fabianism*

The construction of the welfare state in the wake of Labour's election victory in 1945 seemed to bring the translation of the Fabian dream into an only slightly flawed reality. It promised a new society based on a philosophy of gradualism and collectivist solutions organized through the state and backed by the rational analysis of social science experts.

Of course, the key experts who symbolized the great shift in British social and economic policy after the war were not Fabians, but Beveridge and Keynes, both of whom probably shared the overall vision of the turn of the century New Liberals rather more than that of the Fabians. Although both had worked closely with leading Fabians in the past, Beveridge and Keynes presented their policies as ways of defending capitalism – of securing its continued existence. They were what George and Wilding described as 'reluctant collectivists' (George and Wilding, 1976 and 1986). For the Fabians, however, these policies were indications that capitalism was already dead or, at least, well on the way to extinction. The fact that they were being put forward by people who were not socialists merely confirmed that Fabianism was moving with the tide of history. It confirmed the Fabian belief in the almost inevitable triumph of state inspired collectivism.

This disagreement between the positions, however, made little difference to the practical policies adopted or the arguments put forward for them. Having been sharp critics of welfare provision at the turn of the century the Fabians became the most enthusiastic supporters of the Beveridge Report, seeing it as confirmation of their ideas and policies (see the extract by Robson below). And the style of the report was also familiar to them, at least if they had read any of the Webbs' work. Even those who were critical of the Labour Party's leadership for being trapped in Conservative dominated coalition politics during the war echoed the theme of support for the report. Jennie Lee, for example, standing (unsuccessfully) as Independent Labour candidate in Bristol in 1943, emphasized that she stood 'for every word, every letter and comma in the Beveridge Report' (quoted in Addison, 1977, p. 226).

The significance of this should not be lost. Beveridge, the 1945–51 Labour government, and the welfare state became coterminous to such an extent that most of the debates about welfare until the 1970s were dominated by the ghost of Beveridge. Such arguments were about how much Beveridge had been left behind, or even betrayed, by new policies and how far the report's aims could be achieved. While in the 1920s and 1930s references were made back to the Minority Report on the Poor Law, after the Second World War the Beveridge Report cast an even longer shadow. It has become a commonplace to claim that we all became Keynesians after the war, but if it weren't such an unpleasant mouthful, it might be more appropriate to say that we all became Beveridgians. The welfare state entered the popular consciousness far more than demand management ever did, and even the commitment to full employment was far more explicit in Beveridge than in Keynes.

In retrospect one may feel that the enthusiasm which greeted the Beveridge Report was exaggerated, since the report included and institutionalized many of the failings for which the welfare state is now frequently criticized. It assumed the continued subordination of women, even in its espousal of family allowances. It was based on the principle of insurance rather than need. It supported the creation of an extensive professional bureaucracy whose main purpose of welfare provision included within it an explicit concern to police the poor. The unemployed were only to be paid subsistence to ensure that they were not discouraged from seeking work. It was an elitist and patronizing document handed down from above to a grateful people.

Yet it also reflected an important political shift, even if Beveridge was probably right to emphasize its importance as a major pillar of support for capitalism rather than a symbol of creeping socialism as the Fabians suggested. Underlying the report was an assumption of shared citizenship which implied that recipients of benefit received it as a right instead of the grudging charity offered under the Poor Law. A central assumption of the report was that the state would guarantee full employment and this was later developed more fully by Beveridge (1944). Only on this basis, stressed Beveridge, could a minimum level of subsistence be guaranteed, supported by a system of compulsory national insurance with a further safety net of national assistance (now supplementary benefit) if this was insufficient. In the circumstances it is perhaps hardly surprising that the welfare state has found it so hard to cope with the mass unemployment of the last quarter of the twentieth century.

Beveridge on social security and social policy

409. Social security as used in this Report means assurance of a certain income. The Plan for Social Security set out in the Report is a plan to win freedom from want by maintaining incomes. But sufficiency of income is

not sufficient in itself. Freedom from want is only one of the essential freedoms of mankind. Any Plan for Social Security in the narrow sense assumes a concerted social policy in many fields, most of which it would be inappropriate to discuss in this Report. The plan proposed here involves three particular assumptions so closely related to it that brief discussion is essential for understanding of the plan itself. These are the assumptions of children's allowances, of comprehensive health and rehabilitation services, and of maintenance of employment. After these three assumptions have been examined, general questions are raised as to the practicability of taking freedom from want as an immediate post-war aim and as to the desirability of planning reconstruction of the social services even in war.

Assumption A. Children's Allowances

410. The first of three assumptions underlying the Plan for Social Security is a general scheme of children's allowances. This means that direct provision for the maintenance of dependent children will be made by payment of allowances to those responsible for the care of those children. The assumption rests on two connected arguments.

411. First, it is unreasonable to seek to guarantee an income sufficient for subsistence, while earnings are interrupted by unemployment or disability, without ensuring sufficient income during earning. Social insurance should be part of a policy of a national minimum. But a national minimum for families of every size cannot in practice be secured by a wage system, which must be based on the product of a man's labour and not on the size of his family. The social surveys of Britain between the two wars show that in the first thirty years of this century real wages rose by about one-third without reducing want to insignificance, and that the want which remained was almost wholly due to two causes – interruption or loss of earning power and large families.

412. Second, it is dangerous to allow benefit during unemployment or disability to equal or exceed earnings during work. But, without allowances for children, during earning and not-earning alike, this danger cannot be avoided. It has been experienced in an appreciable number of cases under unemployment benefit and unemployment assistance in the past. The maintenance of employment – last and most important of the three assumptions of social security – will be impossible without greater fluidity of labour and other resources in the aftermath of war than has been achieved in the past. To secure this, the gap between income during earning and during interruption to earning should be as large as possible for every man. It cannot be kept large for men with large families, except either by making their benefit in unemployment and disability inadequate, or by giving allowances for children in time of earning and not-earning alike.

Assumption B. Comprehensive Health and Rehabilitation Services

426. The second of the three assumptions has two sides to it. It covers a national health service for prevention and for cure of disease and disability by medical treatment; it covers rehabilitation and fitting for employment

by treatment which will be both medical and post-medical. Administratively, realisation of Assumption B on its two sides involves action both by the departments concerned with health and by the Ministry of Labour and National Service. Exactly where the line should be drawn between the responsibilities of these Departments cannot, and need not, be settled now. For the purpose of the present Report, the two sides are combined under one head, avoiding the need to distinguish accurately at this stage between medical and post-medical work. The case for regarding Assumption B as necessary for a satisfactory system of social security needs little emphasis. It is a logical corollary to the payment of high benefit in disability that determined efforts should be made by the State to reduce the number of cases for which benefit is needed. It is a logical corollary to the receipt of high benefit in disability that the individual should recognise the duty to be well and to co-operate in all steps which may lead to diagnosis of disease in early stages when it can be prevented. Disease and accidents must be paid for in any case, in lessened power of production and in idleness, if not directly by insurance benefits. One of the reasons why it is preferable to pay for disease and accident openly and directly in the form of insurance benefits, rather than indirectly, is that this emphasises the cost and should give a stimulus to prevention. As to the methods of realising Assumption B, the main problems naturally arise under the first head of medical treatment. Rehabilitation is a new field of remedial activity with great possibilities, but requiring expenditure of a different order of magnitude from that involved in the medical treatment of the nation.

427. The first part of Assumption B is that a comprehensive national health service will ensure that for every citizen there is available whatever medical treatment he requires, in whatever form he requires it, domiciliary or institutional, general, specialist or consultant, and will ensure also the provision of dental, ophthalmic and surgical appliances, nursing and midwifery and rehabilitation after accidents.

Assumption C. Maintenance of Employment

440. There are five reasons for saying that a satisfactory scheme of social insurance assumes the maintenance of employment and the prevention of mass unemployment. Three reasons are concerned with the details of social insurance; the fourth and most important is concerned with its principle; the fifth is concerned with the possibility of meeting its cost.

First, payment of unconditional cash benefits as of right during unemployment is satisfactory provision only for short periods of unemployment; after that, complete idleness even on an income demoralises. The proposal of the Report accordingly is to make unemployment benefit after a certain period conditional upon attendance at a work or training centre. But this proposal is impracticable, if it has to be applied to men by the million or the hundred thousand.

Second, the only satisfactory test of unemployment is an offer of work. This test breaks down in mass unemployment and makes necessary recourse to elaborate contribution conditions, and such devices as the Anomalies Regulations, all of which should be avoided in a satisfactory scheme of unemployment insurance.

Third, the state of the labour market has a direct bearing on rehabilitation and recovery of injured and sick persons and upon the possibility of giving to those suffering from partial infirmities, such as deafness, the chance of a happy and useful career. In time of mass unemployment those who are in receipt of compensation feel no urge to get well for idleness. On the other hand, in time of active demand for labour, as in war, the sick and the maimed are encouraged to recover, so that they may be useful.

Fourth, and most important, income security which is all that can be given by social insurance is so inadequate a provision for human happiness that to put it forward by itself as a sole or principal measure of reconstruction hardly seems worth doing. It should be accompanied by an announced determination to use the powers of the State to whatever extent may prove necessary to ensure for all, not indeed absolute continuity of work, but a reasonable chance of productive employment.

Fifth, though it should be within the power of the community to bear the cost of the whole Plan for Social Security, the cost is heavy and, if to the necessary cost waste is added, it may become insupportable. Unemployment, both through increasing expenditure on benefit and through reducing the income to bear those costs, is the worst form of waste.

441. Assumption C does not imply complete abolition of unemployment. In industries subject to seasonable influences, irregularities of work are inevitable; in an economic system subject to change and progress, fluctuations in the fortunes of individual employers or of particular industries are inevitable; the possibility of controlling completely the major alternations of good trade and bad trade which are described under the term of the trade cycle has not been established; a country like Britain, which must have exports to pay for its raw materials, cannot be immune from the results of changes of fortune or of economic policy in other countries. The Plan for Social Security provides benefit for a substantial volume of unemployment. . . .

Assumption C requires not the abolition of all unemployment, but the abolition of mass unemployment and of unemployment prolonged year after year for the same individual. In the beginning of compulsory unemployment insurance in 1913 and 1914, it was found that less than 5 per cent of all the unemployment experienced in the insured industries occurred after men had been unemployed for as long as 15 weeks. Even if it does not prove possible to get back to that level of employment, it should be possible to make unemployment of any individual for more than 26 weeks continuously a rare thing in normal times. . . .

447. The rise in the general standard of living in Britain in the thirty or forty years that ended with the present war has two morals. First, growing general prosperity and rising wages diminished want, but did not reduce want to insignificance. The moral is that new measures to spread prosperity are needed. The Plan for Social Security is designed to meet this need; to establish a national minimum above which prosperity can grow, with want abolished. Second, the period covered by the comparisons between say 1900 and 1936 includes the first world war. The moral is the encouraging one, that it is wrong to assume that the present war must bring economic progress for Britain, or for the rest of the world, to an end.

449. The argument of the section can be summed up briefly. Abolition of want cannot be brought about merely by increasing production, without

seeking to correct distribution of the product; but correct distribution does not mean what it has often been taken to mean in the past – distribution between the different agents in production, between land, capital, management and labour. Better distribution of purchasing power is required among wage-earners themselves, as between times of earning and not earning, and between times of heavy family responsibilities and of light or no family responsibilities. Both social insurance and children's allowances are primarily methods of redistributing wealth. Such better distribution cannot fail to add to welfare and, properly designed, it can increase wealth, by maintaining physical vigour. It does not decrease wealth, unless it involves waste in administration or reduces incentives to production. Unemployment and disability are already being paid for unconsciously; it is no addition to the burden on the community to provide for them consciously. Unified social insurance will eliminate a good deal of waste inherent in present methods. Properly designed, controlled and financed, it need have no depressing effect on incentive . . . (Beveridge, 1942, pp. 153–4, 158–9, 163–4, 165, 166–7).

Enter the Fabians

The next two extracts are taken from a collection of Fabian Society essays on social security, published in 1943, a year after the Beveridge Report but including evidence submitted to Beveridge in preparing his report. The first extract comes from William Robson's preface to the collection and stresses the similarities between the report and the Fabian proposals. It reflects the Fabians' confidence in the application in qualified and trained minds to the resolution of social problems. It may be difficult today to imagine that anyone could have such complete confidence in these methods of developing welfare policies, but in 1945 it was by no means unusual.

Developing a rational approach

Anyone who compares the Fabian scheme with the Beveridge Report will observe a large measure of agreement between them. The unification of administration in a new Ministry of Social Security; the assimilation of unemployment, sickness and disablement benefit in a new standard benefit; the payment of such benefit for the entire duration of unemployment or disability, subject to co-operation by the applicant in measures designed to set him on his feet again; the conversion of workmen's compensation from an affair of private rights, private finance and private conflicts into a publicly administered social insurance, and the assimilation (in 90 per cent of the cases) of workmen's compensation with standard benefit for other disabilities; the provision of children's allowances as an essential aspect of family security; the introduction of maternity allowances for all gainfully occupied women and a maternity grant for all women; the payment of marriage allowances and burial allowances as a normal part of social insurance; recognition of the need to induce old persons to remain at work as long as they are willing and able to do so; an emphasis on the importance of the medical and industrial rehabilitation services, with special reference to training; the provision of a comprehensive medical service available to everyone without charge, and including hospital facilities and specialist treatment of all kinds; the reservation of widows' pensions for widows with dependent children and the treatment of other widows as persons requiring work or training; the replacement of public assistance by a residual service to meet abnormal cases on proof of need – on all these fundamental questions Sir William Beveridge and the authors of our scheme see eye to eye in principle, despite minor variations in detail. . . .

Taking the matter all in all, it is remarkable how large a measure of agreement exists between the Beveridge Report and the Fabian plan. That two bodies so differently constituted should reach identical conclusions in regard to so many of the fundamental issues is an encouraging sign of the times. It shows that, in this sphere at least, the rational method can point the way to a specific and inescapable programme of action. It demonstrates that if persons with qualified and trained minds will apply themselves in a disinterested manner to a great social problem of this kind, the proper principles will emerge so unmistakably that the right solution will cease to be a matter of mere opinion and become a question of scientific knowledge. It implies the beginning of a new outlook in the Social Sciences (Robson, 1943, pp. 2, 4–5).

The second extract, from an article on staffing by John Clarke in the same collection, reflects the Fabians' continued interest in the use of expert trained personnel in managing and running the social security system. Neither here nor in Beveridge was there any interest in developing democratic structures for running the welfare state. As one author puts it, there was a marked lack of 'enthusiasm for popular democratic control of the services' (Mishra, 1984, p. 205). Instead, the issue was how to attract properly trained professional – usually male – staff able to take crucial political decisions, albeit nominally under the control of an elected politician.

Constructing a specialist bureaucracy

A Ministry of Social Security will have to maintain close contact with numerous individual citizens, each of whom will judge the Ministry chiefly by his reception at the local office. It is of paramount importance to the Ministry that he should be welcomed and treated with consideration and interest. The reputation of the Ministry will depend largely on its local staff. These will have to be selected and appointed carefully, and it is essential to consider at the outset what sort of people they must be. But local staff, however suitable and expert, can only act within the framework of their Ministry's policy at any time. If the policy is ill-conceived, no local deftness will cover its deficiency. . . .

On the other hand, in the long transmission belt carrying social policy from Whitehall to the private citizen, it is the interviewing officer who makes final delivery; if he is peremptory, hurried, irritable or stupid he will alienate citizens, and bungle the execution of policy however well thought out that policy may be. A Ministry of Social Security needs perpetual team-work between the planning and administrative Head-quarters staff and the executives in all the local offices; each depends, for final success, upon the intelligent operations of the other. Each will benefit by close liaison – interchange between Headquarters and out-stations staff, Regional and local conferences, provincial officers of Headquarters type and calibre, and Intelligence staff which (among other duties) would explain policy to local staff, and, conversely, tell Headquarters planners how the public had reacted to new policy and what were current social trends.

The thesis of this chapter is that these various functions need persons specially equipped for their performance – that calculating widows' pension rates, relating size of benefits to population groups, estimating the effect of industrial planning on the volume of claims national and local, talking with deserted wives or pushing the malingerer back to work – that all these diverse jobs need special skills and special knowledge, and that both at its Headquarters and in its local offices the Ministry must appoint appropriate persons to exercise appropriate sorts of skill.

This cuts right across existing Whitehall theories and procedures; there seems to be a Civil Service tradition that if you set up tidy governmental machinery and recruit a body of intelligent administrators of high integrity, you can run anything – shipping, Cairo, coal-mines, pensions. The needs of economic planning in a technical age may prove this thesis wrong. Already the majority of higher appointments outside the Civil Service call both for technical specialisation and for background knowledge of economic, sociological, psychological or scientific processes.

How are these sorts of experts to be got into the Ministry? In peace-time some of those who really understand the social sciences are congregated in the Universities; others are engaged on social surveys and research. Since the war many of them are temporary civil servants; they have been called in not only because administration has increased in scope, but because the urgency of war-time planning calls for the right people in the right places. If later we are to plan for national well-being the same criterion must carry over. We must have first-class persons where their skills are needed. We must be prepared to take economists, sociologists, psychologists and statis-ticians into the Ministry of Social Security at the higher salary ranges as temporary staff. We must be prepared to use suitable experts wherever they are to be found in the community. . . .

Recognition of the need for social science experts must be established straight away so that they may be incorporated into the new Ministry as soon as it is formed. 'Good administrators' brought in from the higher ranks of other Ministries to start the new one will not suffice. It is essential that at least some of those who administer at the highest levels should understand the nature and the purpose of the social services (Clarke, 1943, pp. 373–5, 376–7).

Although this call for experts relates specifically to the development of a Ministry of Social Security, the message was relevant to all aspects of the welfare state being constructed in the wake of Beveridge. If experts of one sort were required for the Ministry, professional experts of another sort were required as social workers for the welfare committees and children's departments at local authority level. Fabianism drew clear parallels between the social 'sciences' and technologically based subjects such as engineering, and even the natural sciences. Just as it was possible to identify and implement the best solutions to engineering problems, so, with the help of the social sciences, it should be possible to do the same with social problems.

Implementation by Labour

As Minister of National Insurance, James Griffiths was responsible for translating the Beveridge proposals into legislative practice. In his autobiography he explains how this was done, and incidentally shows clearly how they dominated the political debate within the Labour Party. For Griffiths, the legislation was to be judged not in terms of any explicitly *socialist* criteria but in terms of its closeness to proposals put forward by a social theorist who was a member of the Liberal Party.

The welfare state revolution

1

'A REVOLUTIONARY moment in the world's history is a time for revolution – not for patching.'

This call for revolution came not from Moscow or Peking but from the one-time director of the London School of Economics, Sir William Beveridge, when he presented his plan for social security in 1942.

It was symbolic of the new revolution that the Minister of National Insurance, charged with the task of implementing the plan, and creating the Welfare State, should find himself installed at Carlton House Terrace, once the citadel of aristocratic power.

2

The Webbs, who lived in a world of Blue Books, once lamented that it took as long as thirty years before the recommendations of a royal commission were translated into legislation. The 1945 Labour Government boldly aimed to implement the Beveridge Plan in full within three years, and bring it into operation on the third anniversary of the great electoral victory – 5th July 1948.

This was a formidable task. It would necessitate five Acts of Parliament, scores of regulations and the creation of a nationwide organization. Fortunately one of the five, the Family Allowances Act, was already on the statute book. The Americans have a custom of giving their legislation the names of sponsors in Congress, and it would have been appropriate to give the Family Allowances Act the name 'Eleanor Rathbone Act'. She had fought valiantly, against opposition from many quarters, for family endowment, and I had been one of her supporters in the many debates she initiated in the thirties.

Beveridge recommended allowances in cash at five shillings a week for every child in a family except the eldest, or only, child, and that this should be supplemented by services in kind to the value of three shillings per week.

I decided to bring family allowances into payment as soon as possible. My first job was to find the money, and I made the first of many visits to the Treasury. The Chancellor, Hugh Dalton, gave me the money, 'with a song in his heart', as he told our conference to the delight of our supporters and the fury of his critics.

It was not only in its cover that the [National Insurance] scheme broke new ground but also in the scope and variety of the benefits provided 'from the cradle to the grave'. It provided twice as many separate benefits as the old scheme and incorporated Beveridge's recommendation of a uniform standard for the principal benefits.

The 1946 [National Insurance] Act provided uniform benefits for sickness, unemployment and retirement, with dependants' benefits in each case. In addition it embodied Beveridge's recommendation that the amount of the major benefits should be such as would provide for basic needs, on a subsistence basis. I accept this basis.

The next question was how to ensure that the level would be maintained. This was, and has remained an unsolved problem. One of the practical difficulties is inherent in the insurance principle on which the scheme is based. I shared to the full Beveridge's view that benefits should be paid as of right on the basis of contributions and without any means test. My aim was to provide security with dignity. I considered the possibility of providing benefits on a sliding scale linked to the cost of living. This had practical difficulties in that it would require changes in contributions each time benefits were changed. I was reminded that when after 1918 war pensions had been tied to a cost of living scale it had worked well while the cost of living was rising and was abandoned the first time it fell. In the end, I provided in the Act that the minister should review the scale of benefits every five years with a view to adjusting them to changes in the cost of living and in the standard of life.

In the sphere of the social services the spirit of the administration is as important as the provisions of the legislation. I recognized that the ministry would be dealing with people in adversity, and that the qualities required of the staff were courtesy and dignity. . . .

5

While I was engaged in piloting the Insurance Bill through Parliament, Nye Bevan was triumphantly carrying through his bold and imaginative National Health Service Bill.

In the second session we joined forces in promoting the Bill to establish national assistance. The Bill aimed 'to terminate the existing poor law and to provide in lieu thereof for the assistance of persons in need by the National Assistance Board and by local authorities'. Responsibility for providing assistance in cash was transferred from the public assistance committees to a national board. The responsibility for welfare services for those who by 'age, infirmity or any other circumstances are in need' was to be entrusted to councils' welfare committees. We aimed to provide monetary payments and welfare services which would be different not only in their scope and provision, but also in the spirit in which they were administered. . . .

Beveridge called for a crusade to slay the five giant evils which afflicted our society – poverty, ignorance, disease, squalor and idleness. Within three years of our electoral victory, the Labour Government had provided the legislative framework and created the organization designed to rid our country of all five. To the Family Allowances Act we added four others – Industrial Injuries, National Insurance, National Health and National Assistance. During those same years Ellen Wilkinson and George Tomlinson, at the Ministry of Education, began to implement the 1944 Education Act. The school-leaving age was raised to fifteen, and it was planned eventually to raise it to sixteen.

Together these six Acts of Parliament provide the foundation of Britain's Welfare State. To those of us who were privileged to take part in this work, the Welfare State was not a luxury dependent on what was left over in the national Treasury but the first call upon our resources. To those others who, at that time and now, persist in deriding the security of the Welfare State, I would say as I did to the House of Commons in 1946:

> For a generation I lived with the consequences of insecurity. To those who profess to fear that security will weaken the moral fibre and destroy self respect, let me say this. It is insecurity that destroys. It is fear of tomorrow that paralyses the will. It is the frustration of human hopes that corrodes the soul. Security will release our people from the haunting fears of yesterday, and their gifts to the service of the nation.

In his report Beveridge warned us that 'freedom from want cannot be forced on a democracy, it must be won by them'.

In the nineteen-forties we fought and won a battle for the cause of social security. We rejoice that the present generation knows not the poverty and distress of the thirties (Griffiths, 1969, pp. 79, 80–1, 84–7, 88–9).

For most of those within the Fabian tradition – as Griffiths suggests – the Beveridge Report and its legislative aftermath really were a 'revolution'. The reforms of the 1945–51 Labour government seemed to represent a fundamental break with the past and the start of a whole new period in British political and social history based on wider notions of citizenship. Many believed that the Fabian aim of state-sponsored socialism had virtually been achieved and it became common to talk of managed capitalism or, even, as Crosland (1958) did, of the end of capitalism. Looking back it is easier to see weaknesses but the notion of the welfare state left to us from that period remains strong even today and its legacy stubbornly remains to haunt those who seek to change the direction of British politics. At the time the promise of Beveridge, even in the dry words of an official report, was powerful enough to carry along almost everyone interested in social improvement.

7 · Feminism

The feminist movement of the 1940s does not appear to have been cast in the same radical mould as that of the earlier feminists or suffragettes. The post-war feminists' methods and their political goals seem more respectable and restrained. Their emphasis tended to focus on the unique and valuable role of women as mothers and homemakers. In this respect, they continued a tradition of nineteenth-century feminism which had sought to improve the status of women in their separate sphere, namely the family. And to some extent this theme was evident in the early twentieth-century feminist movement, especially in the work of the Endowment of Motherhood Society which has been discussed in Chapter 4. However, in the post-war period, this theme appeared to become the dominant focus of feminist ideology.

Although some of the original suffrage groups remained active in the post-war era, for example the Six Point Group, the Women's Freedom League, and the Women's Cooperative Guild, newly emergent organizations, which came to symbolize post-war feminism, had a different emphasis to these 'old' feminist groups. For example, the Married Women's Association, which was founded in 1938 by Juanita Frances, had the goal of promoting marriage as an equal partnership between men and women. Similarly the Council of Married Women, founded in 1952, proposed to support the 'stabilization and dignity of marriage as an institution'. It was as if feminism had come to share the view that to ensure the reconstruction of post-war British society, women's primary duty had to be to the hearth and home. The 1940s revealed feminism to be engaging in political debate within the confines of the domestic sphere, rather than expanding their terrain to include the public sphere, or attempting to politicize and transform the structure of personal relationships within the family.

The post-war feminists' response to the Beveridge Report and the subsequent Family Allowance Bill and National Insurance Bill should be understood in this overall context. The feminists accepted that women should assume the roles of wives, mothers and homemakers, but they argued that these roles should be accorded greater recognition and be insured in the same way as the role of the breadwinner. The majority of feminists, therefore, were not so much at odds with Beveridge's perception of the role of married women as with his inadequate proposals to ensure them against hardship. The following extracts from the Beveridge Report make clear where Beveridge himself stood on the position of women in post-war Britain.

In any measure of social policy in which regard is had to facts, the great majority of married women must be regarded as occupied on work which is vital though unpaid, without which their husbands could not do their paid work and without which the nation could not continue. In accord with facts the Plan for Social Security treats married women as a special insurance class of occupied persons and treats man and wife as a team (Beveridge, 1942, p. 49).

That attitude of the housewife to gainful employment outside the home is not and should not be the same as that of the single woman. She has other duties. . . . Taken as a whole the Plan . . . puts a premium on marriage in place of penalising it. . . . In the next thirty years housewives as mothers have vital work to do in ensuring the adequate continuance of the British Race and British Ideals in the World (Beveridge, 1942, p. 52).

On the basis of these principles, Beveridge outlined an integrated social insurance plan which thoroughly disadvantaged married women and ensured their continued dependence upon men and marriage. No sooner had the report been published than the more radical feminist organizations began to identify what they regarded as the major disadvantages of the plan. A main focus was the failure of the plan to secure equal treatment for women and men. The Women's Freedom League (WFL) mounted the strongest criticism through its fortnightly news sheet called the *Women's Bulletin*. On 6 November 1943 they held a conference, drawing together a range of women's organizations. The following extract is from a report of this conference.

Conference of the Proposals in the Beveridge Report as they affect women

The discussion was excellently kept up, and led by Mrs Abbott on the Position of Married Women under the Report proposals: The New Marriage Bar, the Need for direct Insurance of the Housewife, the Position of the gainfully occupied Married Woman, and Pensions. Then Mrs Forster spoke on the Unequal Moral Standard wrongly introduced into an Insurance Plan, and its effects on married women and women 'living as wives'. Miss Pearson spoke on the Single Woman, employed as housewives and on the equal benefit of single woman workers for a lower contribution. And lastly, Miss Challoner spoke on maternity benefits being in reality family benefits and not women's benefits.

A statement proposed by Mrs Munro and dealing with the social security Plan proposed by the Beveridge Report and making definite proposals on the position of women for inclusion in any scheme the Government may put forward when it decides to implement the Beveridge proposals, was adopted. The following are the recommendations made:

1. The same retirement age for men and women.
2. The safeguarding of pension and other rights of unpaid domestic workers by compulsory insurances on their behalf.
3. Direct insurance of the married woman – the housewife – with benefits adjusted to her needs, including cash benefit when disabled by sickness or accident and retirement pension at the normal age.
4. Maintenance of a woman's insurance rights on marriage, subject to general tests of genuine desire and availability for work.
5. No exemption from insurance of the married woman worker save the general exemption for any person earning less than £75 a year.
6. Full normal benefit for the insured woman workers when employed or disabled.
7. Full pension in her own right for the insured married woman.
8. Payment by the single woman of an equal contribution for equal benefit.
9. Removal of all moral tests, especially as applied to women only.
10. Widowhood Benefit to be recognised as and called Temporary Loss of Livelihood Benefit.
11. Maternity Grant to be adequate and this and Maternity Benefit to be recognised for what they are, not individual benefits but Family Benefits designed to safeguard the bearing and rearing of children.
12. The inclusion of the unmarried wife and mother in insurance on a normal and fair basis, entitling her to share in those family benefits, including guardianship benefit.

It was agreed to press these demands on the Government by following the procedure adopted in the Equal Compensation Campaign, that is to form an ad hoc Committee of women's organisations under the chairmanship of a woman MP, so that the political work in the House of Commons is kept to the front, while the women's organisations would lead the campaign throughout the country. It was agreed unanimously to invite Mrs Tate MP to accept chairmanship of the Committee. A strong desire was also expressed that Mrs Abbott and Mrs Bompas who had so ably prepared the work for this conference should continue their valuable co-operation.

In an earlier edition of the *Women's Bulletin* the WFL had also demanded:

That men and women should in marriage not be treated as a 'team' but as individuals each paying equal contributions and receiving equal benefits; and that in every case men and women should pay the same and receive the same benefits (29 January 1943).

This amounted virtually to a call for the disaggregation of benefits to husband and wife and a demand for the social security system to provide for individuals rather than family units via the head of household. This surprisingly radical demand was translated into specific demands for equal treatment but, unfortunately, did not appear in the more radical form in readily available published documents. It would seem, therefore, that the potential radicalism of the WFL did not emerge to influence the feminist movement as a whole. None the less, the report of a discussion between feminists held in 1943, which is extracted below, reveals the extent to which internal debate did cover the whole spectrum of political feminism, from the equal treatment perspective, to the view that status should be enhanced through celebrating motherhood, to the rarer demand for economic independence within marriage. Although the first two positions have become the most well documented, the following passage reveals that economic independence and even an argument for 'wages for housework' were on the agenda for some feminists.

The Economic Status of the Housewife

At the discussion meeting held on 23 July . . . Mrs Billington-Greig (WLF) opened the discussion, stating that the views she was putting forward rested on the general premise that all work should be assessed on its value to the community, and the national wealth to be shared by every member of that community. The community should recognise the work of the housewife and mother as a form of social service and should recompense her for it. Already in its own interest the community has taken many steps to ensure good conditions in the home and this should be the last step; child allowances and payment of the housewife and mother. She considered that marriage should be logically reconsidered as an equal partnership, both parties sharing the means and the responsibilities. *But a wife's share of her husband's earnings or income does not give her true economic independence, because it is an indirect payment through another person for the work she does.* For true economic independence the housewife must be paid direct by the community like any other earner. In return the community should have the right to demand that the housewife and mother should be trained for her job.

Miss Munro said that the Labour Party had no official policy on the question but considered that improved social services would improve the status of the housewife. She considered that payment of the housewife might militate against the freedom of women's economic choice. Personal earnings by women from which to contribute to the upkeep of the home and meet their own expenses has been the only satisfactory solution up to now.

Miss Reeves said that the Liberal Party also had no official policy except family allowances and better social services. She felt it would create a grievance if the wife and housekeeper were paid by the community while there would be no such payment for other housekeepers. Direct wage-earning through professional and other work seems the best way of securing economic independence for the married woman.

Miss Frances spoke of the Married Women's Association policy of the right of a wife to share in the family income and gave examples of hard cases under existing conditions.

Miss Pierotti said that Mrs Billington-Grieg was referring rather to the economic position of the mother than of the housewife. *Payment by the community would probably lead to women being held in the 'job' of marriage*, and also to reduced contribution by the husband towards household expenses. What was needed was to educate women to understand what their status ought to be.

Mrs Spiller asked 'What is economic independence?' He who pays the piper calls the tune and if the state pays the housewife it will hold the woman in the home and limit her freedom in other work. She felt that women need security like everyone else and should get insurance benefits in need, sickness and old age like all other citizens. Children's allowances might relieve the mother from some financial anxiety but would not increase her personal economic independence. Improved housing and social services should free the housewife and mother to undertake paid work, either whole or part time, as this alone would enable her to develop her personality fully and contribute freely to the life of the community in which she lives (*Women's Bulletin*, 6 September 1943, emphasis added).

The idea of a married woman's 'personal economic independence' appeared nowhere in Beveridge's plan for national insurance. Neither did it play any role in his support for family allowances which will be discussed below. Hence, in spite of the work of feminists at the time of the first National Insurance Bill in 1911, by the time the 1946 National Insurance Bill and the 1945 Family Allowance Bill were progressing through the necessary parliamentary procedures, the feminists' argument had made relatively little headway in shifting the parameters of the ideological debate on welfare. Arguably even the Family Allowance Act, which is widely regarded as a success for the long running campaign led by Eleanor Rathbone, was ultimately successful on the basis of arguments far removed from feminist concerns.

This is not to argue that feminists were unsuccessful in getting certain issues on to the political agenda. On the contrary, this formed a major part of the post-war impact of feminism (see Banks, 1981). However, their basic analysis of marriage, motherhood and the impoverishment of women and children in the family did not become a part of the political vocabulary of the 1940s. Part of the reason may have been the general enthusiasm for the Beveridge Report which was welcomed in many quarters including the Women's TUC. Against such clamours of approval and widespread demands for reform and social reconstruction, the more critical feminists undoubtedly became isolated. They were in any case far less powerful than the sections broadly supporting the report and subsequent bill, and they had no clear party political allegiance which might have provided more political influence. Notwithstanding this, in February of 1944, a deputation of twelve leading women's organizations, led by the National Council of Women, went to meet with a representative of the Minister of Reconstruction to press home their views. Moreover, in November of the same year, Dr Edith Summerskill presented a petition to the House of Commons containing 77,000 signatures demanding justice for wives under the proposed scheme.

One of the best examples of the feminist critique of the Beveridge plan is provided by Elizabeth Abbott and Katherine Bompas. Their pamphlet *The Woman Citizen and Social Security* (1943) not only roundly disputes Beveridge's view of married women simply as dependents; it is a clear statement of an ideology which insists that individuals should have individual rights to social security benefits. Its core argument is that women, regardless of their marital status, should have the same rights as men to contribute to, and benefit from, the insurance scheme. However, this individualist/equal rights stance led Abbott and Bompas into some difficulties when considering the position of women who were in a very different structural position to most men, for example the housewife without paid employment or the pregnant woman with special needs for maternity benefits. On the former, Abbott and Bompas were unable to propose an alternative to financial dependence upon husbands – although they implied that it should be possible to devise some alternative. This may be said to be a major weakness in the equal treatment position, because in ensuring the same insurance rights for men and women it presumed that men and women would be in equal positions in the labour market. In fact very few women were in a position of substantive equality with men in 1943.

The latter issue of maternity benefits led Abbott and Bompas to adopt their view that these should be regarded as family benefits rather than women's. This, they argued, would emphasize that children were a joint responsibility. Hence the whole thrust of their argument was to devise a system to treat men and women equally and to remove barriers which prevented women from staying in the labour market after marriage. The difficult position of women at home caring for children received little in the way of constructive proposals in their pamphlet.

The following passages from *The Woman Citizen and Social Security* indicate clearly the main elements of this important variant of feminist ideology in the 1940s.

It is where the Plan falls short of being really national in character, where it shuts out or exempts from all direct participation over nine million adult women, where it imposes special financial burdens on men alone, instead of spreading them equitably over all, that it fails and is open to criticism.

The error – an error which lies in the moral rather than the economic sphere – lies in denying to the married woman, rich or poor, housewife or paid worker, an independent personal status. From this error springs a crop of injustices and complications and difficulties, personal, marital and administrative, involving in the long run men both married and unmarried, and the unmarried as well as the married woman.

Any plea urging the difficulty of bringing the married woman inside the strict rules of insurance is rebutted by the Plan itself. Where women are concerned the ordinary rules of insurance are honoured more in the breach than in the observance by the sequestration of their premiums when they marry, by the possible exemption of a woman worker (however well paid) under a contract of service because she is married, by giving a married woman worker lower benefits for the full contribution, by cutting the fully paid-up pension of a married woman worker when her husband retires, and by various limitations on women's right to insurance based on purely personal considerations. It is possible then to abrogate strict insurance rules to the detriment of women. It would be equally possible to abrogate them in their favour. That, however, is not the suggestion it is here desired to make. The point is that whatever the technical difficulties of bringing the housewife into direct insurance the Plan has not only failed to find a solution, it has refused to grapple with the problem, and is in this respect neither revolutionary nor even wisely evolutionary.

It must be emphasised, then, that it is not upon the denial of equal economic status to women that the Plan comes to grief. Indeed the unmarried woman worker has equal economic status but is divorced from equal responsibility. It is with the denial of any personal status to a woman because she is married, the denial of her independent personality within marriage, that everything goes wrong and becomes unjust and ungenerous, sometimes comic, always unrealistic and inevitably antagonistic to the best interests of marriage and social life. In place of the famous phrase of Blackstone: 'I and my wife are one, and I am he', the author of the Report has substituted his special version: 'Every woman on marriage becomes a new person'. Nearly two hundred years may lie between the two phrases. The thought behind them is the same: that a married woman is not a person at all. Today, as so many years ago, injustice and complication are the inevitable result. That this may be quite other than the aim of the Plan is apparent, since its author refers to the married woman as 'an equal partner', as 'occupied on work which is vital', etc., etc. The tribute of the word is a sad commonplace to women. What is here of concern is not what the Report may say in praise of women, but what it proposes shall be done and the social tendencies which will thereby be encouraged. Far from putting a premium on marriage, as it purports to do, the Plan penalises both the married woman and marriage itself.

Nonetheless it would be unjust and ungenerous not to recognise that some new features and improvements, both evolutionary and revolutionary will benefit women as well as men. The pity is that a Plan which went so far did not go further and in a better direction where women are concerned (*The Woman Citizen and Social Security*, p. 3–4).

Following this introduction, Abbott and Bompas presented a comprehensive list of complaints against the Beveridge proposals. Some of these are extracted here:

Loss of insurance rights in marriage and of all contributions made prior to marriage

These proposals must be unconditionally rejected. The loss of insurance rights and of pre-marriage contributions is not a new proposal. It was put forward and rejected before the introduction of the Anomalies Act. The Report proposes to abolish the Anomalies Regulations for married women

– regulations which were both foolish and unjust – and to substitute a still greater injustice. Onerous and unfair as these Regulations were, the married woman worker at any rate retained her position as an insured person, with right to benefit under certain conditions. The new proposal is that every woman on marriage shall lose her accumulated payments (spreading in many cases over ten years or more) and cease to be an insured person. Should she remain in work or take fresh work, she has to requalify for insurance, and is then put in a position as regards benefit inferior to any other adult worker (16/- instead of 24/-).

The Marriage Grant. This is offered up to £10 as a solace for the loss of insurance rights and accumulated payments on marriage. It is not an integral part of the scheme and should be rejected both in its intention and in the form in which it is offered. The consequences of selling a birthright for a mess of pottage are well known, and women would do well to remember that rights once lost are hard to recover.

If it is desired to encourage marriage, a Joint Marriage Grant to the contracting parties is the proper form for such endowment to take (pp. 5–7).

The real position of the housewife

The new scheme for housewives should be rejected and with it the housewives' policy which is no more than a scrap of paper. Is it not time for the recognition of some plain facts? Though the married woman is not gainfully occupied in the sense that she earns money by salary or by profits from the sale of goods, she is a gainfully occupied person. Her livelihood is the occupation of housekeeping, as a partner in marriage, and in that partnership she has a definite financial share as a worker. In addition to that work which has this definite financial value, she is the mother of the sons and daughters of the nation.

The Report truely says that without the work of such women men could not do their paid work nor the nation continue: and calls upon them to ensure not only the continuance of the British race but the continuance of British ideals in the world. Their value is recognised in words. But there is no practical recognition of the needs of this central figure in our social economy. No independent status is given to her as a citizen and worker, no real amelioration of the difficulties of her life. The woman in the working class home suffers uncomplainingly a vast amount of misery and chronic ill health or subnormal health. A great part of it is due to the undertaking of all the household work far too soon after childbirth: work which is often much heavier and more damaging to health (for instance the family wash tub) and always of longer duration, since it never ends, than many factory and other jobs. These women generally only reach the hospital stage in middle life, there to be patched up as well as may be.

The Report fails to strike a new note, to catch the atmosphere of hope and progress. Here is the old ideal of women as the providers of a comfortable background to life, anonymous and scarcely recognised. Those who make the very life of the community, are to be treated as merely the means to an end. Not so shall the ends be really served, nor can the contribution have its full value. The 'decay of the home' is lamented. Can it be otherwise when the centre of the home – the wife and mother – is to be given no place as an individual in plans made for that future to which the Plan refers: a future of greater freedom, greater justice, greater security (p. 9).

In conclusion Abbott and Bompas wrote:

Practically all the disabilities and anomalies criticised could have been obviated had there been a different approach to the whole subject. At present the Plan is mainly a man's plan for man: it remains selective instead of being truely national. A great part of what is offered to women is in the spirit of that mistaken benevolence from which perhaps more than anything else women need to be emancipated before they can take their place as partners in marriage and in work. Henry James' father once wrote:

> 'I have been so long accustomed to see the most arrant
> devilry transact itself in the name of benevolence that
> the moment I hear a profession of good will from almost
> any quarter I instinctively look about for a constable or
> place my hand within reach of the bell-rope. . . . I do
> hope that the reign of benevolence is over; until that
> occurs I am sure the reign of God is impossible.'

Therein lies a deep truth, upon which every one of us in these days would do well to ponder. One thing is certain. To continue to give women what seems to others to be good for them; to give them indeed anything with an ulterior motive, be it the preservation of marriage and the family – or a rise in the birth rate – is doomed to failure. To respect women as individuals, to give them what is their right as citizens and workers, may, on the other hand, have great and beneficial effect far beyond any immediate object. For both security and progress are rooted in justice (p. 20).

This final passage highlights the post-war feminists' focus on equal rights and equal treatment; an argument which is supplemented by earlier assertions that the main fault of the plan was not in the sphere of the economic but of the moral. Relying on a notion of natural justice, Abbott and Bompas sought to deflect benevolence and paternalism and to establish women as equal citizens. While they were mounting this argument Eleanor Rathbone, with equal conviction, was attempting to do good to women for 'ulterior motives'.

Rathbone's campaign for the endowment of motherhood, or family allowances as they became known, was rekindled during the war. Beveridge was much influenced by her ideas, and his support for family allowances – which he regarded as a basic premise for the success of his proposals – was vital in persuading government departments to support their introduction. In this sense it can be argued that feminist ideas on welfare had become very influential, but Macnicol (1980) has argued that the government introduced family allowances more as a cynical package to control wages and inflation than as a means of preventing child or family poverty. Notwithstanding this argument, it remains highly unlikely that family allowances would ever have been introduced without Rathbone's systematic and long running campaign.

In spite of Beveridge's support for family allowances, he did not propose the same scheme as that outlined by the Family Endowment Society. For example, instead of a truly universal benefit, he proposed that the allowance should only be paid for the second child and subsequent children. In addition he set the level of the allowance considerably below subsistence level for children (this was reduced even further by the government when the Family Allowances Act was introduced). Moreover the Beveridge Plan was agnostic on the issue of to whom the allowance should be paid, allowing the government to decide that it should be paid to the father. This strategy was successfully resisted by the Family Endowment Society, and Rathbone managed to ensure that it was paid to the mother.

This was a very real achievement both in practical and ideological terms. Not only did it put cash directly into the hands of women who were caring for children, and, as an important although unintended consequence, provide mothers with a small degree of economic independence, it also established the basic tenet of the feminist analysis of family economics, namely that the family wage did not automatically go towards the support of the dependent members of the family. The acceptance of the proposal that married women should be entitled to receive benefit direct from the state provided a major plank in the argument that women should not be forced to look to men for their, and their children's, economic survival. The importance of this achievement by Rathbone and other feminists should not be underestimated even if the other campaigns against the anti-feminist element of the Beveridge Plan ultimately has little real effect in modifying the dominant ideologies of welfare in 1945.

8 · *Socialism*

It was difficult for other voices to be heard in the tidal wave of approval which followed the Beveridge Report. The apparent consensus was barely challenged from any quarter and the socialists, too, had little to say. They were dragged in behind the calls for a welfare state and could only add that it should be built faster and have more resources. As George Orwell put it at the time, 'Thirty years ago any Conservative would have denounced this as state charity, while most socialists would have rejected it as a capitalist bribe. In 1944 the only discussion is about whether it will be adopted in whole or in part' (Orwell, 1968b, p. 29). 'Everyone', he said, 'is pro Beveridge – including left-wing papers which a few years ago would have denounced such a scheme as semi-Fascist' (Orwell, 1968a, p. 318).

But some socialists did try to swim against the tide. They remained convinced that welfare reforms were palliatives which did little more than cover up the capitalist system's worst excesses. This is reflected in the first extract below from the Socialist Party of Great Britain. But it also had a wider resonance among political activists in the Labour Party. At the Party Conference in 1944, for example, a resolution was carried which called for the wholesale nationalization of many sectors, including land, heavy industry and banking. It was seconded by Mrs G. Denington of the South West St Pancras Labour Party who argued:

Everybody now can see that anarchic capitalism means unemployment, degradation, malnutrition, and misery, and that any form of capitalism means inevitable war. Sir William Beveridge in trying to put forward a new solution dressed the old wolf in sheep's clothing, but the wolf is still there, and the only way of getting rid of it is to kill it stone dead (quoted in Addison, 1977, p. 256).

A second, probably larger, group felt, like the Fabians, that the Beveridge Report was an acknowledgement of capitalism's past failures and that it presaged a fully socialist transformation of society which could be achieved if sufficient pressure were applied. They disagreed with the Fabians in their reluctance to see Beveridge as a proto-socialist proposal and in their greater suspicion that attempts would be made to undermine it. They saw Beveridge as little more than a stepping stone: something to be implemented and then built on and transformed into a more fundamental challenge to capitalism. Such was the dominance of Fabianism, that this group could barely be distinguished separately at the left end of the Fabian spectrum.

The first extract below comes from a pamphlet prepared by the Socialist Party of Great Britain (SPGB), criticizing the introduction of family allowances. The SPGB has always been a small organization reluctant to be compromised by any contact with the capitalist state. It was the product of a split in the Social Democratic Federation in 1904 and it is unlikely that this pamphlet brought it a wider audience. Indeed the argument probably reflects its isolation at the time. Nevertheless, that isolation allowed it to put clearly some points which link at least one strand of socialism across the periods we are considering. The pamphlet is sceptical about all social reform, although grudgingly accepting that reforms do sometimes improve the position of some members of the working class, at least in a small way. But family allowances, which, as we have seen, play a central part in the Beveridge Report, are dismissed as little more than an attempt to reduce the earnings of individual workers and increase employers' profits. Eleanor Rathbone and William Beveridge are summarily denounced for supporting this. The utilization of Marxist economics by the SPGB led them to take a fundamentally different position to contemporary feminists. Their analysis suggested that equality between men and women could only be achieved through revolutionary change. But their orthodoxy also allowed them to critically assess proposals which, at the time, were receiving little criticism from any quarter.

Beveridge as agent of capitalism

The claim that schemes for social reform can eradicate some or all of the worst evils of Capitalism has often been made in the past and just as often proved to be false. The present war has provided a fertile breeding ground for plans for abolishing the slums, establishing permanent peace on earth, removing the degradation accompanying old age and unemployment, improving the health of the workers and so on. The production of these plans should be expected at a time when many workers are extremely sceptical as to the outcome of the war in connection with their own conditions of life and wondering, in fact, if after this war things are going to be measurably better than they were after that of 1914–18. . . .

In support of Family Allowances advocates claim that their introduction will abolish a major part of poverty, on the ground that the principal cause of poverty is the possession of young families.

We state immediately that no scheme for social reform can remove the poverty endured by the working-class under Capitalism. The poverty of the working-class is as constant a condition of Capitalism as the never ending flow of pettifogging schemes for the alleviation of poverty which the workers are asked to support. . . .

It does not necessarily follow that reforms can never be of any benefit to the workers, although it is true to say that reforms cannot abolish the major evils of Capitalism, nor will they generally be introduced to deal with some of the minor evils except when their introduction is necessary to ensure the continued smooth running of the capitalist system. There are, however, some proposals for social reform which may be harmful in themselves, and perhaps the most obnoxious of all are those which on the surface appear philanthropic, but which in effect work towards a lowering of the already low standard of living of the working-class. We may place in this category the schemes that have been put forward from time to time for Family Allowances.

The Family Allowance advocates claim (to quote one of the best known, Sir William Beveridge, a Vice-President of the Family Endowment Society), letter to *Times* of January 12th, 1940: '. . . the greatest single cause of poverty in this country is young children'.

They further state that as industry in this country is unable to afford a general increase in wages, this poverty can only be abolished by a scheme whereby parents with dependent children would receive allowances over and above their wages. We will deal later with the assertion that industry in this country is unable to afford a general increase in wages, but we challenge immediately the statement that 'the greatest single cause of poverty in this country is young children'.

Professor Colin Clark (*People's Year Book*, 1936) stated that 850,000 persons with over £500 a year shared between them a total almost as great as that which was shared between 12,000,000 people with incomes below £122 a year.

G. W. Daniels and H. Campion (*The Distribution of National Capital*, Manchester University Press, 1936) showed that 1 per cent of the persons aged 25 or over in England and Wales owned 60 per cent of the total national capital of about £14,000,000,000, or on a slightly broader basis 5 per cent owned 80 per cent of the total national capital.

Here is disclosed the real poverty of the working population, besides which the difference in the conditions of those workers with families to support and those without appears trivial and insignificant. The social chasm between rich and poor is thrown into even sharper relief when it is recognised that the vast mass of the impoverished workers perform all of the useful work of society, whilst the privileged minority can be, and generally are, idle and unproductive.

If the advocates of Family Allowances are sincere in their expressed desire to abolish poverty we would draw their attention to this, the 'greatest single', and in fact the only, cause of poverty in the modern world against which they might direct their attacks.

It is questionable, however, whether all of those who have most assiduously supported Family Allowances have been activated entirely by a desire to improve the lot of sections of the workers. Some years ago Miss Eleanor Rathbone, MP, who is chairman of the Family Endowment Society, explained to some of the business men of the insurance world at the Annual Conference of the Faculty of Insurance that in the case of a contributory scheme for Family Allowances the burden would fall on the 'young men and the young women who nearly all are going to get married pretty soon and have dependent children, and who would be expected to be willing to make some sacrifice at the expense of their cigarettes, cinemas, and betting on football to provide for the period when the children are coming along' (*Journal of the Faculty of Insurance*, July 1927). . . .

The problem that Miss Rathbone touched upon in her address to the insurance fraternity was in fact not so much that workers with family responsibilities do not receive enough, but, from the Capitalist point of view the much more serious one that workers without families are receiving too much! . . .

It might at first sight appear paradoxical to assert that a saving in the total national wage bill can be effected by additional payments being made to certain sections of the workers, but in the long run such a saving will result from the introduction of Family Allowances. As soon as the cost (or perhaps more truly the 'alleged' cost) of rearing some or all of the workers' children is considered by the employers to have been provided for outside of wages, the tendency will assert itself for wages to sink to a new level based on the cost of maintaining a worker and his wife, or a worker, his wife and one child as the case may be.

The most obvious way in which this reduction may come about is by introducing Family Allowances at a time when prices have risen instead of granting a general increase in wages to meet the increased cost of living. Sir W. Beveridge admitted this possibility when replying to a question put to him at a meeting of civil servants at Central Hall, Westminster, January 28th, 1943. He said:

> 'I do not see why the provision of Family Allowances should decrease salaries and wages. The possibility that they might lead to wages not going up so quickly is no reason for not providing adequately for children first' (*Whitley Bulletin*, March, 1943).

The recent decision of the Trades Union Congress to support Family Allowances will render it easier for the employers to give an imaginary sop to a small fraction of the workers, whilst, in fact, the large majority have suffered a setback. . . .

But the real issue is not that certain unscrupulous employers may seek to save out of wages amounts paid in Family Allowances, but that once it is established that the children (or some of the children) of the workers have been 'provided for' by other means, the tendency will be for wage levels to sink to new standards which will not include the cost of maintaining such children. . . .

Miss Rathbone thus sees in Family Allowances a means whereby a revolution can be averted and it is beside the point that she attributed to the Labour Party intentions which they themselves would probably be the first to deny. This theme is also touched upon in her book, *The Case for Family Allowances* (1940, Penguin), where she claims that the preservation of family life by means of Family Allowances may quite well be 'a bulwark against certain explosive and disrupting forces. A man with a wife and family may talk revolution, but he is much less likely to act it than one who has given Society no such hostages' (p. 14) (SPGB, 1943, pp. 2, 5–7, 8–9, 11–15).

The force of the SPGB's polemic against family allowances may seem a little odd for us today, since few contemporary socialists would be so critical of the idea of child benefit. But their arguments have clear links both back to the arguments of earlier socialists and to more recent Marxist based criticisms of the welfare state. Like Morris, of course, they stress the inadequacy of social reforms when they argue that revolutionary change is required. Like the SDF, they stress that the real causes of poverty arise from class ownership of wealth and property, which are barely referred to either by Beveridge or the Fabians. Implicit within the SPGB position, too, is the view that it is not possible to detach one small policy area for separate consideration. It has to be set into the wider context of capitalist development. Although the issue is discussed in terms of wage levels, the key point being made is that reforms cannot solve the problems which the SPGB argued were inherent in capitalism. And, as we pointed out earlier (p. 108), recent research seems to confirm that the reduction of wage levels was an important consideration for the government (McNicol, 1980). The kernel of the argument is still important. It suggests that one needs to analyse the development of the welfare state by relating it to the pressures facing capitalism. More recent Marxist debate has tended to look at the development of the welfare state as an essential feature of post-war capitalism; whether in response to demands from below which might otherwise threaten political legitimacy, or because modern production relies on the existence and maintenance of an educated and healthy labour force in order to sustain long-term profitability (see, for example, Gough, 1979; Offe, 1984). The pamphlet was trying to develop an analysis of a new phenomenon (at least in terms of its scale), so it is perhaps hardly surprising that its authors simply focused on the issue of wage levels, instead of going beyond that to identify ways in which the private costs of sustaining and reproducing labour power could effectively be socialized.

No such questions worried the second group of socialists referred to above. As *Tribune*'s ambiguous response to Beveridge in the next extract shows, they saw themselves to be using his report for their own ends rather than acting as uncritical supporters. The language of battle differentiated them from the Fabians if nothing else did. This was not a call for a careful adjustment to new realities, supported by a professional bureaucracy but a call to war using Beveridge as an unlikely weapon, if not ally.

Beveridge as a Trojan horse for socialism

In a general sense the decision to allow a report on social conditions to appear at this time was the work of a guilty national conscience. No return to the conditions of the past were thought possible. The Left were demanding the pledge of a new world. The Right (in the days of military inactivity) realised the perils of withstanding concession. No doubt they believed that a goodly array of burnished platitudes would stay the avalanche of public opinion until they were stronger for the fight and until their conscience had relapsed into its old accustomed inertia. Nothing else can explain the political lunacy (from their own point of view) of Mr Churchill and his friends which has tolerated the publication of Sir William's findings. For the mouse has been in labour and has brought forth a mountain.

Sir William Beveridge is a social evangelist of the old Liberal school. He is an honoured member of the Reform Club, and the horizon of his political aspirations is, therefore, not boundless. He specifically disavows many of the tenets of revolutionary Socialism. But he has a good heart and a clear, well-stocked head, and he has discharged his task with Liberal fervour and even a trace of Liberal innocence.

What kind of world would the honest Liberal like to establish? He would like to make a truce between private enterprise and State ownership. He would like the two to work in harness together, but, above all, he would like, by resolute action, to appease the most obvious pains and to succour the most grievous casualties which capitalism produces. From this dangerous angle Sir William has approached his task. He would like to establish a tolerable minimum standard of security for every citizen, for the injured worker, for the widow, for the aged, for the unemployed, for the sick and for the growing child.

This is a commendable ambition, and the desire to achieve it is certainly not confined to those who have dabbled or delved into Socialism. But the merit and novelty of Sir William is that he has set down with the authority of a statistician and on Government note-paper the conditions which must be satisfied if this modest ambition is to be achieved. Here it is in black and white – a plain description of man's necessities, how much (or how little) he must have in his pocket if fear and want and hunger are to be lifted from his cares and if the grandiloquent phrases of the Atlantic Charter are to be translated into fact. In short, Sir William has described the conditions in which the tears might be taken out of capitalism. We should not be surprised, therefore, if all unconsciously by so doing he threatens capitalism itself.

Sir William states plainly that human claims must come first. The miner choked by silicosis, the worker who loses a finger in his machine, the old man and his wife who have done their lifetime of service, the widow who has lost her husband, the husband whose job has become momentarily redundant, the child whose parents cannot give him the best, none of these and none of the others who have suffered the disabilities of our society in the past must suffer in the future. It is an outrage that men should be the victims of these harrowing fears. To keep their bodies healthy, to ease their minds, to release their souls – these are the first claims on the State. The claim of property must come second. . . .

It will still be a battle, but we must thank Sir William for a weapon. And if it be asked how it happens that a reformer so sedate has been able to fashion a weapon so sharp, and how a Government so timid should have presented materials for its fashioning, we must answer in the famous words of Karl Marx 'that war is the locomotive of history' . . . (*Tribune*, 4 December 1942, Editorial, reprinted in Hill, 1977, p. 48).

9 · *Laissez-faire*

The popularity of Beveridge's proposals for reforming welfare provision and the fact that these proposals subsequently became the basis for constructing the post-war welfare state in Britain have meant that opposition to Beveridge has been lost sight of in the attention given to the post-war 'welfare consensus'. There was, nevertheless, considerable laissez-faire influenced resistance to the Beveridge proposals, which argued against a growing drift to state control and intervention. In particular, such arguments focused on the distinction between wartime and peacetime economies. The state control of the wartime economy and aspects of social life was accepted as a necessary condition of the wartime emergency, but it was argued that these emergency measures should not be extended to peacetime since the costs they imposed on individual freedom and the free market were intolerable.

This individualist opposition to state intervention for post-war Britain surfaced in a number of contexts. When Beveridge was taking evidence prior to the preparation of the report on social insurance, the strongest opposition was provided in the evidence from the Confederation of British Employers who mounted a sustained attack on the main principles of Beveridge's plans. Its Director, Sir John Forbes Watson, urged Beveridge to give up the whole scheme, arguing:

I want to say in here – it will go on the shorthand note but I am not sure that I want to say it publicly – we did not start this war with Germany in order to improve our social services; the war was forced upon us by Germany and we entered it to preserve our freedom and to keep the Gestapo outside our houses and that is what the war means (quoted by Addison, 1977, p. 214).

In the later years of the war, a number of associations were formed – reminiscent of the Anti-Socialist Union of the turn of the century – to propagandize for free market principles. They included Aims of Industry, the Society of Individualists, and the National League for Freedom which declared its intention to 'fight the strong movement now on foot to continue unnecessary official control of trade, industry, business and private lives after the war' (quoted in

Addison, 1977, p. 231–2). Beveridge's plan was a clear target for attacks from these positions, and the right-wing Conservative journal, *National Review*, saw it as reviving laissez-faire's fears of welfare:

The dole is to be greatly increased, so greatly that thousands of people will greatly prefer to do nothing. And an immense scattering of public money under the name of 'social security' is to take place on every sort of occasion (quoted in Calder, 1971, p. 530).

The Conservative Party was divided over its approach to Beveridge. The official leadership was characterized by a lack of enthusiasm for the report, which aroused public scepticism that the plan might be quietly buried. But within the party, a Tory Reform Group was established in 1943 among MPs who were to become significant figures in the post-war development of the party (R. A. Butler, Harold Macmillan, Quintin Hogg), who argued that the party had to address itself to the task of social reform as a matter of urgency. They were opposed by a rather more secretive grouping of Conservative MPs – the Progress Trust – established in 1943 to counter the growing influence of the Reform Group.

As with the Beveridge proposals in general, the subsequent political success of the 'reform' influence in shaping the Conservative contribution to the post-war consensus of 'Butskellism' has left the Conservative mistrust of, and hostility to, Beveridge seeming more marginal than it was during the war. Certainly, the public viewed the Conservatives as a likely stumbling block to the implementation of Beveridge, as a number of Mass Observation and Ministry of Information surveys revealed (see Addison, 1975, chapter 9, and Calder, 1971, chapter 9).

However, the most sustained attack on increased state intervention in the peacetime economy was mounted by the intellectual defenders of laissez-faire. Lionel Robbins, who had been one of the economists drawn into wartime economic planning, wrote in his *The Economic Problem of War and Peace* on the dangers inherent in extending the state control of wartime to the post-war economy. He argued that the collectivist principles necessary to the war represented a profound danger to individual liberties if they were to be continued into the peace.

Individualism, not centralization

But, beyond all this, I must confess to great fears regarding personal liberty under collectivism. Perhaps I have got things out of perspective. But I cannot get out of my head the conviction that there can be precious little freedom, precious little safeguard against arbitrary power, precious little spice and variety, in a society in which there is only one employer and only one property owner. . . . I think, too, of my life as a public servant.

I had an almost uniquely fortunate position, with friendly ministers, the best chief in the world, good colleagues and opportunities of liberty and initiative which can have been the privilege of very few. But I have to recognize that I was seldom unconscious of that sense of unfreedom which comes from the knowledge that, if you fall out with your masters, there is no alternative way of doing what you want to do. I admire more than I can say that priestly caste, the administrative grade of the British Civil Service, whose anonymous self-sacrifice and devotion does so much to preserve order and efficiency in an otherwise disorderly scene. But I think that something quite essential would have gone out of life if we were all to become public servants in peace-time. I should fear this state of affairs as it would bear on the private life of the individual. I should fear, too, the consequences to political and cultural freedom.

For these reasons and for many others which I have not time here to relate, I am still inclined to hold that the goal of progress lies in a direction different from that of over-all collectivism. I am no foe to experiment; and I recognize that there are some fields where collectivist ownership and enterprise may have important functions to perform. But, as a general principle of organization, I prefer the diffused initiative and quasi-automatism which go, or can be made to go, with private property and the market. I believe that the loose institutions of individualism offer scope for the development of a way of life, more congenial to what most of us desire in our hearts, than the tight centralized controls which are necessary if these institutions are greatly curtailed or suspended (Robbins, 1947, pp. 80–81).

Robbins' concerns with the consequences of state intervention and state control were argued in a more extensive and powerful way by the Austrian economist Friedrich von Hayek in his book *The Road to Serfdom* (1944). In this book, dedicated to 'Socialists of all parties', Hayek set out the dangers of which the growth of socialism posed to individual freedoms. Central to Hayek's argument was that socialism was not the opposite of Fascism but its political twin, in that both were committed to the centralization of power and control in the state. He drew extensively upon the lessons of Germany to identify the path along which socialism would lead – a path towards totalitarianism. Our extract from Hayek is a lengthy one – in part because *The Road to Serfdom* was itself the major statement against collectivism in this period, but also because the book has subsequently been related as a prophetic warning by current ideologies of laissez-faire. As we shall see in Part Three, such writers see post-war Britain as having fulfilled Hayek's gloomy prognostications about the growth of the state and its suppression of individual freedom of choice.

Economic security as a threat to liberty

Like the spurious 'economic freedom', and with more justice, economic security is often represented as an indispensable condition of real liberty.

In a sense this is both true and important. Independence of mind or strength of character are rarely found among those who cannot be confident that they will make their way by their own effort. Yet the idea of economic security is no less vague and ambiguous than most other terms in this field; and because of this the general approval given to the demand for security may become a danger to liberty. Indeed, when security is understood in too absolute a sense, the general striving for it, far from increasing the chances of freedom, becomes the gravest threat to it.

It will be well to contrast at the outset the two kinds of security: the limited one, which can be achieved for all, and which is therefore no privilege but a legitimate object of desire; and the absolute security which in a free society cannot be achieved for all and which ought not to be given as a privilege – except in a few special instances such as that of the judges, where complete independence is of paramount importance. These two kinds of security are, first, security against severe physical privation, the certainty of a given minimum of sustenance for all; and, secondly, the security of a given standard of life, or of the relative position which one person or group enjoys compared with others; or, as we may put it briefly, the security of a minimum income and the security of the particular income a person is thought to deserve. We shall presently see that this distinction largely coincides with the distinction between the security which can be provided for all outside of and supplementary to the market system, and the security which can be provided only for some and only by controlling or abolishing the market.

There is no reason why in a society that has reached the general level of wealth which ours has attained, the first kind of security should not be guaranteed to all without endangering general freedom. There are difficult questions about the precise standard which should thus be assured; and there is particularly the important question whether those who thus rely on the community should indefinitely enjoy all the same liberties as the rest.* An incautious handling of these questions might well cause serious and perhaps even dangerous political problems; but there can be no doubt that some minimum of food, shelter, and clothing, sufficient to preserve health and capacity to work, can be assured to everybody. Indeed, for a considerable part of the population of this country this sort of security has long been achieved. Nor is there any reason why the state should not assist the individuals in providing for those common hazards of life against which, because of their uncertainty, few individuals can make adequate provision. Where, as in the case of sickness and accident, neither the desire to avoid such calamities nor the efforts to overcome their consequences are as a rule weakened by the provision of assistance, where, in short, we deal with genuinely insurable risks, the case for the state helping to organise a comprehensive system of social insurance is very strong. . . . But there is no incompatability in principle between the state providing greater security in this way and the preservation of individual freedom. To the same category belongs also the increase of security through the state rendering assistance to the victims of such 'acts of God' as earthquakes

---

* There are also serious problems of international relations which arise if mere citizenship of a country confers the right to a standard of living higher than elsewhere, and which ought not to be dismissed too lightly.

and floods. Wherever communal action can mitigate disasters against which the individual can neither attempt to guard himself, nor make provision for the consequences, such communal action should undoubtedly be taken. There is, finally, the supremely important problem of combating general fluctuations of economic activity and the recurrent waves of large-scale unemployment which accompany them. This is, of course, one of the gravest and most pressing problems of our time. But, though its solution will require much planning in the good sense, it does not – or at least need not – require that special kind of planning which according to its advocates is to replace the market. Many economists hope indeed that the ultimate remedy may be found in the field of monetary policy, which would involve nothing incompatible even with nineteenth-century liberalism. Others, it is true, believe that real success can be expected only from the skilful timing of public works undertaken on a very large scale. This might lead to much more serious restrictions of the competitive sphere, and in experimenting in this direction we shall have carefully to watch our step if we are to avoid making all economic activity progressively more dependent on the direction and volume of government expenditure. But this is neither the only, nor, in my opinion, the most promising way of meeting the gravest threat to economic security. In any case, the very necessary efforts to secure protection against these fluctuations do not lead to the kind of planning which constitutes such a threat to our freedom.

✻   ✻   ✻   ✻   ✻

The planning for security which has such an insidious effect on liberty is that of a different kind. It is planning designed to protect individuals or groups against diminutions of their income which although in no way deserved yet in a competitive society occur daily, against losses imposing severe hardships having no moral justification yet inseparable from the competitive system. This demand for security is thus another form of the demand for just remuneration, a remuneration commensurate with the subjective merits and not with the objective results of a man's efforts. This kind of security or justice seems irreconcilable with freedom to choose one's employment.

Certainty of a given income can, however, not be given to all if any freedom in the choice of one's occupation is to be allowed. And if it is provided for some it becomes a privilege at the expense of others whose security is thereby necessarily diminished. That security of an invariable income can be provided for all only by the abolition of all freedom in the choice of one's employment is easily shown. Yet, although such a general guarantee of legitimate expectation is often regarded as the ideal to be aimed at, it is not a thing which is seriously attempted. What is constantly being done is to grant this kind of security piecemeal, to this group and to that, with the result that for those who are left out in the cold the insecurity constantly increases. No wonder that in consequence the value attached to the privilege of security constantly increases, the demand for it becomes more and more urgent, till in the end no price, not even that of liberty, appears too high. . . . If we want to form a picture of what society would be like if, according to the ideal which has seduced so many socialists, it was organised as a single great factory, we have to look to ancient Sparta, or to contemporary Germany, which after moving for two or three generations in this direction, has now so nearly reached it.

＊　　＊　　＊　　＊　　＊

Within the market system, security can be granted to particular groups only by the kind of planning known as restrictionism (which includes, however, almost all the planning which is actually practised!). 'Control', i.e. limitation of output so that prices will secure an 'adequate' return, is the only way in which in a market economy producers can be guaranteed a certain income. But this necessarily involves a reduction of opportunities open to others. If the producer, be he entrepreneur or worker, is to be protected against underbidding by outsiders, it means that others who are worse off are precluded from sharing in the relatively greater prosperity of the controlled industries. Every restriction on the freedom of entry into a trade reduces the security of all those outside it. . . . There can be little doubt that it is largely a consequence of the striving for security by these means in the last decades that unemployment and thus insecurity for large sections of the population has so much increased. . . .

Thus, the more we try to provide full security by interfering with the market system, the greater the insecurity becomes; and, what is worse, the greater becomes the contrast between the security of those to whom it is granted as a privilege and the ever-increasing insecurity of the under-privileged.

＊　　＊　　＊　　＊　　＊

The general endeavour to achieve security by restrictive measures, toler-ated or supported by the state, has in the course of time produced a progressive transformation of society – a transformation in which, as in so many other ways, Germany has led and the other countries have followed. This development has been hastened by another effect of socialist teaching, the deliberate disparagement of all activities involving economic risk and the moral opprobrium cast on the gains which make risks worth taking but which only few can win. We cannot blame our young men when they prefer the safe, salaried position to the risk of enterprise after they have heard from their earliest youth the former described as the superior, more unselfish and disinterested occupation. The younger gener-ation of to-day has grown up in a world in which in school and press the spirit of commercial enterprise has been represented as disreputable and the making of profit as immoral, where to employ a hundred people is represented as exploitation but to command the same number is honour-able. Older people may regard this as an exaggeration of the present state of affairs, but the daily experience of the University teacher leaves little doubt that as a result of anti-capitalist propaganda values have already altered far in advance of the change in institutions which has yet taken place in this country. The question is whether by changing our institutions to satisfy the new demands, we shall not unwittingly destroy values which we still rate higher.

While it is doubtful whether the spirit of freedom can anywhere be extirpated by force, it is not certain that any people would successfully withstand the process by which it was slowly smothered in Germany. Where distinction and rank is achieved almost exclusively by becoming a salaried servant of the state, where to do one's assigned duty is regarded as more laudable than to choose one's own field of usefulness, where all pursuits that do not give a recognised place in the official hierarchy or a claim to a fixed income are regarded as inferior and even somewhat disreputable, it is too much to expect that many will long prefer freedom to security. And where the alternative to security in a dependent position is a most precarious position, in which one is despised alike for success and for failure, only few will resist the temptation of safety at the price of freedom. Once things have gone so far, liberty indeed becomes almost a mockery, since it can be purchased only by the sacrifice of most of the good things of this earth. In this state it is little surprising that more and more people should come to see that without economic security liberty is 'not worth having' and that they are willing to sacrifice their liberty for security. But it is disquieting to find Professor Harold Laski in this country employing the very same argument which has perhaps done more than any other to induce the German people to sacrifice their liberty.*

There can be no question that adequate security against severe privation, and the reduction of the avoidable causes of misdirected effort and consequent disappointment, will have to be one of the main goals of policy. But if these endeavours are to be successful and not to destroy individual freedom, security must be provided outside the market and competition be left to function unobstructed. Some security is essential if freedom is to be preserved, because most are willing to bear the risk which freedom inevitably involves only so long as that risk is not too great. But while this is a truth of which we must never lose sight, nothing is more fatal than the present fashion among intellectual leaders of extolling security at the expense of freedom. It is essential that we should re-learn frankly to face the fact that freedom can only be had at a price and that as individuals we must be prepared to make severe material sacrifices to preserve our liberty. If we want to retain this we must regain the conviction on which the rule of liberty in the Anglo-Saxon countries has been based and which Benjamin Franklin expressed in a phrase applicable to us in our lives as individuals no less than as nations: 'Those who would give up essential liberty to purchase a little temporary safety deserve neither liberty nor safety (Hayek, 1944, pp. 89–99).

In the 1940s, Robbins and Hayek stood outside the social and political consensus about the future direction of British society. Their warnings about the growth of state power proved largely irrelevant in the context of a popular commitment to post-war reconstruction and the welfare state, which embarked on providing some of those elements of 'economic security' which Hayek rejected so forcefully. But marginal though they were in this period, they were not to be forgotten. By the 1970s, Hayek in particular

---

* H. J. Laski, *Liberty in the Modern State* (Pelican edition 1937, p. 51): 'Those who know the normal life of the poor, its haunting sense of impending disaster, its fitful search for beauty which perpetually eludes, will realise well enough that, without economic security, liberty is not worth having.'

was to be treated as a hero – the man who had kept the flame of laissez-faire individualism burning.

Part Three

Beyond Consensus
(1970–85)

Introduction to Part Three

It has been relatively easy in the two earlier periods to identify the dominant ideologies of welfare – the emergence of the New Liberalism at the turn of the century and the Beveridge influenced Fabianism of 1945 – and to indicate, with the advantage of hindsight, which approaches were declining in significance and which were coming into greater prominence. That is not possible in the same way today.

Certainly, since the late 1970s the New Right (using the arguments of the laissez-faire tradition) has dominated policy making at central government level, pushing forward programmes which undermine the assumptions of Beveridge and which have begun to alter the shape of the welfare state significantly (see for example, Loney, 1986). But the New Right has not succeeded in its self-appointed crusade to overturn received public opinion about welfare which remains fixed in the Beveridge inspired images of the post-war period (see Taylor-Gooby, 1985). Nor, given its direct connection with government, has the New Right been as effective as might have been expected in the policy areas on which it has chosen to concentrate. In the postscript we discuss the ideological basis of the Fowler Review of Social Security (1985). One example of the New Right's difficulty in translating ideology into practice is to be found in the Thatcher government's inability to implement the results of this review, in the short term at least. The structure of the social security system remains difficult to overturn in the absence of a new welfare consensus of the sort associated with Beveridge.

The rhetorical dominance of laissez-faire ideology within and around the Conservative government was by no means complete, was not fully reflected in policy development, and its position reflected the weakness of the other approaches as much as positive political strengths of its own. This last point is crucial to an understanding of current debates. The New Right has been able to set the agenda for these debates in large part because Fabianism's self-confidence has evaporated, only reappearing in rearguard attempts to defend those parts of the welfare state which are under attack. Indeed the Fabian establishment has probably been more effective in defending particular institutions of the welfare state than it has been in defending its underlying purpose. The ideological centre stage has been evacuated, and, despite the revival of the laissez-faire tradition, no single ideology has succeeded in establishing its dominance. Fabianism has not been displaced by a positive alternative with similar strength.

For the first time in this period all four ideologies seem to be competing, if not quite on equal terms, at least as if each was aware of the arguments of the others and was either prepared to consider them carefully or to take them on directly. As the section on Fabianism explains, the approaches to welfare and social policy which were taken for granted for twenty-five years or more after the war, began to face increasing pressure from the beginning of the 1970s. In part this was a reflection of a growing belief that the welfare state had not delivered the promises made in 1945; in part it was a reflection of the practical difficulties of maintaining a welfare state in a period of economic crisis which managed to combine rising inflation and rising unemployment. The combination of Keynes in economic policy and Beveridge in social policy which had seemed to offer so much, now began to look like a recipe for disaster.

Initially, in the late 1960s, the strongest critique of the welfare state – a harbinger of the massive storms to come – came from the explicitly socialist and anti-capitalist tradition. The welfare state was portrayed as a weapon in the hands of the capitalist class which served two functions – first to buy off the working class and ensure that their potentially revolutionary spirit was undermined; and second, effectively to police and discipline the working class through the careful direction of funds and the supervision of officials and professionals, such as social workers.

But these arguments never succeeded in making a significant impact on the practice of social policy, nor even on debates around it. Socialists who became involved in working inside the welfare state and looked for helpful advice within this approach found it difficult to draw direct lessons from it. Their difficulties were explicitly theorized in work such as *In and Against the State* (London Edinburgh Weekend Return Group, 1979) in which the possibilities of working within, yet undermining and potentially transforming the existing (capitalist) state were explored. Bolger *et al.* (1981) tried to show how socialist social workers might operate within 'the local state'. Links were also forged to the growing feminist movement – for example through the feminist inspired *Beyond the Fragments* (Rowbotham *et al.*, 1979) – and attempts were made to draw lessons for a new socialist programme of welfare. The feminist focus which has challenged traditional divisions (so important to the laissez-faire view, in particular) between the public and the private, the political and the personal, appeared to offer new possibilities for social intervention which might not immediately involve a direct confrontation with the state.

The feminist wave of the 1970s produced some of the most perceptive and confident critiques of the existing welfare state. It also began to present potential alternatives, both through campaigns directed towards the state – for particular provision or against negative changes – and through challenges to social relations within the family. While socialism was nervously picking its way through the wreckage of Beveridge, feminism was developing an independent position, stressing the need for self-activity and autonomous agencies.

If the 1970s were a period of uncertainty, division and debate within social policy, their legacy now seems less divided. The strength of the laissez-faire critique which questioned the certainties of a state paternalism, seen by the poor as oppressive in practice and by the better-off as wasteful, has meant that the welfare state cannot simply be rebuilt in the image of the past. Even the Fabians recognize this, as Glennerster comments in a Fabian collection on the future of the welfare state: 'We begin from the belief that all is not well in the welfare state as we know it – and not just because of Mrs Thatcher's cuts' (Glennerster, 1983b, p. 1).

Indeed, such a starting point is now so widely accepted that there is a danger of a new orthodoxy emerging in which all the differences we have explored are buried once more in broad and bland generalizations. There appears to be broad agreement that state centralization is a bad thing and conversely that decentralization and community care are good things. The value of voluntary activity also seems to be recognized and stressed across the political spectrum. But it should be clear, in considering the sections which follow, that the interpretation of these policies by the different groups are not likely to be the same. The same term may be used to have quite distinct meanings. In the case of 'decentralization', for example, it is rather misleading to use the same term to describe what for laissez-faire writers is virtually a synonym for privatization; what for some in the Fabian tradition is a way of organizing collective provision more efficiently; is for socialists a way of undermining the power of capitalism through collective action; and for feminists involves a shift of power away from male dominated institutions in areas of direct concern to women. Similar difficulties arise with most of the key terms in the debates about the reconstruction of welfare.

It is very easy to become involved in debates which appear to start from shared assumptions and yet lead to surprising conclusions. In this final section it is important to note which assumptions really are shared and which are not, in order to clarify the extent to which each is compatible with different ends. In spite of renewed ideological conflict, the seductive language of policy debate at present tends paradoxically to obscure political and ideological division. Ideas tend to be absorbed within existing professional debates so that approaches which fundamentally challenge existing structures become absorbed and reinterpreted in such a way that professional agencies can manage and deal with them.

This helps to explain the continued underlying strength of the broad Fabian approach to welfare, since, however battered it has been, it seems to make the most sense within the 'caring' professions, because of its stress on practical expertise and client support. The other approaches may nibble at the edges, but cannot offer the prospect of quite the same relatively unified professional model. Indeed, all of them in one way or another actually threaten the system. As a result, despite high level political support, even laissez-faire approaches have found it difficult to make headway, although major shifts in spending patterns have taken place in the last ten years, and in practice, the move to community care has often meant a shift to private provision (e.g. in the care of the elderly), or an increased emphasis on 'caring' within the family. Socialist and feminist approaches are likely to find it still more difficult to achieve any major impact. Even if they are taken up within some local authorities it is often managerially easier for the forms to be adopted and run in traditional ways. Decentralization of social work services, for example, is often presented as a means of more effective area management and control over resources by senior officers, at the same time as being sold as a socialist policy to those at lower levels.

The central tradition of Fabianism is beginning to reconstruct itself in the face of political and economic change. It remains deeply rooted in Britain's welfare state, picking up lessons from rival approaches and at the same time forcing them to fight on Fabianism's own terms, imperceptibly – particularly in the case of the socialists and feminists – having to borrow the methods of Fabianism and arguing for particular reforms and piecemeal change.

Fabianism has had a protean existence. From a sharply critical force at the turn of the century, with an identifiable socialist vision, and a support group for Beveridge in the post-war period, it became an orthodoxy, with little of its socialist origins on view, until facing fundamental challenge at the end of the 1970s. It is now showing that it is capable of adjusting to the changed economic realities of mass unemployment and that the obituaries were premature. Indeed some of the approaches which developed out of criticisms of Fabianism in welfare are finding themselves forced into its arms for support once more.

10 · *Laissez-faire*

During the post-war period, laissez-faire ideology remained marginal to the public, political and intellectual discussions about the welfare state. It existed outside of the political consensus which accepted the mixed economy and state welfare as the preconditions of government in Britain. Its flame was kept burning by individuals and organizations who were viewed from within the consensus as anachronistic and idiosyncratic. Hayek, and organizations such as the Institute of Economic Affairs (IEA) and the Adam Smith Institute, continued to assert the primacy of the free market, and warned of the dire consequences of 'state interference'.

The Heath government of 1970–4 represented the first real opportunity for laissez-faire ideologists to 'come in from the cold'. Heath's commitments to controlling trade union power and freeing the energies of private enterprise offered a chance for the reassertion of free market individualism. In 1971, the Conservative MP Rhodes Boyson edited a collection of articles which attempted to apply the lessons of 'individual responsibility in a free society' to welfare issues. This collection – entitled *Down with the Poor* – contained contributions from individuals who were to become central intellectual figures in the subsequent rise of the New Right: Alfred Sherman, Ralph Harris (of the IEA) and Milton Friedman. Boyson's own contribution to the volume outlined the attack on state welfare which was to be developed over the following decade.

Farewell to paternalism

The present welfare state, with its costly universal benefits and heavy taxation, is rapidly producing a similar economic and spiritual malaise among our people. Planned, introduced and encouraged by good men who believed that state intervention would bring both economic and spiritual returns, the end-product is completely different.

The National Health Service was introduced by men of compassion who wished to improve the health of the poor and to remove the worry of medical bills. The end result has been a decline in medical standards below the level of other advanced countries because people are not prepared to pay as much through taxation on other people's health as they would pay directly on their own and their families'. Long queues in surgeries, an endless waiting-list for hospital beds, and the emigration of many newly-trained doctors are among the unexpected results. Small wonder that more and more people are looking to some form of private insurance to give them wider choice in medicine and surgery.

Unemployment schemes and other social security benefits have been universalised and increased to their present level because people remembered the millions of unemployed and the poverty and deprivation of the 1930s. The 'means test' is still a dirty word despite the fact that all of us in paying (or not paying) income tax regularly face a means test, as do others in seeking legal aid or applying for any of dozens of allowances or rebates which give preference to poorer people. Those of us with children at university face regular means tests.

There is also encouragement for the lower paid with large families to become unemployed or to go sick. Similarly, millions of workers are encouraged to break the monotony of factory routine by strikes when meagre strike pay can be augmented by supplementary benefits to their families and tax rebates for themselves. The reliable and industrious worker looks with irritation and animosity at his idle fellows whom he helps to maintain, and the general sense of responsibility and personal pride declines. National economic strength and personal moral fibre are both reduced. Officers administering supplementary benefit and unemployment insurance are so afraid of complaints being made to newspapers and MPs about harsh treatment that rules are bent, and scores of teachers even in London are paid unemployment pay whilst there are vacancies in the schools. Thus teachers trained at considerable national expense and now desiring more exotic careers in professions, rarely if ever recruited from employment exchanges, are encouraged to waste their teacher training. . . .

Housing subsidies and rent controls, also introduced by good if short-sighted and muddled men, have produced the appalling slums and homelessness of the present day. Many working-class families are virtually prisoners of their council houses since they would lose the subsidy – and perhaps a roof – if they moved elsewhere. The larger tower blocks with their tragic effect upon young and old inmates would never have multiplied in a free market where the producer has to take careful account of the preferences of the sovereign consumer. . . . Larger local government units have removed officials and councillors from contact with the ratepayers as people, and every increase in size of local authorities transfers more power to officials concerned more about their professional advancement than with satisfying the ratepayer. Hence the fashions which run through professions are immediately perpetrated upon the innocent citizen.

Meanwhile the landlord penalised by restricted rents allows his property to deteriorate and the stock of houses to rent continues to diminish. The prices of large and modern houses are increased because, on high incomes, tax relief obtained against building society mortgages is one of the shrewdest forms of capital gain in an age of inflation.

We can all recall that Mr Crossman's grandiose scheme for national superannuation would have drastically widened the breach in national insurance by requiring that present 'contributors' (for which read 'taxpayers') should pay for present pensions in the hope that 'future contributors' (for which read 'future taxpayers') would pay for future pensions. This would have been a further confidence trick on the contributors made possible only by the bemused state of the electorate after five years of continually increasing governmental imposts.

The result of all this extra interference financed by taking over 50 per cent of the gross national product in taxation has been not the production of an economically viable society but what might be called rampant stagflation, that is to say stagnation in production and raging inflation which further destroys belief in the future. The moral fibre of our people has been weakened. A state which does for its citizens what they can do for themselves is an evil state; and a state which removes all choice and responsibility from its people and makes them like broiler hens will create the irresponsible society. In such an irresponsible society no-one cares, no-one saves, no-one bothers – why should they when the state spends all its energies taking money from the energetic, successful and thrifty to give to the idle, the failures and the feckless?

Religious philosophy holds that man is moral only when he can freely exercise his choice between good and evil. This requirement is the basis of free will. The same applies equally to economic, social and family life. A man will grow to full moral maturity only when he is allowed to take risks, with subsequent rewards and penalties and full responsibility for his decisions. Yet in Britain the state now decides how half or more of a man's income shall be spent, how his family should be educated, how their health care should be organised, how they shall save for misfortunes and retirement, what library and in many cases what cultural provision they should receive, and where and at what cost they should be housed. . . .

Not only is the present welfare state inefficient and destructive of personal liberty, individual responsibility and moral growth, but it saps the collective moral fibre of our people as a nation. John Stuart Mill wrote 'The worth of a state, in the long run, is the worth of the individuals composing it.' Disraeli in another context declared, 'We put too much faith in system and look too little to men.' The truth is that a strong, free country can be built only on strong, free men and the weakness of our foreign policy and defence provision over the last few years is not only a reflection of weak government but is symptomatic of an enfeebled people. Samuel Smiles wrote 'The solid foundations of liberty must rest upon individual character; which is also the only sure guarantee for social security and national progress.'

In *Down with the Poor* we are concerned to point towards a society which will be more efficient on the one hand in abolishing poverty and want because it will give equal priority on the other hand to building up the strength of the individual and the family as good in themselves and essential to a strong country. Some people look with amusement or even horror at the self-help of the Victorian age, but its virtues of duty, order and efficiency have been replaced in the muddled thinking of our age by a belief in individual irresponsibility: a neglect of our responsibilities to the past, to our fellow citizens and to the future. The predictable outcome is seen in disorder, crime and lack of civic duty, and the palsied inefficiency so often visible throughout the public service, nationalised boards and even private industry. We have been heading for economic and moral bankruptcy. . . .

The massive increase in taxation since Victorian days has crippled voluntary welfare, while permitting poverty to linger unnecessarily. Where poverty remains it is the fault of politicians whose double sin has been to spread benefits too widely and raise taxes on a scale that hinders the increase in the national income. It is significant that during the six years of the last Labour Government there was an increase in the number of families living below the 'poverty line' despite an unprecedented increase in taxation, public expenditure and the bureaucratic machine. . . .

Down with the Poor shows how resurgence of the past pride and responsibility of our people, bringing a rapid increase in the gross national product linked with the concentration of aid on the deprived and handicapped, will eliminate poverty and the poor.

On many occasions the freedom of the world has depended upon our courage, efficiency and love of liberty. We must build these virtues anew in our people so that we shall not be found wanting in any future crisis. As in higher self-help we owe this not only to ourselves – it is part of our duty to all men (Boyson, 1971, pp. 1–9).

The 'failures' of the Heath government were ascribed by the New Right to a loss of nerve (economic U-turn and the defeat by the miners) and betrayals of principle which, they argued, meant that Heath failed to break the post-war consensus. The electoral defeat of Heath in 1974 led to his replacement as leader of the party by Margaret Thatcher, who, together with Keith Joseph, promoted the party's 'conversion' to monetarism, free-market principles and a laissez-faire view of the state. In this creation of a new political 'home' for laissez-faire ideology, the role of the previously 'marginal' individuals and organizations became more central. The IEA and Adam Smith Institute were accompanied by other 'think tanks' such as the IEA's Social Affairs Unit, and the Centre for Policy Studies, in the promotion and promulgation of laissez-faire views of state policy.

Before considering the specific arguments about welfare, it is worth detailing some of the more general positions about the relationship between the state and the economy in this revival of laissez-faire ideology. One central theme is the freeing of enterprise and initiatives from the interference of the state. This interference takes a number of forms. Government intervention in the planning and regulation of the economy acts to inhibit and block the most efficient operation of the economy (i.e. market forces) – because no government could ever hope to co-ordinate economic forces as efficiently as the normal workings of the market do. Second, government interference also takes the form of excessive taxation used to fund public spending. Taxation – it was argued – blunts initiative by removing the economic incentive from risk taking and economic effort. Third, public spending is not 'wealth-producing', whereas private sector economic activity is. Therefore the growth of public sector activity hastened economic decline, both by the fact that it did not generate wealth, and by taking the wealth producing private sector.

In the following extract, Sir Keith Joseph argues for the changes that need to be made in the relationship between the economy and the state:

Monetarism is not enough

Cuts in state spending are essential both to make way for the revival of the wealth-creating sector and to achieve a deceleration of the growth of the money supply. Cuts in state spending of sufficient magnitude to reduce inflation substantially will require strong nerves. But the alternative would be accelerating decline in standard of living and in employment within the next few years.

To hold down the growth of the money supply to a level commensurate with the expected growth in productive capacity, and to keep it there, is part of the cure for inflation. If the whole economy were private, then all firms would be subject to the resulting constriction – and only the unsound would need to go. But the whole economy is not private. Nearly two-thirds is statist, and insensitive in itself to contraction of the money supply. It is fed with money which is expanded automatically to maintain given levels of expenditure in real terms – 'funny money', as Samuel Brittan calls it. Indeed, while money supply is contracting, budgetary spending is expanding.

So the state sector bids up interest rates, bids off funds, bids away manpower and leaves the force of the monetary contraction focused on the private sector. While the activity rate is low, and stocks have run down, as now, the private sector feels the pinch of lower demand and increased costs but, though there are record levels of bankruptcies, the sector as a whole can temporarily increase its liquidity. . . .

In other words, the monetary process is both a cause of inflation and a link in a wider chain of cause and effect. Contraction in a mixed economy strangles the private sector unless the state sector contracts with it and reduces its take from the national income.

Hence my title 'Monetarism is not enough'. Detaxing and the restoration of bold incentives and encouragements to business and industry are necessary too. Until the state contracts, and indeed until enterprise is encouraged both by this contraction together with some assurance that it will stay contracted, and by less destructive taxation and intervention, there will not be the confidence nor the climate for entrepreneurship and risk-taking that will alone secure prosperity, high employment and economic health.

Cuts mean cuts. At present, we have learned, actual government expenditure has outrun projected by several percent of the GNP. We shall need to cut it back by several percent. Pseudo-cuts of future programmes will not be enough. We shall need to cut state employment and subsidies to rail, steel, housing and the supported sector. We shall need to explain that subsidised employment is not really saving jobs because the subsidies have to be paid for and the paying for them loses more jobs than are saved. We must demonstrate that state spending – including subsidies – is a cause of many smaller firms cutting their force or going out of business. . . .

Our monetary problems reflect the underlying weaknesses of this man-made chaos, the divorce of work from production, of cost from benefit, of reward from performance, the greatest government spending spree of all time which is designed primarily to keep people busy instead of useful. . . .

That is going through the motions, keeping up appearances, window dressing a fraudulent facade. Behind the facade, the private sector that produces the goods which people want is restricted by controls, over-taxed by local and central government and harassed by officials. Our monetary arrangements are bound to reflect this dichotomy. Hence the public sector's 'funny money', which, we now learn belatedly, has led to massive state overspending, while the ever more constricted wealth-producing sector has to conduct its accounts, taxes and dividends in terms of an increasingly threadbare pound. . . .

Monetarism is not enough. This is not intended as a counsel of despair, but a warning note. Government's intention to contract the money supply is welcome and potentially beneficial to all. But it is not enough unless there is also the essential reduction of the state sector and the essential encouragement of enterprise. We are over-governed, over-spent, over-taxed, over-borrowed and over-manned. If we shirk the cure, the after-effects of continued over-taxation will be worse than anything we have endured hitherto. Our ability to distinguish between economic reality and economic make-believe will decline further. We shall experience accelerated worsening of job prospects, the growing flight of those with professional skills, talent and ability to other countries, and an increase in the shabbiness and squalor of everyday lives.

That is why, by itself, the strict and unflinching control on money supply though essential is not enough. We must also have substantial cuts in tax and public spending and bold incentives and encouragements to the wealth creators, without whose renewed efforts we shall all grow poorer (Joseph, 1977).

In addition to these economic costs, the expansion of the government's sphere of action, induced by the post-war consensus approval for state intervention, was leading to the breakdown of government caused by an 'overload' of pressures and demands on the government. Because the principle of state intervention contained no inherent limits, the tendency was for more and more special pleading for 'needs' to be met through state action, to which political parties had to respond to maintain their electoral viability. The New Right argued that this 'electoral bargaining' (trading political support for state action in response to interest group demands) was destabilizing democracy, and producing a constant expansion of state intervention as more interest groups identified more 'needs' which had to be met.

These arguments for 'rolling back the state' underpinned the more specific arguments about the state's role in welfare provision. Welfare exemplified the errors of excessive state interference, and represented one area in which 'market' alternatives could be constructed. There are three main areas of debate around the welfare state which the New Right opened up. First is the nature of state provision itself. Not only did state welfare require heavy taxation, but provision of welfare by the state also involved 'economic waste'. Because welfare services were provided by state 'monopolies', they were insulated from the efficiency-inducing pressure of market competition. This monopoly position meant that welfare services were more likely to serve the bureaucratic and professional interests of their staff (sometimes described as bureaucratic and professional imperialism) rather than the needs of their consumers (clients). In addition, welfare consumers were denied any choice in the way their welfare needs could be met. Rather than being allowed to decide how they wanted to invest in their own welfare, welfare consumers were forced to accept what the state provided. Thus, state welfare constrained the freedom of the individual in two ways – first in the guise of the taxpayer being forced to pay for wasteful welfare systems, and second in the guise of the welfare consumer being forced to accept 'monopoly suppliers'.

The second area of arguments concerned the social and economic effects of state welfare. The expansion of state welfare provision had led to a growing population dependent on state benefits. The stress here is on 'dependent'. Just as in the turn of the century debates on the Poor Law, the concern is with the creation of dependency through state benefits, which leads to an expectation that needs will be met by the state. State benefits were held to be undermining 'work incentives' by being paid out too readily and at levels which made waged work unattractive. Initiative and enterprise was, in yet another form, being undermined by the 'nanny state'. The extreme form of this state – induced dependence – was the growth of 'scrounging' – the abuse of state liberality by the work-shy. In the pre-1979 election period, the scrounger became once again the major figure in public concerns about welfare benefits (see Clarke, 1983). State welfare was undermining the sense of responsibility of the individual. The responsibility which should have led him to safeguard his own interests and those of his family could be surrendered to the state in the secure knowledge that the state would 'pick up the tab'. The following extract develops these arguments about the effects of social insurance on the will to work. It is taken from the preface to a pamphlet on social insurance by Hermione Parker, and was written by Arthur Seldon, the Advisory Director of the Institute of Economic Affairs:

Self-help not state help

Mrs Hermione Parker's *Monograph* is a massively documented examination of the extent to which the 40-year-old British social security system of national insurance, supplementary and other state benefits has impinged on and weakened the labour market to the detriment, not least, of working people. Her detailed examination and examples indicate that the original purpose of helping people in times and conditions of distress has been overlaid by the effect, foreseen or unforeseen, intended or unintended, of altering relative income from the state when out of work and from industry when in work. It is now increasingly rational for increasing numbers of the traditionally conscientious, law-abiding and self-respecting British people to avoid work, since they and their families are better off out of work.

That development cannot benefit the British economy, its social coherence, family life or individual integrity. The dilemma is not easily resolved. Helping people weakens the will to self-help. That is not criticism but a recognition of human nature. Moreover, if help is provided for particular circumstances and conditions, the number of people who tend towards those circumstances and conditions increases. That again is no more than the natural response of human nature to increase supply in response to a rise in price or an improvement in income. But it is true, to varying degrees, of all conditions that humans can influence, from unemployment and even sickness to the number of children in normal two-parent families and the number of oddly described one-parent families.

The source of the impasse in social policy is the concentration of politicians, conventional sociologists and the caring fraternity on the income effects and their total neglect of the price effects of social benefits. Experience amply demonstrates that price effects assert themselves in all social systems, socialist or capitalist, except where they are suppressed by coercion or terror. The higher the benefits, the larger the number qualifying for them. That is supply-and-demand economics that applies no less to state benefits than to payment of labour in industry (Seldon, 1982, pp. 7–8).

Beginning from these criticisms, the New Right began to develop a series of alternative conceptions of how welfare ought to be provided. Central to the New Right's approach to welfare is the idea of 'privatization', involving the opening up of welfare provision to the private sector and market forces. In Britain, privatization has contained three main elements. First, it has involved the encouragement of 'private' alternatives to state supplied systems of welfare benefits and services – medical insurance and services, private education, private pension schemes and so on. Second, it has involved pressure on state services to 'contract out' some of their tasks to companies in the private sector, such as cleaning and catering, laundry services, refuse collection, etc. The third sense in which the New Right has striven to promote privatization is a more complex one, since it concerns the overlap between two different meanings of 'public' and 'private'. The first two aspects of privatization rest on a distinction between the private (commercial) sector of the economy and the public (state) sector. But there is also a distinction between the private (familial) sphere and the public world which is important to the New Right. Privatization has also involved the attempt to *remoralize* the family – to restore to it the responsibilities for its own welfare and to revive the traditional virtues of family life.

Our next extract highlights the connections between these different meanings of privatization. It records an exchange between Dr Rhodes Boyson and Professor Patrick Minford during the Department of Health and Social Security's review of benefits for children and young people. Professor Minford, one of the leading proponents of privatizing state services, is giving evidence about the relationship between benefits and the prospects of privatizing services:

Privatization and the family

Dr Rhodes Boyson: Could I centre on the question of children and young people? I know you are dealing with an overall want. We all pass through the stage of being a child and young person, as it were.

Some of the material you put out will be attractive to certain people in my own party and other parties. You mentioned the question of moving so much more to the free market which puts more responsibility upon the parents as the responsible beings at that time for young children in the market. You mention the question of spending a minimum on the education of children. How would you see the movement to a more free market-oriented society affecting a parent's involvement with his children, both on the question of their education and where they work and also on the question of their training between the ages of 16 and 19?

Professor Minford: Now you are turning to my proposals for reducing public expenditure in effect and privatization of large parts of the state sector.

Dr Rhodes Boyson: That is right. Could I centre on how this will affect the family and how it would not actually disadvantage the large family compared with the small family to an extent that society was not prepared to tolerate, if I can be the devil's advocate.

Professor Minford: My proposals are designed to safeguard and in fact improve the position of families because, as Professor Townsend mentioned, I propose that the additional cost that would have to be borne for educating children and so forth under the privatized set up would be met by a rise in child benefits. So, therefore, the families would not be disadvantaged by the move to privatization. At the same time, I believe that it was necessary to have compulsion in the taking out of health insurance, education and so on.

On your general question of the effect of privatization on the position of the family, turning now from the purely financial to the other issues, what I would argue is that it gives the parent more choice. Since there is greater competition in the provision of education and health, there will be better quality at all – and this is the point I always feel is missed in many parts of the public debate – types of education and in all neighbourhoods; that is to say, competition is no respecter of neighbourhoods. It applies just as much to academic type education as to vocational type education. It applies to education for the handicapped as much as it applies to education for the very advanced and intelligent and so forth.

Therefore, I would argue that the principle of competition would, by bringing better value for money to a whole spectrum of the population, improve the quality of family life substantially (DHSS, 1984, p. 27).

At the core of these arguments about the need to restore and remoralize the family lies a very traditional conception of the nature of the family unit. In a speech to the Conservative Party Conference in 1977, Patrick Jenkin (subsequently to become Secretary of State for Social Services) made it clear that this concern with the family embodied an equally traditional view of the sexual division of labour within the family:

Quite frankly, I don't think that mothers have the same right to work as fathers do. If the good Lord had intended us to have equal rights to go out to work, he wouldn't have created men and women. These are biological facts. . . . We hear a lot today about social work – perhaps the most important social work is motherhood (Jenkin, 1977).

Paul Johnson, once a socialist but a subsequent convert to the merits of individualism, set out an eloquent description of the relationship between the family, the economy and the state in western capitalism, which explains the centrality of the family to New Right arguments:

But once the West . . . finally produced a clear definition of marriage (and so family) law, it became an enormously important element in the rise of stable political and dynamic economies. The rule of law, and the clear definition of legal rights and responsibilities, is essential to wealth creation. Legal certainty is the basis of investment and capital formation. And a stable law of property must be centred in a clear and universal doctrine of marriage, legitimacy and inheritance. . . . The monogamous bourgeois family unit provided the social framework within which capitalist lift-off was achieved and the rapid climb to late-twentieth century living standards was made possible.

It is true, of course, that the family has its oppressive aspects – and necessarily so. Human beings have lawless and destructive instincts, as well as orderly ones. Civilised societies require institutions which restrain our passions and supplement our shortcomings. The three principal ones are the family, organised religion and the State. The more society can be policed by the family, assisted to some extent by the voluntary Church, and the less by the State, the more likely it is that such a society will be both orderly and liberal.

Unfortunately, the decline both of family solidarity and religious practice have thrust more and more of the burden of social control on the State. This means both growing antagonism between the public and authority (chiefly the police), and more crime. The State is overburdened and it shows.

The State is overburdened, too, in coming to the rescue of inadequate individuals. . . . The notion of the state as the sole source of welfare is not only morally abhorrent, but, as we are discovering, wasteful and impossibly expensive.

In my view, family, Church and State are complementary institutions,

both of control and of charity. The ideal society rests upon the tripod of
a strong family, a voluntary church and a liberal, minimum State (Johnson,
1982, p. 27).

The passage is an interesting one for the way in which it links
New Right criticisms of the over-burdened and over-intrusive state
with a theory of human nature (our 'orderly' and 'lawless'
instincts). The family has emerged as an institution which can
harmonize human nature, the economy and social order. The
centrality of its 'restoration' in contemporary laissez-faire ideology
rests on this idea of the family's ability to link self-discipline and
social discipline.

We think it is worth drawing attention to two other themes in
the New Right's reworking of laissez-faire ideology in the 1970s
and 1980s. The first involves a substantial change in the 'language'
of welfare. The Beveridge reforms and the post-war welfare state
had talked about the individual as a *'citizen'*, drawing on the ideas
of New Liberalism about the reciprocal relationship between the
state and the citizen. The citizen in this conception had both rights
and obligations. The rights were rights of access to welfare benefits
and services; the obligations were to contribute to the maintenance
of those services through national insurance, taxation and rates (for
services provided by local authorities). The New Right, however,
focused mainly on the citizen's obligations – talking about
taxpayers and ratepayers, and the need to protect their interests
against exploitation (either by 'public waste' or 'scroungers'). The
intended reciprocity between rights and obligations was dissolved
and forgotten. When the New Right did consider the rights to
welfare, it did so by talking of the citizen as *'consumer'*, i.e., in
terms of an implicit market relationship. Even here, there were
distinctions between 'legitimate' consumers and 'illegitimate' ones
such as the scrounger. But the identification of the public as 'tax/
rate-payers' put the emphasis heavily on the *cost* of welfare, discon-
nected from its benefits.

Second, there was an undercurrent in the New Right discussions
of welfare and the state which expressed dissatisfaction with the
democratic machinery of political control and decision making in
a number of ways. We have already considered the argument about
'electoral bargaining' leading to excessive state intervention and
government overload, and this unease about the political process
was reflected in a number of other arguments. As you can see in
the following extract from Arthur Seldon, one of these was the
argument that the market provided a better test of the public's
wishes and demands than the political process, being a constantly
responsive process rather than occasional competition between a
limited number of choices. This echoes Hayek's view of the market

as the most sophisticated means of co-ordinating information about wants.

True and false measures of public preferences

In Britain there are only two ways of measuring what the public wants: in the ballot box and the market. The ballot box records votes by crosses cast for this or that party, policy or politician. The market records votes by money paid for this or that commodity, service, brand, firm or business man.

The ballot box is crude compared with the market. The ballot box is used locally every three and nationally up to five years: the market is used every day or few days (for food, newspapers, transport, etc.), every few months (clothes, books, etc.) or years (furniture, homes, etc.).

The ballot box says: 'This is my list of 57 varieties: take it or leave it.' The market says: 'This is my one item: pay for as much or as little as you want.'

The ballot box says: 'This is what we promise.' The market says: 'What you see before your very eyes is what you take away if you pay.'

The ballot box says: 'Aren't our party slogans splendid!' The market says: 'Judge us by your experience of our product.'

The ballot box says: 'We are saints, public-spirited, selfless and honest. The other are devils, in the pay of vested interests, selfish, dishonest.' The market says: 'We are the best. Compare our value, quality, price.'

The ballot box says: 'Look! Benefits galore! All Free!' The market says: 'All our goods are priced: tax shown separately.'

This contrast is over-simplified but basically right. Even if allowance is made for advertising, the persuasion of people to try this rather than that breakfast cereal, washing powder or newspaper is infinitely harmless contrasted with the persuasion to 'buy' this or that political slogan, promise or policy. You can, with little loss, change from one cereal, powder or paper to another every few days. But you are stuck with the wrong political policy for years or a lifetime (no matter how bad it becomes, the NHS will go on and on and on).

Although the ballot box is very much a second best to the market, it must be used for public goods because opinion on, say, how much and what quality of defence, cannot easily be measured in the market by individuals voting with their money. But even where there are private benefits, the ballot box is still used because wrong thinking brought it into being and vested interests keep it going even where it is inferior to the market (Seldon, 1977, Appendix 1).

This concern about the workings of democratic political processes was given a sharper twist when the 1983 Conservative government was preparing its plan to abolish one tier of local government – the Greater London Council and the Metropolitan Counties. Roger Scruton, editor of the *Salisbury Review* (an influential journal of the New Right), wrote an article suggesting the proposed abolition plans did not go far enough in the reform of local government. He invoked the figure of 'the ordinary middle-class Londoner, who bears the principal burden of the rates' confronted by local government which embodies all the hated elements of state provision:

For consider how the remaining 8 per cent of his rate bill is spent: on the ILEA – to whose schools he would never dream of sending his children if he could help it; on the social services – which, far from confining themselves to natural measures of charitable relief, are dedicated to the task of creating an empire of ungrateful dependants; on the local planning department – with its tyrannical power both to compel work and prevent it, and with its arbitrary relation to any moral or aesthetic standard comprehensible to the ordinary citizen.

Scruton argues that what is necessary to 'protect local government' is to abolish many of its undesirable and unnecessary elements:

. . . the greatest single cause of the disaster of local government must be removed. I mean the elected councils. . . . Far better . . . to abolish elections altogether, and to return to local government on the medieval model – by the sovereign's command. If attendance at council meetings were a duty, like jury service, imposed upon citizens of sufficient public standing for a limited period and with no prospect of reward, then the result would be precisely what the Conservative Party is seeking. Local government would begin to dwindle at once, and the quantity that would eventually remain would be just sufficient to ensure that the local community, upon which the officers depend for their public standing, flourishes according to its local conditions (Scruton, 1983, p. 9).

These doubts about democracy – and the very different alternatives put forward by Seldon and Scruton – highlight a tension within the ideology of the New Right: a tension between free-market liberalism and moral authoritarianism. While espousing economic theories which emphasize individual freedom of choice, the New Right has also been concerned with 'moral issues' and has celebrated traditional moralities which run counter to the stress on individual freedom. There has, for example, been a sustained attack on the 'permissiveness' of the 1960s for encouraging excessive freedom, self-indulgence and for undermining traditional authority (respect for the police, parents, the law, family life, etc.). Although the links between the New Right and morality have been more explicit in the USA with the strong connections between President Reagan's Republicanism and the organized 'Moral Majority' movement, they have also been a consistent theme in the revival of laissez-faire ideology in Britain. The reassertion of the need for discipline, self-discipline and respect for authority have been combined with attacks on 'permissiveness', 'lax parenting', the liberal professions (social workers and teachers, for example) and those who subvert respect for established authority (critics of the police, for instance).

Although this contrast between morality and free market

individualism represents an intellectual tension in the New Right it is not a new one, nor peculiar to the recent revival of laissez-faire ideology. The 'Victorian values', so extensively praised by Margaret Thatcher, exhibited just this combination of a commitment to individual freedom and a profound moral authoritarianism. Part of the explanation for this co-existence of economic liberalism and moralism lies in the way that laissez-faire is as much a social theory as it is an economic one. It combines economics with morality in two distinctive ways.

First, laissez-faire has always viewed 'freedom' as circumscribed by law ('freedom under the Rule of Law'); seeing the law as a means of controlling the excesses which might occur if individuals were simply allowed to pursue their own selfish interests. So, although it has a commitment to the 'minimal' state, laissez-faire has always believed that the minimal state must be a strong state, capable of policing 'lawless instincts'.

Second, laissez-faire ideology has always treated the market (and the competition between individuals in the market place) as a means of promoting discipline and moral character. 'Self-help' is both economically productive and creates good character. You may remember that in Part One, nineteenth-century laissez-faire ideology was concerned to ensure that poor relief was not 'abused' to allow those of poor moral character to escape their responsibilities to compete in the labour market. The same fear of creating 'dependency' and sapping moral fibre characterizes contemporary laissez-faire ideology, too.

The promotion of 'independence', therefore, is supposed to bring about a whole array of beneficial consequences. It re-invigorates the economy; it promotes competition; it fosters moral strength and character; it removes the need for the 'nanny state'; it revitalizes the family and regenerates self-discipline. Laissez-faire, in this sense, appeals to a natural harmony of society – the individual, the family, the economy, the nation, all co-exist happily and to each other's mutual satisfaction. The revival of laissez-faire ideology in the 1970s and 1980s has been dedicated to the restoration of this natural harmony – and the overthrow of the interfering state which has disturbed its balance.

11 · *Feminism*

The 1970s witnessed a new wave of feminism in the UK. Although this phenomenon has now been well documented (Coote and Campbell, 1982; Banks, 1981) it is none the less important to consider the nature of this 'new' feminism in order to appreciate its place in the debates on welfare.

First it should be recognized that 'old' forms of feminism never disappeared. The focus on equal rights and treatment continued, and the work of individual women inside the parliamentary process was vital in maintaining a vigilance over women's issues (e.g. Renee Short and Edith Summerskill on the Divorce Reform Bill, Jo Richardson and others on equal pay legislation). But the 'new' feminism developed outside these institutional forms of political life. Certainly many feminists came from left-wing political groups, but these tended to be far removed from established political groupings. In any case, many of these women left these groups precisely because they rejected their sexual politics and their organizational structure.

The 'new' feminism was a grass roots movement with, ideally, no leaders and no hierarchies. Traditional forms of feminist activity, namely through lobbying, were therefore not a major part of the new wave – although at various stages, such as with the Sex Discrimination Bill, legislation on abortion or on family allowances, feminists did organize lobbies and campaigns as well as major demonstrations. Much of the early work of feminists was taken up with exploring the dimensions of the oppression of women and developing means of explaining, and, hopefully, eradicating it.

Feminist writings began to proliferate, from academic texts to political news sheets, but the core of feminist activity, in the form of consciousness-raising groups and conference workshops, was not documented. Yet it was these groups which identified the main concerns of the movement, from financial and legal independence, to free 24-hour nurseries, to the right for women to determine their own sexuality. But, as Mary McIntosh (1981) argues below, the early discontent over lack of nursery provision, the cohabitation rule or the lack of provision for women within the National Health Service was not initially formulated into a specific position on the welfare state. This position, in as much as there can be a homogeneity in such a broad movement, did not emerge until major works on the welfare state by feminists such as Hilary Land (1976, 1978) and Elizabeth Wilson (1977) became available. These served to focus the discontents and helped to provide both a feminist critique of welfare as well as formulating demands to be made of the welfare state.

Key concepts in the formation of these more coherent analyses of welfare and social policy were the dependent family and patriarchy. The former focused on the economic vulnerability of wives and children in ways close to the ideas of the early feminists; but in the 1970s this was combined with a major critique of traditional family life and its values, and a rejection of the institution of marriage. This form of feminism embraced an ideology of individual rights which still coexists uneasily alongside its collectivist sentiments (i.e. living in communal households, sharing childcare). The other key concept, namely patriarchy, differentiates this late feminism quite clearly from its earlier forms. The concept of patriarchy which has been defined in a variety of ways, from the power of the father to a system of male oppression over women, has served to unify the discrete experiences of oppression experienced by individual women (Beechey, 1979). Regardless of the often heated debate over the definition and exact nature of patriarchy, feminism in the 1970s developed a range of theories of women's oppression which made it possible to link apparently disparate issues. Feminism became a much more coherent system of thought, or ideology, and less a collection of *ad hoc* responses to instances of discrimination or oppression. With this development it became possible to associate the cohabitation rule, women's low pay, the lack of nursery provision, the lack of married women's rights to state benefits and so on, with a re-emergent recognition of the poverty of women and a coherent critique of the formation of the modern welfare state. This process is best explained in the following extract from a paper by Mary McIntosh (1981).

During the 1970s feminists developed a critique of the welfare system that was both sophisticated and damning. It began in a fragmentary way in the early seventies with specific protests about issues like the 'cohabitation rule' and the 'tax credit' proposals. There was a growing awareness that women figure prominently among the clients of social workers, the inmates of geriatric and psychiatric hospitals, the claimants of supplementary benefits – despite the fact that married and cohabiting women are not eligible for many benefits. There was resentment about the degrading way that women are treated when they need state benefits and state services.

The first responses were most clearly articulated by libertarian feminists, who could express vividly what women know of the conditions under which welfare is granted. They know the queues and the forms, the defence, the anger, the degradation, the sense of invisibility and the loss of autonomy. They see the mean, witholding face of the state and can readily take up the negative cry of 'smash the state!' But the cohabitation campaign also raised deeper issues. It was not just that the 'SS' were 'sex snoopers' who prevented women claimants from drawing their benefit if they were suspected of living with a man. They also tried to force women into prostitutional dependence on the man they slept with. This raised the whole question of women's dependence on men and the fact that women were second class citizens. The Women's Family Allowance Campaign against the Tory Government's 1972 tax-credit proposals focused on the same problems. The family allowance, paid directly to a mother, was preferable to the same, or even greater, amount paid in tax credits through a father's pay packet. The model of the couple as a financial unit bore little relation to reality as many women experienced it. In the end, after we had defeated this aspect of the tax-credit scheme, the trade unions' reluctance to accept the loss of the child tax allowance that accompanied the improved child benefit only verified what we already knew: that money in a husband's pay packet was not equivalent to a direct payment to his wife.

In the context of the women's liberation movement, the developing awareness of women's relation to the welfare state was crystallised at the national conference in 1974. Elizabeth Wilson's pamphlet *Women and the Welfare State* (1974) was launched there and a new demand, the fifth to be adopted by the movement, recognised clearly the relevance of the state in solving the problems of women's dependence upon men. [This demand was the demand for Financial and Legal Independence] The other demands (concerned with equal opportunities in jobs and training, equal pay, nurseries, abortion and contraception) all had a bearing on women's independence in their different ways. But this one, as the paper calling for it to be adopted expressed it, 'highlights the links between the state and the family, and the way in which the state systematically bolsters the dependent-woman family' (Gieve *et al.*, 1974). It saw the relevance of state policy not merely to those categories of women who receive or are denied state benefits of various kinds – not merely to mothers and non-mothers, wives and non-wives, earners and non-earners – but to women as a whole category. For it saw how state policies play a part in constructing that category and in constructing the idea of the family in which it exists. *All women suffer from the stereotype of the woman as properly dependent upon a man. But all women suffer in quite practical terms from the fact that there are few viable alternatives to such dependence.* . . .

The welfare state is . . . not redistributive as between the social classes, but makes the working class pay for its own casualties . . . it does not even eliminate poverty at the end of the scale . . . it is not the harbinger of socialist provision according to need – neither in its style nor in its effects – and . . . it is an instrument of bourgeois control, forcing people to work and imposing standards of morality, decency and household management. To this, feminists add that the welfare state is especially oppressive to women, in that it harnesses them into the team that pulls the whole welfare charabanc along (McIntosh, 1981, pp. 32–4, emphasis added).

As McIntosh makes clear, feminists identified women's need for welfare provision while recognizing that the provision as presently constituted is part of women's oppression. Since 1981, when McIntosh wrote her article, the social and economic situation facing women has further deteriorated as a consequence of government policies and, to some extent, the wider economic recession. Concern has grown about levels of unemployment, poverty, poor housing, homelessness and health care. In such a climate the potential influence of a feminist analysis of welfare and the effects of feminist policies once again become limited. Long term unemployment is inevitably identified by policy makers and politicians as a male problem, the difficulties faced by young people leaving school are seen in terms of a youth group which is constituted solely by young men. In response to this dominant view of poverty and unemployment – which in turn produces 'solutions' which inevitably also exclude women – feminists in the 1980s have argued that poverty itself is a women's issue and that women's poverty is not simply massively under-reported but that it requires separate analysis to that of male poverty.

What is much less generally recognised is the increasing extent to which women are represented among the world's poor. 'The feminisation of poverty' is the phrase used to describe the fact that a growing proportion of families below the official poverty line are headed by women alone. It is seen as one of several manifestations of the economic hardship caused by recession and cuts in public spending. The treatment most frequently prescribed is the expansion of public assistance to poor mothers and children, and the provision of training that will enable women without skills to become better providers.

In spite of the attention to the problems of poor women in the press, by public agencies, and even by some politicians, it frequently proves necessary to defend the very concept of the feminisation of poverty from attacks on both the right and the left. Often these overlap in a curious way. Women's poverty, it is argued by the right, is due to the instability of the family (often, specifically the black family) and a pervasive moral laxness that produces teenage pregnancies and children born outside marriage. On the left it is held that to talk about the feminisation of poverty is to divert attention from issues of class and race, that women's poverty cannot be discussed separately from men's poverty. What I hear both sides saying is that there is nothing wrong with women that an employed husband could not cure. . . .

Sociological literature offers us packaged explanations to the effect that poverty is influenced by class, race, nation, economic region, ethnic group and gender. This is an ideologically impeccable conclusion that can never get you into trouble but also does not leave you much the wiser. In fact, considerable academic research has been done on the role of the first five factors in determining who is poor, the sixth is a recent afterthought. Yet gender cuts across all the others. Women are poorer than men in all the first five categories. Surely this says something about the power of gender as a way of getting a handle on the whole issue of poverty (Scott, 1984, p. vii–ix).

Feminism's contribution to the debates on welfare has therefore moved substantially from the early position which regarded the state as a neutral dispenser, or witholder, of the resources required by women either living with their husbands, having the care of children or looking after the elderly. In contemporary feminist ideology the state is fully implicated in the structure of family life, the labour market and hence in constructing the very poverty of women which in turn causes women to make demands of the state for welfare benefits. Although this is something of an oversimplification of feminist theories of the welfare state, it is none the less the existence of such theories which so clearly differentiates feminism in the 1980s from feminism in the 1910s or 1940s. In this sense feminism as a whole in the UK has moved to the 'left' of the political spectrum and although there are still a great many equal rights or libertarian feminists, the movement as a whole is influenced, however indirectly, by radical, revolutionary or Marxist thought (see Delphy, 1984; Barrett and McIntosh, 1982).

Throughout the 1970s a major concern of feminists was the problem of women's dependent status. Unlike earlier feminist ideologies, a central plank to modern feminism was the aim of undoing the dependency entailed in marriage or cohabitation. This led to a number of demands. One was for wages for housework, another was for a guaranteed minimum income and a third was for disaggregation in the social security and personal taxation systems. These were all means of providing an independent status and income for women, but they were based on different analyses of the role of the state in the oppression of women, and on different ideas of how women should be liberated. The following extracts will reveal some of these differences.

The first extract comes from a pamphlet produced by the Campaign for Legal and Financial Independence in 1975. This group became known as the Fifth Demand Group because, as Mary McIntosh has outlined above, this demand was the fifth to be ratified by the 1974 National Women's Liberation Conference.

What dependence means

The independence demand is concerned with the battered wife who may be forced to stay with her husband or else lose all right to the marital home because the Council had insisted in registering it in the husband's name alone. Or the sixty-year-old woman who, divorced in middle age, discovers fifteen years later that she is entitled to no provision at all; the law, expecting her to depend on her husband's payments, has discredited her own National Insurance contributions.

It is also concerned with the less dramatic and more mundane, but nonetheless crippling, effects. Such as the married woman who loses her job and discovers that although her contributions are the same as a single woman's, her unemployment benefits are one-third less – simply because she is married. Or the working woman who has to go to her husband for money, after the Inland Revenue has automatically sent her tax rebate to him. Or the woman who works while her husband stays at home caring for the children; this family is entitled to neither full unemployment benefit, full pensions in old age, nor Family Income Supplements. Such benefits are reserved for either single women, or families with a male breadwinner.

This web of state regulations serves to hinder the development of women's social, psychological and economic independence by enforcing their dependence on men – or making their lives intolerable if they try to rebel individually. A woman is tied down by a system which makes any experimentation in social and sexual relations virtually impossible for her. The only way in which she can achieve any degree of independence is if she remains unmarried and childless, or has the backing of an independent income. . . .

But women's legal and financial independence is determined by laws imposed by Parliament and its agencies. Unless these laws and regulations are abolished, the movement cannot be effective in bringing about practical change in women's status as dependants. Women's dependence on men is underpinned by legislation at every point. It is extremely difficult for women to even envisage themselves as people in their own right when in reality their full personhood is continually contradicted by state policy. In short, IT IS IMPOSSIBLE FOR A WOMAN, SINGLE OR MARRIED, TO ACHIEVE INDEPENDENCE UNDER THE LAWS OF THIS LAND (*The Demand for Independence*, March 1975, p. 1–2).

At the same time as feminists were developing their analysis of financial dependence and the role of the state in maintaining this dependency, another campaign was growing around the use of family allowances. In 1972, the Conservative government produced proposals to abolish family allowances and to replace them with a system of tax credit to be payable through men's wage packets. This proposal engendered a massive response from the 'new' feminists as well as the older established bodies such as the Married Women's Association, the Women's Institute and the Conservative Women's National Committee. For a section of the women's movement the demand to keep family allowances developed into a wider demand for wages for housework. The following passage comes from a pamphlet produced by the Women's Family Allowance Campaign in 1973.

The family allowance under attack

The Women's Family Allowance Campaign began as a defensive response to the Government's attack on a right that women already have: the right to some money from the State paid to all women with two or more children. But, taking strength from the fact that many women already felt strongly about the need for financial independence from men, it quickly became an offensive campaign, a fight not only to keep but extend the State's payment to women. . . .

What do we want?

The proposals they make for us limit us all over again. The demands we make should be for things that would help us to break out of our roles and structures that confine us. No one demand, or group of related demands, can indicate all we want. But the Family Allowance Campaign has expressed our desire for financial independence from men in a new way. We know how important economic independence from men is if we are to live our own lives, and if they are to have a chance to move without the burden of having to support us. But in the past, demands for money for women have been expressed in a way that has simply led to more work for us. They have been in terms of getting a job outside the home, without seriously challenging the burden of work we do *in* the home – which has remained as our other 'hidden' job. The Family Allowance Campaign has given practical expression to the idea of extending payment from the State for work women already do, work in the home.

We are beginning to get a sense of how crucial the work done in the home is to the economy, and how reluctant the State is to pay for this huge quantity of 'hidden work'. But just because it's not on their agenda, it doesn't mean that we shouldn't put it on ours. A demand for money for that work can do two things. It aims to bring us economic independence without bringing us more work. In doing so, it challenges the idea that 'home-making' is just a 'natural' expression of our femininity, a god given part of our relationship with children and men. It underlines the fact that housewives, in servicing men and rearing children in our society, are working for capital.

The threat to the Family Allowance, the threat to the little money that the State now pays to women, has highlighted how important that money is for women. The fact that such a small sum of money is so important gives us some idea of what a difference it would make if, instead of a pittance, we could make the State pay women a proper income (Fleming, 1973, pp. 1 and 6).

This pamphlet barely hints at the demand for wages for housework which became a major demand of one part of the women's movement in the 1970s. The majority of other feminists rejected this demand, however, because it appeared to be a demand for payment to keep women at home clearing up after men. This difference between various feminist groups became a major element in the development of ideas on social policy at this time. But it was not a new division; it reflected some of the arguments between Eleanor Rathbone and the National Union of Women's Suffrage Societies (see Chapter 3), namely the debate over whether policy should improve the existing position of women in the family or whether it should radically alter the sexual division of labour between men and women.

The importance of the Wages for Housework Campaign was that it focused attention on the invisible, unremunerated work of women in the private sphere of the family. At the same time the Campaign for Legal and Financial Independence demanded a recognition of the different and competing interests of individuals inside the family and challenged the assumption that there should be simply 'family benefits' or 'family services'. In spite of their difference, both sought to undermine the assumption that the family and marriage should, or could be, an adequate source of social security for women. The campaign for 'Disaggregation Now!' was a direct result of this view of the family and women's dependence. It sought to give married and cohabiting women the right to claim benefits in their own right and not as dependents of their husbands (see ROW 1979). This was to be achieved by ending the practice of 'aggregating' entitlement to benefits in the case of marriage or cohabitation. At the same time there was a major campaign to end the cohabitation rule which forced women into financial dependence on the men with whom they had intimate or sexual relations. This campaign produced a Private Members Bill in the House of Commons (introduced by Jo Richardson) which was unsuccessful but at least put the cohabitation rule on the wider political agenda.

If the focus of feminist campaigns in the 1970s was financial independence, the early 1980s produced a slightly different emphasis. Building on the earlier work, feminists came to recognize the significance of 'caring' for women, not just the care of children, but the care of the elderly and the disabled. Of considerable importance in the development of this perspective has been the work of Hilary Land. In the following extract she outlines the cost of caring for women.

The costs of loving care

Caring for a disabled or infirm person, even in the context of a loving relationship, is costly in terms of time, opportunity and resources. It is not an experience confined to a tiny minority of families. On the basis of a national study carried out in the 1970s it was estimated that 'one half of the housewives between 35 and 64 can expect at some time or another to give some help to elderly or infirm persons'.

Apart from financial hardship, all the evidence suggests that what these families need is some relief from the daily and often nightly strains of caring. A small study conducted in 1980 looked at the amount of time spent caring for an elderly relative. The majority were spending between four and six hours daily. On average women were spending over three hours a day in caring activities, helped by their husbands for an average of thirteen minutes.

Cuts in domiciliary services, like home helps, day centres, or holiday relief schemes, which sadly the previous Labour Government set in train in 1976, and to which this (Conservative) Government has given a vicious momentum, makes the work of caring within the family even harder. It is quite clear that it is too little, not too much state provision which undermines a family's capacity to care.

To assert that families, meaning of course mainly women, could and should do more in the context of major cutbacks in community welfare services, is an insult to those hundreds of thousands of women who do care and do so often at great cost to themselves and other members of their families. As for those who have no immediate family (and again they are mainly women – only a third of the over 75s and a quarter of the over 85s are men) what of their needs? (Hilary Land, 1983, pp. 20–1).

The work of Hilary Land is also a good example of the way in which feminist analysis in the 1970s and early 1980s has drawn together all the apparently discrete areas of women's oppression into a critique of the state.

Why then, do the state's income-maintenance schemes still only support men in the role of chief breadwinner and woman as man's dependent housewife? The answer must lie in the fact that there are enormous advantages to the economically powerful groups in our society in sustaining the belief that men are breadwinners and women, at most, are supplementary earners, whose primary duties lie in the home. In this way work incentives for men are preserved even among low-wage earners whose wives also have to work to support the family. At the same time it justifies paying women lower wages than men. Women when they enter the labour market do so in the belief that they do not need as high a wage as a man. Moreover, their paid employment must take second place to their unpaid work in the home. They, therefore, form a very cheap, docile and flexible section of the labour force and the majority confine themselves to the less secure and less rewarding jobs. At the same time they continue to care for husbands, children, the elderly and the infirm at a minimum cost to the state. However, it should not be forgotten of course, that when we talk of economic advantages, we have, as Eleanor Rathbone pointed out forty years ago 'an economic structure devised by and for men' (Land, 1978, p. 142).

The feminist movement of the 1970s and early 1980s faced serious political problems in attempting to move from a purely critical stance on the welfare state to making proposals for a system of welfare based on feminist principles. Dependence on the welfare state was identified as more acceptable than dependence upon individual men in the family. However at the point of formulating this preference and subsequent demands (disaggregation, free nursery provision etc.) the very nature of the welfare state began to change. Previous victories or advances (i.e. Employment Protection Legislation, Child Benefit legislation, equal treatment in entitlement to benefits etc.) were increasingly undermined. The fundamental principles inherent in the Beveridge Report and the basic values of the welfare state were increasingly subject to attack. In consequence the feminist movement was faced with a dilemma, whether to continue to attack the patriarchal structure of the welfare state, or whether to defend it against the attack from the right. For Elizabeth Wilson, the answer was to remain true to the feminist critique of welfare.

At a time when the welfare state is under savage attack from the right it may seem political madness to challenge it from the left. Yet we must. For the Labour Party future programme for welfare still harks back to the vision of 1945. When the whole base of welfare is being hacked away, it is tempting to return to the familiar comfort of the well-tried formula. But we can't. For the truth is that the way in which the welfare state went wrong is complex and the way in which we must reconstruct it is also complex (Wilson, 1982, p. 6).

In the 1980s the women's liberation movement is once again fighting for rights for safe contraception, for adequate health and social services for women, for adequate maternity benefits and child benefit. It realizes that these are demands to be made of all political parties. It has also rightly recognized that the dismantling of welfare (albeit that it is an inadequate system) where women as lone mothers, pensioners and carers are the main recipients of welfare benefits and services, is a further step in the feminization of poverty or, put another way, the impoverishment of women.

12 · *Socialism*

As the foundations of Fabianism as the semi-official ideology of the welfare state began to crumble in the face of economic crisis and political attack, socialists, too, became increasingly critical of Beveridge and his legacy. Socialist critics have rediscovered an uneasy independence which seemed lacking both in the immediate post-war period and in the following years when 'left' social administration was simply an accepted part of political (and academic) life. In general, the welfare state was taken for granted and the argument was about the ways in which it could be defended or improved.

Some aspects of the new socialist critique have been particularly forceful since many of the critics have refused to take any blame for what went wrong, turning their full hostility on to the Beveridge system. They have argued that, far from being the unalloyed benefit to the working class which has usually been assumed, the welfare state has helped to undermine moves towards fundamental political change and to encourage detailed and intrusive 'policing' of the poor. More recently there have been frequent echoes of feminist arguments about the ways in which social policy systematically reinforces the oppression of women.

Friend and Metcalf criticize those who see the state as a potentially liberatory force, arguing instead that it has operated in an ambiguous way: providing welfare support, but only in return for oppressive supervision of the working class by professionals which discourages any understanding of the broader (and more fundamental) reasons for their poverty. In this there is a clear echo of Morris's arguments in Part One, but they go further by highlighting the negative aspects of state intervention in practice. Links *could* also be drawn with some of the points made by laissez-faire thinkers, but Friend' and Metcalf's criticism of the welfare state is not that it hampers the positive operation of the market, but rather that it reinforces the negative features of the market. It protects capitalism from effective challenge and encourages the subordination of the working class.

Welfare state against the working class

In its social role the state operates in an uneven way providing nothing but a subsistence income for some, giving aid such as housing to others, and in some situations throwing in a whole apparatus of investigation, control and regulation.

This unevenness flows directly out of the cross-class origins of what we now call 'the welfare state'. Its main provisions on social security, pensions, education and health arose out of a convergence of working-class demands and the calculations of the more long-sighted political representatives of capital. The latter were also conscious that an educated, healthy and adequately housed workforce would aid post-war growth. Social democracy was the matchmaker and the course of the marriage since then has expressed the strains of the original union.

Although the welfare state emerged from the convergence of the politically articulated demands of distinct classes, it was not the product of an equal partnership between those classes. Working class needs, while recognised, were subsumed into alien institutions which were never under working-class control. Capitalist social relations are produced through the processes of the welfare state in a number of ways.

The welfare state's institutions and the services they provide are grounded on the view of society which stresses that it is composed of citizens, equal under the law, with mutual rights and obligations. Such a view fragments the working class into either isolated individuals seeking services or special interest groups lobbying for more attention from the state. The state thus relates to the population as 'citizens, voters, taxpayers, patients, social security claimants, employees, smokers, non-smokers, on a host of different bases but never on the basis of class, never on the basis which would raise explicitly the question of exploitation and class domination'. It also reproduces the capitalist social relations through the way in which it oversees and intervenes in the family – the cradle of those relations. By looking at the situation of . . . children in care, we will gain a clearer picture of the ways the subordination of the working class is an integral part of the welfare state's activity. . . .

The state's relationship to the family with growing children shows its intervention into working-class social life in one of its most developed forms. The architects of the welfare state understood the central importance of the family as the cradle of social relations. The Beveridge Report was unambiguous:

> In many measure of social policy in which regard is had
> to the facts the great majority of married women must
> be regarded as occupied on work which is vital though
> unpaid without which their husbands could not do their
> paid work and without which the whole nation could
> not continue.

From all quarters attention was now directed at mothers and their children, by psychologists like Bowlby, the child guidance clinics and educationalists and by the armies of social workers who were being trained in family case work. The social services have come to devote a large proportion of their budgets and their most skilled workers to regulating the reproduction of the next generation of wage labourers.

In its open regulation of family life the welfare state shows itself to be centrally concerned with the reproduction of capitalist social relations. And this concern is evident not only in its most authoritarian and repressive bodies, but in every sphere of its activity. Even in the state's most obviously 'progressive' acts, as when it moves to prevent child battering, it does so in an essentially authoritarian and bureaucratic fashion – denying the rights and needs of the children involved as it resolves the problem institutionally – through children's homes or often randomly assigned foster parents. The network of children's homes has expanded as family and community life has decayed, but the state as parent has proved all too often incapable of meeting the children's emotional needs. . . .

The state, in its welfare aspects, presents us with a familiar dilemma: we need its services for there are no other forces which can intervene to protect children, provide meals on wheels, or supply special schools for disabled children. But its cross-class origins, the bureaucratic framework in which the services operate, their overall strategic orientation, make them at best a distorted shadow of their potential for human liberation – and at worst a cudgel to enforce the sort of social relations government decides are in the best interests of capitalism as a whole. The evolution of the welfare state in the post-war period, the proliferation of its institutions under the control of the professional middle class, tended to reinforce the illusion that the state is a neutral body doing its best to balance conflicting, legitimate interests in a difficult situation. . . .

We need a break with an economistic approach to the welfare state which emphasizes the need to simply increase the quantity of the services to the working class. We have to challenge the very nature of these services and the ways bureaucratic agencies define, and impose their definition, of the social services' needs of any particular district. We have to raise the question of the local working class defining its own needs – and in that process – redefining the nature of the services which are required.

Within the labour movement itself, it is beginning to be accepted that the mass support for Tory policies at the (1979) election and the apathetic response to subsequent economic cuts, indicates the deep disillusionment amongst the working class towards the welfare state. An approach which seeks to maintain the status quo by defending the existing level of services cannot reverse such apathy and hostility. Nor can the problem be overcome by arguing for increased public spending on social services, if the welfare state's features of bureaucracy, control, and regulation of the social life of the working class are not challenged . . . (Friend and Metcalf, 1981, pp. 136–45).

Like Morris, Friend and Metcalf seem stronger on criticism than its resolution, although their reference to locally based decision-making shows at least some continuity with the arguments presented earlier by Quelch. Bob Deacon deals with similar problems indicating some possible new directions without finally attempting to present any clear blueprint for a socialist social policy. Again, the break from Beveridge is explicit and the defining characteristic of a socialist approach is presented as a search for collective rather than individual solutions.

Developing socialist alternatives

Only *collective* struggle for and over the form of social welfare services can counteract the tendency of the New Right to capitalise on the dissatisfactions consumers feel as *individuals* about inadequate or inappropriately run services. The disenchantment of the individual council tenant faced with high rents and no repairs; the worry of the individual patient suffering a depersonalising experience within the NHS; the competitive concern of an individual parent with regard to the inadequate schooling of her or his child; the isolated distress of a claimant left without an expected Giro: all these experiences have to be counteracted by those of collective challenge to, and increasing control over, these services which are at present causing people to suffer. The tenants' association negotiating with the direct labour force over repairs; the women's health centre providing mutual reinforcement in the challenge to sexist medical practice; the gathering of parents and teachers realising the hopelessness of individual competitive education in a context where not even the 'best' school leaver can find a job; the claimants' union demanding redress for maladministration: such activities have to be multiplied to counteract those which feed the New Right.

The goal of transforming the social relationships of welfare, which includes the aim that people should feel collectively in control of their services, must also be reflected in the method of struggle over social welfare issues. It is here that the notion of *prefigurative* forms of struggle has arisen. In Tosh Flynn's words, 'Throughout the individual struggles in which we engage socialists must press for forms of popular decision making and control, production and distribution of use values for need not profit, workers' control of the labour process, the transformation of social relations' (Flynn, 1981, p. 126).

There are, however, a number of problems that arise in the development of prefigurative welfare struggles. First, localised prefigurative examples of transformed social policy might become no more than a new form of provision capable of being co-opted into, or permitted to run alongside, the predominant state welfare form of service.

Second, prefigurative struggle over welfare issues might not actually be a form of struggle that can abolish capitalism. Capitalist welfare is a highly centralised system, backed up by an efficient oppressive arm of the state. Much socialist theory and experience in other countries suggests that a high degree of nationally co-ordinated strategy is necessary to defeat it, and that this may impose requirements very different from those of prefigurative struggle (which may need to be experimental and tentative).

Third, struggles over welfare issues, particularly those initiated by state employees, are often embarked upon with no thought of transforming the relationships of welfare. On the contrary, they may well be defending the particular sectional interests of employees in the present form of state services. These struggles are often most successful because of the industrial action that can be taken. But how can a socialist strategy for welfare, which has as one of its goals the liberation of the mutual ability to care for each other's welfare needs at the level of the local commune form of organisation, be achieved through the defence of disabling (for the majority) professional and bureaucratic jobs in state welfare agencies?

Fourth, those struggles that *do* have as a more-or-less articulated goal the transformation of the social relationships of welfare are often conceived and led by groups such as women and youth and blacks, who have less to gain from the defence of existing forms of welfare provision. The power of such groups to effect change is likely to be less because it is not derived from their employment within existing services.

It is often the case, for example, that feminist perspectives on the welfare state are more closely allied to a truly emancipatory socialist perspective than the blinkered defence of current welfare state practice articulated by one or other section of the trade union movement. But however much women may, as a result of their oppression, be more conscious of the need to transform the social relationships of welfare, their power, as women, to bring this about is probably limited compared with those (men and women) with 'industrial' muscle as employees.

There are therefore contradictions, between forms of struggle that are prefigurative and forms of struggle that challenge the power of the central capitalist state. There are also contradictions between prefigurative forms of struggle and those that are based on the sectional interest of employees in present state welfare services. Political strategies in the field of social welfare may or may not take account of these conflicting and contradictory requirements. At worst, it is possible to imagine a strategy which loses sight of the need to abolish capital, is based solely on the sectional demands of those who stand to gain from employment on present terms in existing state welfare services, and is not informed by a conception of the socialist transformation of the social relationship of welfare. This has been the dominant form of struggle over welfare issues over the past 30 years.

In opposition to this it is possible – and necessary – to conceive of demands and struggles that are genuinely transitional. These would involve both the workers in and the users of the present welfare state. They would provide for a shift, in the course of the struggle, in the consciousness of the workers in the service away from a narrow sectionalism based on the need, under capitalism, to defend their own jobs. The shift must be towards an understanding of the need to transform the social relationships of welfare and the realisation that such a need can truly be met only if the constraints of capital that generate their sectionalism are abolished. Such a strategy is likely to involve at some point the construction of alternative workers' and women's welfare plans, the full implementation of which requires the abolition of capitalism. The socialist 'utopia' has to be made concrete, graspable and convincing if it is to be desired by enough people to make it realisable. Alternative workers' plans, so well illustrated in the industrial sector by the Lucas Aerospace Combine Committee's ideas as to how they could put existing Lucas resources to better use, need to be extended into the sphere of social welfare. No illusions must be spread, however, that such plans are entirely realisable under capitalism, or that the struggle against capital does not also require at some point a nationally co-ordinated response to the determination of capital to resist changes of this sort, by force if necessary.

There are, therefore, four requirements for a strategy for achieving a socialist social policy. It should be concerned to overthrow capitalism; to combat, at the level of the state, the forces that will defend capitalism; to embody in its aims the transformation of the social relationships of welfare; and finally, to prefigure these aims in the course of struggle over welfare issues (Deacon, 1983, pp. 244–7).

The revival of independent socialist approaches to social policy has not been straightforward. There is no simple, clear socialist 'line': some writers seem close to the left Fabians (such as Townsend, see pp. 173–6) while others seek to distance themselves from all the legacies of Fabianism. Coming to grips with the ambiguities identified by Friend and Metcalf is not easy and one should perhaps not be surprised if the attempts by socialists to do so sometimes appear tortuous and uncertain. They are trying to reinterpret a cornerstone of post-war British politics, which has usually been associated with the left and to begin to construct an alternative approach, often borrowing ideas from feminism and (less consciously, perhaps) from the Fabians as well as building on their own analysis (see also, for example, Gough, 1979). The tension identified in Part One between socialism's strength as a critique of capitalism (and a call for revolutionary change), and the desire to present proposals which are realizable even before such change, is particularly noticeable in contemporary debates.

In the extract below, Alan Walker attempts to bring the two together in his call for a wider conception of social planning (more fully developed in his book, Walker, 1984). His approach turns traditional socialist ideas on their head by suggesting that the driving force of a socialist programme should be its social policy. A socialist social policy, he argues, should influence economic policy, instead of being influenced by, or even being the product of, economic policy. He challenges assumptions that changes in the organization and ownership of productive assets will necessarily lead to social changes heralding a reduction in inequality and poverty. He argues instead that it is necessary first to adopt and develop a social policy pledged to such aims and then to ensure that the social policy will be supported by changes in economic policy.

What is the Left's social strategy?

The subjugation of social planning to economics follows from the dependence of social policy on economic policy and helps to account for the underdevelopment of social planning in Britain. The main form of social planning is public expenditure planning, or more correctly, public expenditure control. Nationally then social planning is always conducted within the framework of economic planning and what is more, the latter is narrowly interpreted by the Treasury as financial planning. Thus in Britain and other capitalist societies too, the social and economic spheres have been artificially separated and the separation institutionalised through the state's social and economic planning machinery.

Preoccupation with ownership

As well as the economic hegemony which dominates capitalist societies, the failure of the Left to give sufficient attention to social policy must also be attributed in part to the excessive concentration by some Marxists on certain economic relations within the cycle of reproduction. Quite properly emphasis is often placed on the basic structural relations formed within the social division of work: ownership and to a lesser extent power and knowledge. But other relations, such as those formed in the spheres of distribution and consumption, are rarely considered at all. Moreover some of the manifestations of the fundamental relations of production, such as the sexual division of labour and the sort of work that is actually carried out, are similarly not discussed or are made a subsidiary matter for social policy.

My point here is that because of the narrow focus . . . on ownership of the means of production there is a risk that a change in the ownership of key productive sectors will be taken to be the end of the struggle for socialism. Nothing could be further from the truth. Nationalisation would represent a step towards a socialist economy only if it also entails the replacement of production for profit with production for social need. . . .

Planning for social need

The question confronting social planning is can we reform the minimum rights/subsistence approach to welfare which stems from the Beveridge Report and which has characterised the postwar welfare state? The answer is no, because the conception of physical need on which it is based is outmoded and also because it has created and sustained fundamental inequalities, such as the subordinate position of women to men. The economic and ideological functions of the system constructed in the immediate postwar period, including labour discipline, suggest that only limited advances can be secured without a radical re-appraisal of the principles underlying distribution, not only in the public sector but also in the occupational sector. The elimination of widespread poverty and social inequalities rests on the transformation of the systems of production and distribution so that they reflect social need.

This sort of structural change requires democratic control over systems of distribution in *both* of the so-called public and private sectors, that is over the direct distribution of resources through wages, dividends, non-wage benefits and so on, as well as over the redistribution of resources through the tax and social security systems. A 'participation' standard of income could be established which would allow the full participation in family and community life of every individual, regardless of sex and marital status. Income would vary principally on the basis of need, such as family size and disability. Wealth too would be equalised both through the dispersal of the ownership of capital and through increased public ownership under democratic control. Thus for example, housing rights might be shared more equally between owner-occupiers and tenants. Ultimately individual ownership itself would be abolished in favour of local community ownership with the safeguard of strong occupier rights. As a first step the local community might be given the power to restrict certain luxurious forms of owner-occupation and to subdivide large properties. Large holdings of land would be transferred to the local community. A more progressive wealth and capital gains tax would be required in the short-run.

Planning for need also requires the democratic discussion of an equitable income structure and differentials. A statutory maximum as well as minimum wage may well be another short term option. Collective bargaining at industry and plant level would be circumscribed by these measures and discussions and, following the development of a less hierarchical distribution of incomes, would be more concerned with the social organisation of work than with earnings. A more equitable tax system would accompany changes such as these in the distribution of income. Universal rights to employment, adequate wages, social security, health provision, personal social services, housing and education, coupled with the local democratic control of these institutions, would help to overcome inequalities based on sex and race and also reduce the power of professional groups to control access to these services.

Democratic methods

A major change in the social organisation of health care would also be required under a system aimed at planning for need. This would entail a reorientation of health and welfare services away from institutions towards the community and away from curative medicine towards preventive action. This means a wide range of measures to control drugs, pollution, to reduce accidents and improve diets. It also means less professionally qualified high status jobs and many more less specialised community-based health workers. Private hospitals would be made illegal and the pharmaceutical industry would be strictly controlled. Residential institutions for groups such as the mentally handicapped and elderly would be abolished also, and replaced by smaller nursing units and sheltered purpose-built housing fully integrated with other forms of housing.

These are some of the long term policies towards which a socialist social strategy might be set in order to reduce social inequalities and thereby establish the conditions for socialist evolution. It is according to these social ends that the shape of economic policy and economic planning should be determined. It is, in other words, not a matter of proposing reflation to create more jobs or growth to create more resources, but of asking what are our social goals and which social and economic policies are compatible with them. Some indication of the scope for redistribution without growth can be gauged from the fact that if the incomes of the top one-tenth of earners were reduced to 75% of their current share, and those of the next two-tenths to 90% of what it is now, this would realise some £19,000 million a year in 1980–81 terms or roughly the amount that was spent in the entire social security programme in that year.

I have described these policies in some detail because this makes it easier to discuss them and any alternatives which might be proposed, as well as the sort of measures necessary in the short and medium term to achieve them. The policies are included for illustrative purposes, it would be quite wrong at this stage to propose a detailed manifesto. As well as having socialist goals, socialist social planning should also employ democratic methods. There have been a series of innovations in planning over the post-war period – including social reports, social accounting, cost benefit analysis, a Department of Economic Affairs and proposals for a Department of Social Planning – all of which have been concerned predominantly with centralised, expert activity and which, furthermore, have accepted both the methods and seniority of orthodox economics. In socialist planning goals are inseparable from methods. Utopias elaborated in great detail by experts and imposed on people from above cannot be expected to meet with much success and in the first instance, cannot be expected to attract widespread support at an election.

Oppositional planning

Rather than being an expert or bureaucratic activity, socialist social planning should be diffuse and democratic. Thus social planners would be locally based workers, subject to local control and charged with the task of initiating a planning dialogue. Democratic participation in and control over the planning process is essential also to avoid the growth of corporate power. Thus the social organisation of planning would be an important means of dispersing power. This would entail increased powers for local government in social and economic planning, greater local autonomy and control over resources and devolved powers from local government to smaller geographical areas and groups of citizens.

Socialist social policies of the sort discussed here and a transformative planning system clearly are not compatible with a bourgeois government and state; their introduction therefore rests on the election of a socialist party to power. But the alternative social strategy cannot pin all of its hopes on the election of a Left Government. Large sections of the working class are currently oppressed by unemployment, poverty, inequality and powerlessness. Moreover the working class is divided and now is the time to form political alliances to re-establish the common interest between the poor and the rest of the working class. So the planning process must begin at once in a wide range of groups within and outside of the labour movement – trade unions, women's groups, tenants' groups, claimants' unions and so on – to discuss and formulate socialist policies. Following the election of a socialist government the planning process would be institutionalised by the appointment of social planners and the establishment of local and central planning machinery.

For the present and immediate future our social planning will take an oppositional form as isolated struggles against capitalist institutions and particularly those of the state. Again it is in the realm of the welfare state that these struggles are most frequently manifested but they occur everywhere the contradictions of capitalism are experienced. There is for example, the social security claimants arguing with supplementary benefit officers about their need for money to feed their children and attempting to overcome individualising and demeaning services by gaining common strength, the workers trying to persuade their employer to improve working conditions and the tenants trying to get basic repairs carried out by their landlord.

As well as arguing for an alternative social strategy it may also be possible to *demonstrate* albeit in limited ways, how certain elements of it may work. Professional individuals – doctors, social workers, teachers – can attempt to share power. Similarly in inter-personal relationships. Collectively too there is some scope for the practical demonstration of socialist relations. Some local authorities, such as Sheffield, have begun in recent years to develop small-scale initiatives in socialist planning. Local authorities are also well placed to encourage socialist evolution through for example, the promotion of collective activities such as child care, the reorganisation of services to reflect more directly the needs of citizens and the inclusion of the clients of services in their management. Collective activities can militate against individualism and consumerism.

Socialist social planning is already underway in the form of oppositional struggles against capitalist state institutions and relations. Also in the building of 'oppositional practice' socialists working *within* the state machine are discussing and mentally constructing alternative social relations. The urgent task for the labour movement is to actively support and extend these separate struggles and thereby begin the process of constructing an alternative social strategy, which arises directly out of the experiences of those served by and also those working in state services (Walker, 1982, pp. 27, 28–9, 30–1).

Unlike Walker, many other socialists would continue to focus on the *economic* system of capitalism as the main cause of social inequality and social ills and would suggest that his inversion of traditional approaches was inadequate and inappropriate. Changes in economic policy may not solve all of society's problems, but if substantial improvement is to be achieved, they would argue, a challenge to the basic economic structures of capitalism must still be central to the socialist project. If Walker's approach were taken up as the basis of a political programme in the absence of more fundamental economic change then – as Deacon implies earlier – his new structure is likely either to be transformed in practice into a semi-corporatist dependence on capitalism (perhaps in the form proposed by Mishra, 1984) or else remain as utopian a dream as other social blueprints of the past.

Almost all of the critiques, proposals, ideas and blueprints presented in recent socialist writing include a call for more democratic involvement in one way or another, usually coupled with a call for more localized or decentralized approaches. Blunkett and Green (1980) criticize 'top down' approaches to social policy, claiming that 'bottom up' community based decision making is more appropriate and more socialist – and incidentally, suggest that it already happens in Sheffield.

Building from the bottom

How, for example, will council tenants be won over to the nationalisation of the building industry if their weekly experience of the Council's direct labour organisation is that it is inefficient and remote from their control? They will not be persuaded by the theoretical arguments of an incoming

Labour Government if their local experience tells them otherwise. Equally, a central Labour administration will lose support unless it draws in the everyday experience of working people: not just the general opinions they hold on a range of issues, but the skills they can offer because they have applied socialist principles locally. Steelworkers know what is wrong with the steel industry, because they have worked in it: they would resent any central state intervention which did not build on their experience. Women who have experienced the physical battering of husbands and lovers have worked out locally some solution or temporary refuge: they would rightly criticise any government, local or central, which, in co-ordinating a broader response, ignored the lessons of their local struggle.

A start in making the connections between local experience and wider economic and social strategies can be made in local government. It will not always be the best place to continue the fight, but with a hostile central government and a trade union movement currently enmeshed in a defensive economism because of the great economic slump, it gives us a singular opportunity. For the central questions cannot be ignored in our towns and cities. In levying a local rate each year on industrialists and house-holders we are obliged to reconcile our traditional responsibilities for education and welfare with our distintegrating local economic base. The connection between the local economy and social expenditure is a live political issue. All local authorities are necessarily concerned with demo-cratic accountability. Labour controlled councils must be especially concerned that there is not a mass upsurge to defend either local services or local democracy: how they defend their very existence cannot be post-poned. Sheffield Labour Party's 1982 manifesto shows that defence is also an opportunity to explore how to build mass support for a socialist administration.

> We intend with the commitment and co-operation of those who work for us and those who receive services to change the way in which services are delivered to make them more sensitive and responsive. We intend to extend democracy within the workforce to generate ideas and the power to implement changes. We intend to harness the needs of the community to the productive capacity of local industry; to link the industrial worker with those providing essential services in the public field. To this end our industrial and employment policies, which reflect a modern version of the pioneering work done by our predecessors, will take the democratic framework of local accountable government into the fields of manufacture and service industries. We will thereby link the process of democracy at work with the ends of the local community in their widest sense.

. . . [Labour controlled councils] must rebuild popular support not only through the Party machinery, but by internal reorganisation too, by continually re-examining how best to relate their resources and organis-ation to the community outside the Town Hall. They are currently failing (with notable exceptions like South Yorkshire buses) to attract mass support for the services they provide, whether they be housing, welfare, education, recreation or transport. A major problem is the way they are 'delivered'. We have not provided services *with* people, we have provided them *for* people. Therefore our commitment has been to some sort of paternalistic socialism where we say 'Give us a chance and we will do it for you'. We have done that at national level and at local level. We end up being defensive. We are defensive about the role of so-called 'clients'. Central and local government services end up being something given to people out of the grace of our good hearts and not something they are participating in and feel to be theirs.

If we are going to get a coherent policy we need to talk about the way we deliver what it is that we are supposed to be doing on behalf of the people. As socialists, we need to think about the relationship of those we employ with the community for whom they work and to examine the relationship of those who are elected to represent that community with those same people. The interface between the people who are getting something and those who are delivering it, either as elected members or as paid workers, is vital.

If we take social services as an example, we should examine how we deal with the provision of services for the elderly. Are old people's homes somewhere that is separate and isolated from the community in which they are placed, a kind of retreat that people are put into when they are no longer able to cope in their own homes, away from their friends, neighbours and family on whom they normally relied in what we now call the 'community network'? Or is a community home literally that – an actual part of the community, a living part, where people are coming in and out, helping, supporting: where residents are treated as human beings and not as clients. The same question is being raised at national level about how social workers relate to community action and community work. Are social workers part of the community or do they come in from outside as professionals, delivering their expertise to people? (Blunkett and Green, 1983, pp. 5, 6, 21, 22).

Seabrook goes further, in a discussion of new initiatives in Walsall, to argue for the decentralization of local authority welfare provision to local (neighbourhood) offices as a key weapon in recreating the unity and collectivity of the working class which he believes has been undermined by the post-war growth of welfare capitalism.

Rebuilding working-class communities

What was not foreseen in the struggle by the labour movement for a more secure and dignified life for working people was the possibility that the very basis of the industry which had created these poor and haphazardly built little industrial towns and villages that now make up Walsall might itself one day be seriously eroded. And it is in this context that we have to consider the attempts to regenerate a sense of community – something that was an organic part of the growth of these towns and settlements in the nineteenth-century. In some parts of the area – Darlaston, Willenhall – there are acres of dismantled machinery and rusty metal, twisted girders and heaps of rubble from the bigger factories that developed much later –

many of the companies that owed their prosperity to the car industry and which have suffered in the wake of its contraction; many of them firms taken over by multinational companies who have found it more profitable to divest themselves of the machinery and the workers alike. With this intensified disintegration of the whole reason for experience of these older industrial areas, it becomes far more difficult for people to unite than it was against a more tangibly harsh and oppressive system. It is harder to bond together in the face of an *absence* than it is in the direct presence of exploiters and oppressors. When the people who employ us or disemploy us are removed to remote boardrooms in Texas or Osaka, it is far less easy to perceive the ways in which we remain subject to the whim of the market forces which they also serve. It is as though the system has become a great impersonal machine, in which we are all powerless, insignificant figures.

While the old factory boss lived in his neat Victorian villa (or, in Walsall, he was just as likely to live in the shabby dwelling near the works where he could keep an eye on everybody, keeping his money in a greasy cashbox and counting it by candlelight at night), it all seemed so much more straightforward. But when everything depends on vast international transactions of which we can see nothing; when capital, noiseless, winged and infinitely mobile, can withdraw stealthily like a thief in the night and take up its abode in other, more profitable parts of the world, where the working class is more docile and disposed to accept low wages and inferior conditions – there seems to be very few points of contact with it and its agents. It all seems much more powerful; and we are less inclined, because we feel less able, to combat its mysterious and invisible power; even though it rules our lives with the same iron necessity as it did when these towns were thrown up in the wake of the industrial revolution.

But in this absence of immediately identifiable enemies; and in the face of that impersonal system which even the welfare state seems to have become (that great prize won by labour, with its embodiment of the best of the working class ideal of mutual support and caring); and given the consistent assault on brotherhood and sisterhood, the unrelenting attack on the values and institutions of the working class, it isn't surprising that people have tended to lose their sense of belonging, of cohesiveness and community. It shouldn't surprise us that the migrants from the Third World into the towns readily became identified as the *cause* of that loss of cohesion, even though the recent newcomers to Walsall came in the same migration in search of a better life for themselves and those they love, as the original inhabitants of the town – those who came from Wales and Ireland and the villages of Staffordshire and Shropshire a century and a half ago came on the same quest.

The tendency has been, not for people to intensify their unity and solidarity against these new forces that seem to govern our lives, but to break against them, to turn inwards, to absorb the ideology of capitalism and seek personal salvation. This is done, where possible, by buying our way out, retreating to the suburbs; and, where this isn't possible, by turning away, locking our door against an incomprehensible world, barring the entry to strangers, buying a stronger lock against all the intruders and aliens and muggers and rapists which, the press assures us every day, the world has suddenly become full of.

It is in this context that the Neighbourhood Offices have been set up. That they run counter to the whole temper of the times makes it more difficult for them to succeed. How much harder it is to create a sense of unity, when faced with great indifferent systems, where even a benign idea like 'receiving benefit' sounds like a threat, where immovable functionaries sit behind barred windows and administer bare subsistence, where any kind of labour, no matter how demeaning and degrading, looks like a rescue from the impotence and futility of unemployment. It is so much easier to blame the people we see around us, real flesh and blood with its frailties and weaknesses, than the distant manipulators of our destiny in their remote fortresses. It is so simple to blame the blacks for being here, the young for having it so easy, the old for living too long, the unemployed for being idle, the employed for being greedy; it is even simpler to see a husband as selfish, a wife as indifferent, children as too demanding, parents as too busy, friends as unreliable, comrades as a burden, neighbours as an intrusion; and, in this way, we can see the furthest effects of a brutally damaging individualism into the lives of those who have nothing but their solidarity to fight the assault of capital. We see ourselves as struggling, isolated individuals, pursuing our lonely way through life, panting after all the wonders and promises with which capitalism taunts us and which never seem to go round far enough, which never quite live up to the promise, no matter how much money we may lay our hands on.

It has to be asked whether it is possible to create the kind of unity that is required to fight these forces in our lives; especially since it sometimes seems they are so abstract and beyond our reach, vague and distant shadows. There is no sense in underestimating the work that waits to be done. For it is within a very painful and difficult setting that the people who have set in train the regeneration of neighbourhood have gone to the heart of the way we live now. It is only a beginning; a first and tentative step in the cementing of a solidarity that is the only weapon of those who have nothing but their labour – and their spirit and heart and intelligence – and who are called upon to fight the great global empire which capitalism controls in the declining years of the twentieth century (Seabrook, 1984, pp. 143–7).

Many socialists would disagree both with Seabrook's vision of a past working class unified in the collective fight for immediate survival, and with his argument that the state needs to intervene to rebuild confident working-class communities capable of challenging the blandishments of welfare capitalism and the pressures of multinational capital. The former seems unnecessarily romantic to many, while the latter seems rather patronizing. Nevertheless, running through his argument is a theme which consistently recurs in the writing of socialists, namely a concern to link social policy to a wider process of fundamental political change. The arguments about the ways in which this might be achieved and indeed the overall ends in view are hotly contested among socialists. If a socialist social policy is to be developed it will be the product not only of debates like these, but also of individual battles over particular issues out of which more general lessons may be drawn.

13 · *Fabianism*

By the mid 1970s, the older certainties of traditional Fabian welfarism were under severe challenge, not only from the ideologues of laissez-faire on the right, but also increasingly, as we have seen, from the women's movement and the socialist left. Fabianism may never have been as hegemonic – or as unified – as it seems through the rose-tinted spectacles of retrospective myth, but its weakness and uncertainty in recent years are certainly new. It began to crumble from the inside as well as being threatened from the outside.

Fabianism triumphant was based on an assumption of sustained economic growth guaranteed by economic management by the state. It was the social policy counterpart of Keynesian economics. The failure of post-war British economic policy to rescue Britain from first recession and then deeper crisis has been accompanied by a similar failure of social policy and the welfare state. The costs of welfare are supposed to be covered by economic success which never came, and economic failure – with increased poverty and unemployment – has itself helped to impose additional costs on the welfare system. Some (such as Bacon and Eltis, 1976), have even argued that the rising costs of welfare have themselves been the cause of economic decline, because they have added intolerable burdens to the existing costs of industry and have helped to reduce incentives more widely.

In the wake of economic crisis, it has become more and more difficult to sustain the set of class compromises – the negotiated settlement – on the basis of which the British welfare state was constructed between 1945 and 1950. Since Fabianism had played a major part in providing the ideological justification for this political compromise, had been identified with, and had identified itself with the welfare state, it is hardly surprising that its collapse was accompanied by a fundamental fracturing of Fabianism as a coherent intellectual system. Of course, it would always have been wrong to imply that Fabianism – at least as we have defined it – was ever a totally unified or enclosed approach, but until the last decade it has been possible to identify some sort of political and intellectual core. That is no longer the case. Instead, different groups are now seen to be fighting over its legacy.

For that reason, in this section, we have chosen to look at some of the different directions in which writers and politicians within the Fabian tradition have moved in recent years. A central issue is whether this period marks the end of Fabianism as a force in the development of social policy – as Mishra suggests, 'perhaps the most revealing thing about the Fabian response [to the crisis of the welfare state] is that it is virtually a non-response' (Mishra, 1984, p. 123) – or whether instead it offers the possibility of reconstructing the Fabian approach on a new basis, as Deakin suggests in an article marking the hundredth anniversary of the Fabian Society (Deakin, 1984, pp. 356–8).

Two principal concerns have been central to the Fabians' reassessment of their welfare state: first, an appraisal of its failure to provide an effective redistribution of income and wealth within society; and, second, a response to criticisms of the excessive power of state bureaucracies and an increased sympathy for more decentralized and, by implication, more democratic structures. In this ungainly process of self-criticism, the range of alternatives produced has been striking and the boundaries between Fabian and other approaches have increasingly lost their significance as ideas have been borrowed and transformed to remake old traditions.

Although it has been forcibly argued that state welfare spending since the war has had significant and positive redistributive effects (see, for example, O'Higgins, 1983, pp. 171–82) the extent to which these have been successful has been very disappointing to many within the Fabian tradition (see, in particular, Le Grand, 1982). An end to poverty and moves towards greater equality seem as distant as ever.

In the following extract Adrian Webb considers the record of the personal social services (defined as 'the work of local authority social services departments and of voluntary and informal care and provision for similar client groups' (Webb, 1980, p. 279) particularly in the light of the experience of the 1974–9 Labour government. He argues strongly that, despite their stated aims, they have failed conclusively to reach these ends.

The search for equality

A concern for equality has characterised the personal social services throughout the past decade or so, despite the lack of quantitative studies of redistribution. The impact has been on the ideologies and nascent theories which underpin practice rather than on specific or general objectives. An increase in resources could remove some of the disappointments. Both residential and community care services could be extended, improved in quality, and made more flexible. The status of 'simple' care could be enhanced by focusing more attention on the role of domiciliary, day and informal care. An enhanced share of training opportunities for care staff would be a key to such improvements. Similarly, greater imagination and collaboration, backed by extra resources, could bring more advisory, supportive and socially and culturally enriching care to the handicapped, the mentally ill and to the elderly. Resources are a necessary means of moving away from the 'emergency service' syndrome which afflicts this most neglected of the social services.

A second issue, that of charges and means tests, raises a problem which has not been made explicit, that of equity between consumers and potential consumers. If charges are a source of stigma and non-uptake of service, they offend against one of our concepts of equality; if they enable service to be extended, they may promote equality. The personal social services include a variety of different contexts in which charges are, or can be, applied. Charges for residential care for the elderly primarily represent a substantial transfer of resources from the social security system to local authorities and are comparatively non-controversial. Those imposed on the parents of children in local authority residential care are potentially far more controversial and may represent a source of additional stigma for families who are reluctant users of child care services. Charges on domiciliary services occupy a middle ground: they are controversial but they do not contain 'punitive' overtones. Charging policies differ enormously and there is unfortunately little factual evidence, as opposed to assumptions and assertion, on which to base policy. Even the economic viability of charging for some services (such as home helps) is unclear. At present, the question of charges poses an apparent and unresolved choice between the equality to be achieved through a possibly more extensive, but means tested, service and that achieved through a universal, free, but admittedly under-financed, service.

A third problem – that of territorial inequalities – is by no means simple or receding. The national concern for inner city areas reflected in the rate support grant formula may be an appropriate redistributive strategy, but not all shire counties have the resource base from which to provide good services in rural areas and by no means all of those which have, do so. Rural deprivation has been greatly neglected and it bears heavily on the personal social services in many county districts. The physical isolation induced by declining rural transport services exacerbates the problems of the elderly and disabled in particular and adds to the cost of maintaining services. Since local government reorganisation in 1974, most shire counties have been faced with inequalities of service between the old county and the old county borough areas and territorial justice has been a key policy issue for some of the new social services departments.

A fourth example of complexity centres on the growing enthusiasm for informal and voluntary care. At worst it is unreflective jingoism, but this worst manifestation was a predictable reaction to 'resource shock'. The potential, and the limits, of alternatives to state services are beginning to attract more serious attention. Whether the right questions are yet being asked in a coherent way – from the equality, or other, perspectives – is another matter. The danger presently remains that these alternatives could be developed and used with too high an expectation of saving money in the state sector. To paraphrase Richard Titmuss's famous dictum on selectivity, we most urgently need to establish that infrastructure of universal, publicly financed provision which will enable the non-statutory alternatives to grow in appropriate ways. This is profoundly a matter of philosophy and objectives and not merely of giving a bit more public money to voluntary agencies or beseeching families and neighbours to do more for the socially dependent.

One final problem for the future arises from the tendency of an inadequately financed policy of community care to transfer the burden of care to the families, neighbours and friends of the people in need of care or to volunteers. Surprisingly, there has been little attempt to document the extent and consequences of this phenomenon.

Nevertheless, there is a sense of failure and disillusionment among many personal social services staff – admittedly counter-balanced by optimism and sheer determination – which is too fundamental to be explained wholly by the shortage of resources. It is intimately connected with the concern for equality.

Even at the level of general philosophy, some problems were already apparent from the beginning of the seventies. A structural view of causal processes and policy solutions is highly likely to lead to frustration: structural change depends essentially on the effectiveness of social and economic policies outside the control of the personal social services. The paradox of commitment and impotence surfaced in the Community Development Projects, and more indirectly in corporate planning and the growth of community work within social services departments. Impotence in the face of frustrated hopes has been a large part of the experience of personal social services staffs throughout the seventies.

This experience has raised a fundamental question of legitimacy. The structural view of causality was sufficiently widely accepted for the wider failure to fund egalitarian policies to undermine the legitimacy of much social service work from within. The experience of failure to achieve the more ambitious hopes of more optimistic days has been generalised. The attempt merely to ameliorate inequalities – material and social – tends to be derided or undervalued. But amelioration, in context, is a legitimate and necessary function of the personal social services.

Similarly, by reference merely to the raised expectations of visible outcomes instead of the underlying causes and increased social stress, public and political reactions have signalled a lack of confidence in these services from without. The problem which these reactions highlight is partly one of morale, but also one of theory and philosophy and of a lack of widely shared understandings. The personal social services are beginning to reverberate to the question: what are we achieving with the use of even those scarce resources we possess? Part of the response must be the evolution of a more sophisticated analysis of the different types of egalitarian objectives which can appropriately be pursued through the personal social services (Webb, 1980, pp. 279–80, 286–95).

Webb's response to the problems of the personal social services clearly leaves him within the central Fabian tradition. He notes that 'mere' amelioration has been undervalued, argues for more resources, but also stresses the need for 'a more sophisticated analysis' which will allow more appropriate decisions to be made on the allocation of those resources. In other words, for past failures to be overcome it is necessary to develop a more systematic and effective process of assessment, an argument which has strong links back to the Webbs' stress on coherent programmes and expert supervision.

Peter Townsend, in the next extract, starts from the same failure to achieve equality but explicitly argues for more fundamental social and political changes. Instead of arguing that there is some under-lying and universal rationality of which all people of good will can be persuaded or that more modest aims would be appropriate, he argues that problems of poverty stem from existing economic and social structures which have to be challenged directly.

The need for structural change

An alternative strategy has to be comprehensive if it is to have any chance of being successful. The creation of a mass dependent under-class is by no means inevitable. It must be fought intellectually, socially and morally: society *can* have more say in deciding what forms of employment deserve to be developed, who should have the right to access to paid employment and how the wage system within employment might be reorganised according to certain guiding principles. Society can also have more say in broadening rights to the inheritance and accumulation of wealth and dramatically increasing taxes from wealth. Such arguments about employ-ment, the wage system and wealth tend in the years since the war to have been ignored in arguments about poverty, and yet our analysis of the growing extent of poverty must bring us back to them.

Beveridge recognised the importance of full employment in the war and that became an accepted objective of policy in the following two decades. But the concept of 'full employment' as traditionally adopted as the goal of economic policy might properly be replaced by one described as 'employment for all'. People who want paid work, including women, older people and disabled people, must be guaranteed rights to employment. Moreover, society must play a much more positive role in defining the type and conditions of employment. We must debate what kind of production and what kind of society we want to build. A Labour Govern-ment will need to promote new forms of industry on a large scale, but it will also need to foster the expansion of employment in the public services, particularly social services like home nursing, home help and day care centres. The mixture of youth opportunity and job creation programmes which have been developed since the mid 1970s have only been temporary, peripheral and largely self-defeating gestures rather than something which could properly be called a programme of permanent employment for all. In place of a strategy designed to give least offence to the private market, a strategy has to be evolved to define the kind of employment which deserves to exist in a socialist society. This necessarily would involve trade unions, social security claimants and many other sections of the population in creating socially useful, productive and satisfying work.

In reconstituting employment the definition of objectives has priority. Greater equality of employment deserves to be established. Merely to reduce registered unemployment to tiny dimensions would be an insufficient expression of that policy. A substantial section of the popu-lation who would like to work are not in the labour market at all. They do not register for work because they know their chances of getting a job are minimal or non-existent. Women of all ages, middle aged and elderly men, and many disabled people are included. In the past they have been treated as a labour 'reserve' to be drawn upon when demand is high and turned back when the economy moves into a downturn. It is wasteful and short-sighted to disregard the productive and socially useful roles they could play.

In the early stages the Government would play a major part, through industrial investment and the reorganisation of public services, in creating millions of new jobs, establishing 'industrial democracy' and experimenting with different forms of work organisation. At a second stage, having explored viable new forms of social management and work relationships of production, the social ownership and direction of the economy can be confirmed.

The reconstitution of employment holds the key to the equalisation of income. If assumptions can be made about greater equality of status at work as well as outside work then public support can be found for a more equal system of income. There would be two kinds in action. The differences between the income of those inside and outside employment would be reduced, as would the differences between those at the top and the bottom of the pay structures of employment. The unpaid social responsibilities of women could be properly recognised for the first time. People outside the traditional labour market would be recognised as playing a very constructive part in society, and, accordingly, would enjoy higher living standards. Within the traditional labour market, retrenchment of top and upper middle salaries would help to provide better pay, and respect for, the jobs performed by many manual workers. I do not think proposals for a minimum wage are likely to be successful unless there is considerable control over the whole structure of earnings. It would be possible for a government to specify a maximum permissible earnings level of, say, four times the average wage. The trade unions could play an important part in devising the principles of a national incomes system while leaving themselves considerable scope for local and plant bargaining over pay within specified ranges. The approach suggested here will of course depend also on corresponding action internationally to improve some of the lowest wages in the Third World and elsewhere, by means of collaboration between trade unions and between government and to control the movement of jobs, capital, and professional and other workers.

Action to reduce the dispersion of wealth must also involve allocation and accumulation and not just taxation. In the short run a ceiling could be placed on the wealth that can be owned by an individual as well as the gross value of assets that may be inherited. Decisions would have to be made about the transmission of ownership and the social use of different forms of property. An opportunity would be given to local communities, where appropriate, to contribute to such decisions, and objections (on the part of property-holders) to be heard. Agricultural land, housing, paintings and sculpture, antiques, stocks and shares would come into different kinds of ownership. A ceiling might be placed on personal overseas holdings too, and this restriction related to rights as citizens. Corporate holdings with specific personal use or value would have to be redefined and legally counted in total personal wealth. Plans would have to be made not only for the smooth transfer of major assets, but efficient social management. A blanket form of old-style nationalisation would be undesirable. Groups in each region working through the lists of the major holdings of each property, being properly accountable for their recommendations, and creating public holding corporations to receive different types of amounts of resources might be envisaged. All this would be bound to take a period of years and would have to be brought into effect by stages, possibly beginning with the largest holdings of personal wealth and property.

In the meantime, a Labour Government should introduce an annual wealth tax. Such taxes already operate in many other advanced industrial countries. It should be accompanied by a progressive accessions tax. This would differ from the current Capital Transfer Tax because it would be paid by the recipient of the wealth rather than the donor. Tax would be levied at a progressive rate according to the amount of wealth received by that individual in gifts or bequests, during their lifetime. The accessions tax should be combined with the annual wealth tax to encourage property holders to pass on their wealth more quickly, as proposed by the Meade Committee on tax reform (Meade, 1978), a body which could hardly be attributed with revolutionary intentions. On receiving a gift or inheritance, a progressive accessions tax would be levied. At the same time, an additional tax would be payable on the annual value of the wealth over the period that the recipient was expected to hold the wealth, perhaps his or her life expectancy. An annual wealth tax would thereby by paid in advance, a rebate being made if the wealth changed hands sooner than expected.

A society built on principles of equality and collaboration would be one in which incomes and wealth would be more widely shared. A basic untaxed income could be paid to, or on behalf of, every member of the population, and this social income might represent the bulk of personal income available for distribution, leaving to remuneration in employment a kind of 'topping up' role.

This is not the place to go into all the possibilities in detail. The nature of the exercise is such that a beautiful blueprint, complete in every detail, cannot be offered. When a society chooses to reconstitute itself on the basis of new social values there is bound to be experimentation, endless discussion and unapologetic revision of initial false steps. The goal is equality with participation. This means structural change and not piecemeal reform. Thus a first step must be to establish *social planning*. As critics of present modes of planning – like public expenditure planning and corporate planning – have increasingly recognised, good social planning must ultimately involve different forms of participation on the part of workers, residents, tenants, clients, rate-payers and consumers. Social objectives have to be defined in some detail and the administrative apparatus to control and monitor social planning needs to be set up so that the management of the economy can be properly informed. This is the single most important act for a government which seeks to lay claims to socialism. Any study of the evolution of taxation policy, the social services and, above all, the relationship between the distribution of income and wealth, and incomes and wealth policies under successive Labour administrations shows the want of planning. While it is true that we cannot entirely control the internal conditions of our own society, we cannot let the definition of what those internal conditions are and how they might be overcome go by default. In saying this we do not want power to plan to grow only at the centre. There must be a dialectic. Development has to be coordinated according to socialist aspirations and principles but it must also be allowed to prosper locally. Power to organise services and plan employment and recreation must be devolved to local communities. A big effort to communicate information about Government policies, foster discussion regionally and locally and represent public opinion on particular issues, has to be made (Townsend, 1984, pp. 31–4).

Few would challenge Townsend's status as a major writer and campaigner within the Fabian tradition. And even in this extract his deep roots in that tradition remain clear. He remains principally concerned with fairer distribution rather than challenging capitalism as an economic system. His policies may, in the end, lead towards a socialist society, but that is not their immediate (or even medium-term) intention. But his language, and the means he suggests, certainly take him beyond the normally accepted parameters of Fabianism. His is hardly an acceptance of gradualism, nor does he see 'permeation' as a useful approach. He calls for radical change if poverty and inequality are to be removed.

If Britain's economic and political crises of the 1970s have driven some Fabians like Townsend towards dramatic demands on the existing system, they have also encouraged others to break with some of the Fabian traditions in rather a different direction. There was a major split within the Labour Party as Roy Jenkins, David Owen, Shirley Williams and others left to form the Social Democratic Party, explicitly breaking the old alliance forged in the first two decades of the century between middle-class radicalism and the trade union movement. But there was no intention of completely breaking with the traditions of the past and the SDP has even created its own Fabian Society in the form of the Tawney Society. In the extract below David Owen sets out his view of the problems of inequality and ways of solving them.

Developing the social wage

Any government that wants to construct a strategy for the reduction of inequalities must analyse the pressures which inhibit its freedom to distribute wealth. It is in many ways a diversion to concentrate only on the pressure of the very wealthy or of top management. Those pressures do exist, and have influenced Labour governments as well as Conservative governments, but it is an illusion to pretend that they have been the dominant or even a very influential force. Labour governments have been more influenced by the resistance to paying tax among their own voters; Conservative governments influenced most by middle income taxpayers. The way through these often conflicting pressures can only lie in the democratic process of publishing the facts, arguing for the priorities which the facts support and constantly challenging vested interests wherever they are. It means ensuring that the debate about inequality does not centre only on income but also on access to services: and that the debate on the provision of basic services – those available to all as part of the social wage – is not just a question of simply looking at money quantities without also taking into account how that money is allocated and the quality of the services.

The quantity of services has become a vested interest in that it provides jobs, and with the public service unions naturally concerned about this aspect as well as wage rates, it is important that their pressure is counter-balanced by pressure over quality. If the quality of service falls then resistance to paying taxes and rates will rise among the very people for whom public services could provide a measure of real improvement in their overall standard of living. We must enable people to choose quality.

The only way of achieving a more equitable distribution of income in a democracy is to secure a greater awareness by the mass of the population of the facts about poverty, and by greater diffusion of wealth-holding. The cost for the social security system of an effective anti-poverty strategy will be very great and the taxes necessary to provide for such a social strategy will be very high. Unless more people can feel secure and satisfied by their present and future standard of living they will resist paying such tax levels. Additional incomes from a share in profits and the security afforded by an ownership of assets is still the prerogative of the few. What is needed is to widen the definition of standard of living from a comparison of income to a concept that embraces asset-holding, whether in terms of home ownership, secure rented accommodation, shares or savings, and sees security as the ability to benefit fully in our society from access to a good education service and health service – and to have confidence in the financial and care provision available in old age, sickness or disablement. It is this wider concept of the social wage, where the taxpayer sees his or her standard of living in broader terms than the after tax figure on the wage slip, that will cause the voter's resistance to paying tax to alleviate the poverty of others to be moderated. Nationalization is neither a necessary nor a sufficient condition for social change of this kind: reliance must be placed on changing people's attitudes, on promoting industrial democracy, and on industrial co-operatives, wider share ownership and above all, wider home ownership (Owen, 1981, pp. 246–7).

Unlike Townsend, Owen stresses the need to persuade people of the need to pay increased taxes and avoids any suggestion that poverty may be caused by structural factors which have to be challenged. In some ways, his approach fits better with past political and social administration orthodoxies since it goes on to consider various technical alternatives without – except in the broadest way – considering political obstacles to change. For all its apparent careful reasonableness, in fact Owen's approach is almost utopian in its belief that all groups can be persuaded of the need for greater equality and that there are few fundamental obstacles to such a consensual approach to welfare. His optimism sits uneasily by the side of Townsend's harsh realism in analysing obstacles to equality, even if Townsend's proposals seem equally difficult to achieve.

Towards a new consensus?

There is wide agreement even among those most closely associated with the Fabian tradition that the post-war welfare state has neither significantly reduced levels of poverty, nor generated greater equality. The responses to this apparent agreement have, however, as we have seen, varied widely. A second aspect of Fabian self-criticism, stemming from a similarly wide agreement that welfare provision has suffered from over-centralization and bureaucratization, has begun to encourage a response which is rather more unified. It also finds a reflection in the other three approaches considered in this book. A new set of assumptions about the value of decentralization, devolution and 'democratization' seems to be taken for granted on all sides. Centralization, bureaucracy and professionalization have, it is argued, made it more difficult for poor or disadvantaged people to make their voices heard or to act independently.

Hadley and Hatch are among those who have put the case against centralism most strongly.

Liberty and fraternity as well as equality

Today we are ruled according to the tenets of a centralist faith. The country is governed by a powerful complex of centralised political institutions, and its social services are amongst the most collectivised and bureaucratic in the Western world. Their main features have been determined by national legislation and they are administered by central and local government departments remote from the recipients of the services. A premium is placed on the attainment of standard-quality services over the country as a whole. Autonomous activity by the people, whether the informal care exchanged between family members, friends and neighbours, or the work of formal voluntary bodies, receives little attention in the design of government policies and is poorly integrated with the statutory services.

The system is based on a firm belief that the central government is not only legally responsible for shaping detailed policies for the management of the country but is also best equipped to oversee their administration. Even the present Conservative government, which is committed on paper to reducing the scope of the state, has not been able to resist the temptation to curb the autonomy of the local authorities when it seemed that it was being used to mitigate the effects of central government expenditure cuts. . . .

The reorganisations of the statutory services have made decision-making more remote from the ordinary consumer. But in response to this tendency efforts have been made to strengthen the voice of the consumer, through such devices as tenants' associations, placing parents on the managing bodies of schools and the establishment of community health councils; while the spread of community action in its many forms indicates that the consumers of public services are becoming more articulate. However, it would appear that these developments are more by way of reactions to the lack of popular control, rather than expressions of effective participation in decision-making. The provision of more services by authorities ultimately subject to the sanction of the ballot box has not done much to make those services responsive to their intended beneficiaries or to redistribute power more widely.

Liberty and fraternity, as well as equality, are other general criteria for judging the social services, but ones which are difficult to operationalise. In a general sense freedom from want is of course a prerequisite for the exercise of freedom to choose. But more specific issues can be raised by asking what choices individuals are actually able to exercise. Choices most obviously exist within further and higher education – between both courses and institutions – and these choices have been greatly extended by the expansion of post-school education. But in primary and secondary education, in health, in housing and in the personal social services the opportunities for choice are more limited: indeed, allocation rather than choice is the more appropriate term for describing how people come to receive one service or facility rather than another. As already argued in relation to equality of power, there has been a growing recognition of the desirability of responsiveness to consumers: but it is difficult to find evidence of anything beyond marginal changes resulting from this. A substantial increase in freedom would come about by extending the private sector and improving the terms on which individuals can opt out of statutory services; but this would be at the expense of equality.

Fraternity can be given various meanings. Interpreted widely, it embraces unilateral, impersonal gift-giving, as of blood through the trans-fusion service, as well as collaborative relationships between people regarding themselves as equals. Both kinds of activity can be valued for themselves as well as for their contribution to social cohesion and soli-darity. It is difficult to envisage fraternity being as direct and explicit a goal of social policy as equality. Nevertheless, the way in which policies are designed can either encourage it or discourage it. There is little by way of fraternity in the supplementary benefits office, or in the usual doctor's waiting room or in the way that local authorities allocate their housing. In essence, services that follow the normal bureaucratic pattern of dealing with individuals in isolation from each other are inimical to fraternity, and much of the expansion of the social services during the past two decades has taken this character. It is voluntary associations that are the natural vehicle for co-operative activity, and only with the encouragement of community development and volunteering during the 1970s have official policy-makers begun to show signs that fraternity has any place in their thinking (Hadley and Hatch, 1981, pp. 5, 54–5).

They argue that Britain's representative system of government itself encourages a dangerously hierarchical structure:

The elected member is seen as the sole legitimate repository of authority and the social services (as with other instruments of government policy) are designed to carry out policies determined by him. Administrators and professionals are seen at any rate in theory as servants of the representative assembly and are expected to adhere strictly to these policies. The citizen in his role of consumer, is assumed to have a largely passive role, and is expected to accept the services provided for him (Hadley and Hatch, 1981, p. 147).

They go on to argue for alternative methods.

A *participatory*, rather than a representative, model of democracy. In such a system, while the general directions of social policy are still determined by the elected members of central and local government, the ways in which the policies are developed and applied are open to discussion and amendment by both social services staff and clients, for their involvement is regarded as indispensable if available resources are to be maximised and variations in need/demand are to be recognised.

It is now possible to begin to identify some of the more salient characteristics of social services organisation implied in participatory organisations and to compare them with the features of the currently dominant system, based on bureaucratic and professional criteria derived from the representative model of democracy.

The *underlying function* of the bureaucratic social service organisation is to carry out the delivery of a predetermined service to a well-defined client group. In contrast, the participatory organisation operates with much wider terms of reference which encourage a co-operative and entrepreneurial approach. Aims are defined in collaboration with staff and users. The most is made of whatever resources are available in carrying out the aims including volunteers.

Authority in the bureaucratic model clearly reposes in the organisational hierarchy. The only exception is where a professional has been given an area of discretion and his professional knowledge and status are the source of his right to take decisions. In the participatory model authority is only based in part on formal position and qualifications. Practical knowledge, personal commitment and position in the community are also sources of authority. In the fostering of adolescents, for example, the knowledge and experience of the foster parents may soon be superior in some respects to those of the social workers, and in the care of the dying, untrained carers may acquire special insight and understanding through their accumulated experience.

In bureaucratic social service organisations *roles* of staff tend to be clearly defined. Their relationships with users are typically meant to be detached, void of personal feeling. In most circumstances the role of the user is supposed to be passive. Patterns of behaviour in participatory organisations of the kind described in this chapter sometimes differed markedly from these prescriptions. Staff roles tended to be flexible and to blur at the edges. Personal involvement of staff with individual users was a feature of most of the schemes reviewed. And the active involvement of users is an important feature of the participatory system.

Innovation within bureaucratic organisations is relatively rare since the formal authority to change structures and procedures resides at the top of the hierarchy, and most employees are likely to feel bound by their tightly defined roles. In contrast, participatory organisations tend to be much more innovative both because they have more freedom to introduce change and because the wider interaction of different grades of staff and of staff with users is likely to produce more criticism and more ideas for change . . .

In bureaucratic social service organisations *indicators of performance* tend to relate to input factors such as the investment in buildings, the number of hospital beds, the number of meals delivered. This reflects in part the upwards responsibility of staff and the need for 'objective' and 'concrete' measures to meet the needs of the political heads of the organisation. Participative social service organisations are not immune to such pressures but they are likely to give much greater weight to users' views. . . .

While any major changes in the framework of the social services will require substantial alterations in policy . . . it is possible to obtain a fuller picture of the shape and operation of a more comprehensive approach in one corner of the existing social services: the development of community-oriented teams in certain social services departments.

The main features of an alternative system would be:

1. Plural provision. A greater proportion of all forms of social service would be provided by voluntary organisations, the one major exception being social security. Thus instead of expanding the statutory services, there would grow up alongside them a variety of community based initiatives.

2. Decentralisation and community orientation of statutory services. The predominant mode of statutory provision would be the community-oriented one, implying flatter structures, a different interpretation of professionalism and reinforcement as opposed to replacement of informal sources of care.

3. Contractual rather than hierarchical accountability. In return for funding and the contracting out of more services to voluntary organisations, government, both local and central, would exercise a stronger monitoring and inspection role than at present. Thus there would be more emphasis on maintaining accountability through contractual agreements as opposed to the exercise of authority within hierarchies.

4. Participation in representation. The counterpart of greater monitoring and inspection would be the participation of consumers and providers in statutory decision-making. Thus the representatives of users and providers would sit on local authority committees, and in the absence of, say, parents' organisations to represent parents on the education committees, nominations could be accepted from the generalist neighbourhood councils. This would mean a substantial dilution, or perhaps rather enrichment, of the pure doctrine of representative democracy: legitimacy would cease to reside exclusively with representatives selected by existing methods (Hadley and Hatch, 1981, pp. 166–7).

The position put forward by Hadley and Hatch fits in well with the wing of the Fabian tradition earlier identified with David Owen – what he might call the social-democratic tradition – although they (and Owen) explicitly criticize the Webbs. Instead, they claim to be building historically on Cole and the more decentralized guild socialist tradition. Since Hadley and Hatch seem to have rejected the revolutionary aims and the peculiar blend of collectivism and syndicalism which were important to the guild socialists, perhaps this search for historical roots should not be taken too seriously (see, for example, Cole 1917, particularly chapter 2). Like the Fabians, they are concerned with giving practical advice to the state. But they do not share the guild socialists' aim of trying to construct a new society within the straitjacket of the old as a first step to breaking with the old one completely. Their emphasis on voluntary organizations could be seen to link them with some of the new right, who seek a return to charitable rather than state provision. Certainly, what Owen (1981, chapter 12) calls the 'enabling state' has little in common with the demands of William Morris, who is quoted approvingly on p. 19 of his book, or of the guild socialists. They were decentralizers – in the case of Morris even close to anarchism – who wanted to undermine capitalism. Hadley, Hatch and Owen are explicitly seeking new ways to shore it up, preferably more cheaply than in the past.

Nor can the social democrats claim to be the sole voice within the Fabian tradition calling for decentralization, despite their attempts to present matters in that way. Even the much reviled Webbs had traditionally based much of their argument on local (municipal) provision as well as that of a centrally organized state machine. In contemporary debates it has often been Fabians (and more explicitly radical socialists sometimes using a Fabian platform as in the case of Blunkett and Green – see Chapter 12) who have tried hardest to develop decentralized provision, even if they stress, rather more than the social democrats, the need for continued state involvement.

In the following extract from a Fabian Society collection assessing and evaluating the welfare state in the 1980s, Deakin outlines practical ways in which local government might become involved and involve communities in the development of social policy.

Towards social programmes for local government

To launch on the preparation of a programme outlining priorities for social policy suggests that we have the equipment to define such priorities and are broadly clear what the options are. However, to embark on any seriously intended programme of consultation is usually to upset any preconception on either of these scores. In particular, any attempt to categorise need groups by priority ranking – a potentially helpful line of advance – runs into the basic difficulty that priority allocations are likely to differ radically as between different interests in the community. Even so basic a proposition as trying to achieve some degree of priority for education or more broadly still for children may run into problems in a highly deprived neighbourhood with a disproportionately large number of single people, old and young, and childless couples. This might have mattered less when programmes were still incremental and resource decisions were about where to distribute the additional expenditure; but in a situation like the present where real cuts are being made all round, priority for (say) the disabled can only be achieved at the expense of other groups in need. Remembering Donnison's account of the letters of protest he received about supplementary benefits rates from the working poor, it is difficult to exclude the possibility of a backlash affecting local government services equally strongly.

Periods in opposition can be helpfully employed in a review of programmes across the whole range of social policies. Some useful models are already in existence. Such an expertise necessarily involves forming a clear concept of what is politically possible – not abstracted from the political debate any more than from the economic imperatives. Equally, its authors should be prepared to be open-minded about some of the issues that have acquired totem significance in the social policy field in some sectors of the labour movement (council house sales, comprehensive school sixth forms and, rapidly assuming the same touchstone status, cheap fares). Against this background, the outline of an agenda might look something like the following.

First proposition

A review should be undertaken of all existing services on a need group basis, involving all the activities of relevant agencies. The objective is to establish at the outset the effects of current policies on the position of the groups identified. It is capable of being extended to other groups besides ethnic minorities – for example, it should almost certainly now be accepted that the long-term unemployed form a distinct group of this kind. Consequences of existing policies for the young family could also be explored in the same way. Once the distributional effects of such policies for the elderly or the mentally handicapped have been established, a set of priorities for action became feasible, if three further conditions can be satisfied:

a The record needs to incorporate the activities of all agencies with relevant responsibilities, not only in the statutory sector but also voluntary bodies;
b There needs to be a parallel process of identification of resources available for possible new initiatives – not only those immediately available to local authorities in main programme areas, but also special grants (particularly relevant in the case of ethnic minorities) and possible sources of funding in the private sector;
c Serious attempts should be made to obtain the views of the consumer groups for whom the services are intended. This should cover not only the introduction of new programmes but modification in existing provision.

Second proposition

The decentralisation of the machinery of service delivery to the maximum extent feasible should be an intrinsic part of any social policy programme. This has already been attempted on a substantial scale in a number of social service departments as part of the so-called 'patch' approach, which decentralises administration to small area level and provides a unified range of services operating out of a single office. A similar approach is being pursued by a number of housing authorities. By extension, an attempt could now be made to cover a variety of services, both locally and centrally run. The pedigree of proposals for 'miniature town halls' is admittedly rather mixed; it goes back to the early 1970s and the initial attacks on 'centralised bureaucracy' associated with the community development projects. The experience of Community Development Projects (CDPs) was not a happy one, either for the immediate participants themselves or the host agencies, but some of the ideas first developed in the CDP context, notably their work on equipping neglect groups with the resources needed to assert their claims, deserve another airing. The possibility of associating local budgets with decentralised multi-service centres would also repay further examination. . . . Conscience at the national level, fades almost to vanishing point in the local context. If the test is to be free consent of the majority to a line indicated in advance, the Apathetic Tendency have commanded a majority in most local authority areas for the past decade. More seriously, the mandate theory allows no scope for mid-course correction, in circumstances which are likely, if the past decade is any guide, to be exceptionally volatile. The importance of establishing measures of the effectiveness of policy that go beyond a simple record of money spent or political objectives met is therefore central. One of the Tory Government's rare virtuous deeds in its dealings with local government has been its insistence on the wider availability of information on local authorities' affairs. The social accounting movement that this initiative has helped to get back on its legs is a thoroughly healthy development and should be extended as rapidly as possible to cover similar assessments of the local performance of the agencies of central government (Deakin, 1983, pp. 217–22).

Taken in conjunction with arguments considered elsewhere in this chapter, it would be difficult to find any writer or politician in the field of social welfare who would argue (fundamentally) against decentralization. It has become an unchallengeable 'good things', even though its precise implications remain unclear. The danger for those within the Fabian tradition is that decentralization may undermine universal rules and encourage unequal provision. But it should also allow for more accurate identification of problems and, in practice, closer involvement by professionals or trained volunteers which has always been a central concern within Fabianism.

The extent to which an overall consensus looks achievable, however, is probably an indication that, like Beveridge, it is possible to read quite different implications into what appears to be the same policy. For Owen, Hadley and Hatch, decentralization implies an increased role for the voluntary sector and a still greater focus on the individual (the possibility of an *escape* from collective action and the chance of cutting spending); for Townsend and Deakin it offers the chance of a revived and more successful Fabianism avoiding the bureaucratic excesses of the past; for Seabrook, Blunkett and Green a policy with the same name implies a greater role for collective organization by the poor and indeed potentially the rebuilding of a class conscious, united working class. As the policy gets translated through the layers of professional policy, our guess is that the former approaches are more likely to dominate in practice than the latter – so that decentralization becomes a means of reconstructing Beveridge on the cheap with a more or less human face rather than a means of challenging capitalist priorities. But that remains to be proved in practice in Sheffield and Islington, East Sussex and Northamptonshire, Strathclyde and Cleveland. It will be the result of decisions by government departments, local authority social workers and action by 'client' groups, as well as the result of debates between proponents of the ideas outlined in this book. We shall be able not only to watch what is happening but also to help determine its outcome.

Part Four

Back to the Poor Law?

Back to the Poor Law?

The summer of 1985 marked a watershed in the conflict between different ideologies of welfare. The welfare state, most particularly in the area of social security, had been for the previous decade the butt of mounting criticism from the right and left of the traditional political spectrum as well as from feminists and claimants. By the 1980s there were few who would give unconditional support to the remaining edifice of the Beveridge structure, although the nature of criticism varied widely. Into this context the Secretary of State for Social Security, Norman Fowler, launched his review of, and subsequent Green Paper on, the social security system. This document was a clear indication of the demise of any consensus that might have survived from the days of Beveridge.

This concluding chapter takes a different form from preceding ones. The inclusion of this section on contemporary politics of welfare is intended to document an attempt by a political party in government, to transform a specific ideology into a set of concrete policy proposals. The breakdown of consensus over welfare in the 1980s has produced an historical moment when a specific ideological position has the potential to go beyond mere critique to the formulation of policies radically different to those celebrated in the post-war decades. Hence this chapter will focus on the Conservative government's review of the social security system and its subsequent proposals for radically restructuring the welfare state. We will, however, not be concentrating on the details of the proposals, but on how the Green Paper celebrates a particularly narrow laissez-faire ideology of welfare and imposes a coherent but oppressive world view of the role of the state and the place of public support on to a demoralized population.

The rise of unemployment from 1979, the declining value of Beveridge's cornerstone of income support (i.e. national insurance benefits), the deepening poverty of women and ethnic minorities, the alienation of the young, and the effects of an economic recession have all contributed to the creation of a 'two nation' Britain. The divide between those in work and those outside paid employment and living on state benefits has widened – not only in economic terms but also in ideological terms. Under such conditions it has become easier to blame poverty on the poor once again, to reassert the distinction between the deserving and the undeserving poor, and to reintroduce old concepts of Poor Law relief (i.e. less eligibility) in the form of a new, more acceptable terminology (e.g., targeting, 'genuine' need, incentives to work, and so on). Yet it is significant that the Green Paper retains some of the methods of Fabianism (namely through establishing a public review and the collection of evidence) as well as laying claim to elements of the 'Beveridge tradition'. There has not been a complete break with the successful rhetoric of 1945, but as the following passages reveal, there is a discernible shift of emphasis.

Fundamental to this approach is a belief that the system of social security provision should be based on a clear understanding of the relative roles and responsibilities of the individual and the state. In building for the future we should follow the basic principle that social security is not a function of the state alone. It is a partnership between the individual and the state – a system built on twin pillars.

Most people not only can but wish to make sensible provision for themselves. The organisation of social security should encourage that. It should respect the ability of the individual to make his [sic] own choices and to take responsibility for his [sic] own life. But at the same time it must recognise the responsibility of government to establish an underlying basis of provision on which we as individuals can build and on which we can rely at times of need. . . .

State provision has an important role in supporting and sustaining the individual; *but it should not discourage self-reliance or stand in the way of individual provision and responsibility* (Green Paper on Social Security, vol. 1, 1985, p. 1, emphasis added).

The social security system affects almost all of us during our lives. It grew out of Beveridge's clear concept but has developed into a leviathan almost with a life of its own. The proposals in this Green Paper *will bring the social security system firmly back under control*. Social security will be based on twin pillars of provision – individual and state – *with stronger emphasis on individual provision than hitherto* (vol. 1, p. 45, emphasis added).

It is the final sentence in the above passage which identifies a common theme in the areas of health, education, social security and employment, namely privatization. The rhetoric of privatization has come to dominate social policy in the 1980s. It heralds a shift away from services and provision by central and local government towards provision by private firms and industry. Hence there has been a growth in such areas as the private provision of health care, of private homes for the elderly, and of profit-making services such as catering and laundering in public hospitals. But the process of privatization is not limited to a question of state versus private ownership or provision; it also denotes a shift away from collective provision in favour of individual provision. Hence in the fields of social security and the social services, individual provision (through the thrift of the 'breadwinner') and familial responsibility (through the extension of the caring work of wives and mothers) have become political ideals in themselves. The process of privatization does not simply mean that private industry will provide necessary services in the place of public provision, it means that individuals and families will only be able to benefit from such services if they have taken the appropriate steps to insure themselves at an early stage or earn sufficient money to buy the services when required.

Such developments considerably weaken the position of individuals outside the labour market or on low pay. Moreover, they intensify the problems that feminists have identified in relation to the dependent family. Put another way, this process means that the more that access to essential services like nurseries, health care, day care, pensions and so on, are linked to a full-time, regular wage or income, the more carers (who are predominently women), children, the elderly, and the disabled must depend on the 'breadwinner' to secure essential facilities. In effect, those who cannot buy services or insurance policies for themselves will be disinherited from access in their own right, and must establish their dependence on a wage-earner to qualify. It is precisely this dependence and personal insecurity that feminists and special interest groups have been struggling against.

The process of privatization has one further dimension. The reduction in public services to the very young, the disabled and the elderly puts pressure on individuals to provide where formerly there was some degree of state provision. Hence women are increasingly forced to adopt the 'caring' role instead of the state, to give up paid work or to work only part time. This in turn intensifies their dependency on the 'breadwinner' and lessens their opportunity to buy into private provision for themselves.

The growth of the ideology of privatization is based on the theory of the minimal state, so familiar in the Victorian and early Edwardian periods, combined with the dogmatic purpose of cutting public expenditure (Hall, 1985). It is clear from the shifts in welfare policy since the Conservative administration of 1979, that the future of welfare had become subservient to monetarist economic policies closely associated with the Treasury. Notwithstanding this, the Treasury has not been as successful in cutting spending by the Department of Health and Social Security (DHSS) as originally planned, not least because the rise in unemployment has increased spending on unemployment benefit and supplementary benefit. The review of the social security system must therefore be understood in this context. On the one hand, the Treasury was looking for cuts in expenditure, and the DHSS made it clear that any reforms to the system would be 'revenue neutral' (i.e. would not involve any additional expenditure). On the other hand, there was the growing rhetoric of privatization and the celebration of Victorian values.

The ideological starting point of the review was clearly apparent in the consultation documents produced by the review panels set up by the DHSS. The overall review was divided into panels with 'independent' members (although all were notably right wing) to take evidence on the four areas of supplementary benefit, benefits for children and young people, pensions and housing benefit. (Maternity benefit was dealt with by civil servants in an internal review procedure.) Each panel took written and oral evidence from the public and submitted their conclusions to a central review team. This in turn produced the Green Paper. In spite of this elaborate procedure, the final outcome of the review process could be closely predicted from the consultation documents published before the review began. For example, the individuals and groups who gave evidence were asked to submit 'revenue neutral' proposals and to focus their responses on the following issues.

* How should the [supplementary benefit] scheme deal with incentives to claimants for self-help? Can there be better incentives for claimants to take part-time work, while retaining incentives for full-time work? How should claimants' capital and resources be treated to retain the incentive to save?

* Whether there are alternative ways of providing means-tested help for several million people?

* Those commenting are asked to bear particularly in mind the contribution towards the stability of families which may be made by social security arrangements and also to consider opportunities for simplification . . . in the range of benefits . . . (DHSS, 1984).

In spite of the fact that the proposals emanating from the review process might have been regarded as foregone conclusions, it is important to realize that the government was able to mobilize very strong antipathy to the welfare state in order to justify its radical approach to reform. On one level, hardly anyone supported the welfare state as it stood in 1980, at least not until the Tories began to dismantle it. But the government was able to use the abundant critiques of welfare, whether from socialists or Fabians or feminists, to argue that there was a consensus of dissatisfaction which demanded radical action. The fact that all these different critiques demanded very different forms of action was glossed over. The grounds for dismantling the remaining edifice of Beveridge had been established.

In many ways the Green Paper marks a revival of the Victorian Poor Law, not only in relation to its strong ideological commitment to a minimal state, but also in its reintroduction of distinct elements of charity. Beveridge's plans were popular for their emphasis on a *right* to benefit through the insurance or contribution principle. Flawed as this was, its aim was to move away from the stigma of charity. The Green Paper, however, proposed to reintroduce the principles of charity under the recommendations for extending the scope of means-tested benefits and the introduction of a social fund which would be used to top up the basic means-tested income support in cases of proven genuine need. It was proposed that this need would be assessed by a combination of specially trained DHSS officers, social workers, and health professionals. Its administration would be entirely discretionary with no legal framework and no right of appeal. Moreover local DHSS offices, which would administer the fund, would be given a limited annual budget as a means of keeping tight control over any inclination to be too charitable. The Green Paper outlines these proposals in the following way.

The Government recognise that, alongside the new income support scheme (a revised form of supplementary benefit), it will be necessary to provide for the exceptional circumstances and emergencies faced by a minority of claimants and to help those who find difficulty in managing their resources and budgeting. At present these problems are dealt with ineffectively through single payments and urgent needs payments. These systems have become unacceptably cumbersome and expensive. They are subject to complex regulations and instructions as a result of which help is often dependent more on intricacies of interpretation than on genuine assessment of need. These arrangements will be replaced by a new social fund. It will be administered by DHSS local offices on a discretionary basis so that appropriate and flexible help can be given to those in genuine need. The fund will have an annual budget and its operation will be monitored to ensure that it is being used appropriately. Staff will be specially trained to assess individual need, to offer help with budgeting problems and to assist the more vulnerable groups who face special difficulties (Green Paper, vol. 1, p. 32).

The aim of the social fund was to make the distribution of small sums of money conditional upon compulsory counselling, advice on how to budget and debt management, and surveillance by the social services and other professional groups. While means-testing and its indignities were not new in 1985, the idea of the social fund grafted the worst aspects of the Poor Law on to the worst aspects of the Beveridge structure. For Beveridge, means-tested provision was meant to be a safety net for the few. In the Fowler proposals, the many would be required to live on means-tested benefits, and those who fell though this inadequate safety net would be caught in another net to be subjected to further tests of eligibility. Eligibility for assistance would rest on a system of subjective evaluations of proven need rather than on legally protected rights. In brief, it signalled a new attempt to pathologize and stigmatize the poor by treating them as 'inadequate'. In addition, the monies paid to the 'genuinely' needy from the fund would be in the form of loans which the recipient would have to repay in cash. In this way the values of thrift would be instilled into the poor.

The concept of the social fund epitomizes the traditional laissez-faire ideology of welfare, albeit that it is dependent upon a bureaucratic and professional infrastructure unimagined during the Victorian era. But it sits uneasily alongside the newer, radical right view that a system of social security should be clinically efficient and streamlined rather than based on ambiguous value judgements and 'moral' counselling. This view, propounded most influentially by the Institute for Fiscal Studies (IFS), is reflected in some parts of the Green Paper. But on the specific question of defining eligibility and methods of mean-testing the poor, the IFS adopted a different perspective to the government. They state,

What is offensive are specific and potentially humiliating enquiries into the affairs of poor households which discriminate between them and the population as a whole. The intention of [our] proposals is to effect a considerable reduction in these enquiries by utilising much more extensive information which is, or could be, collected through the tax system (Dilnot, Kay and Morris, 1984, p. 117).

There are, therefore, tensions apparent in the shift to the right in the field of welfare. While there is no question about whether poverty should be eradicated, or whether the system should be redistributive, there is debate about whether the poor should be subject to a different regime of management and entitlements simply because they are poor.

The specific proposal for the social fund is reminiscent of the Poor Law, but there are also a number of other ways in which the Green Paper significantly shifts the debate on welfare back several decades. These are in relation to the young, to women and to the celebration of the dependent family. The proposals for the abolition of the universal maternity grant, the transformation of the state earning-related pension scheme (SERPS), the abolition of family income supplement (FIS) which is usually paid to mothers to be replaced by family credits payable through the (male) breadwinner's wage packet, all herald a further twist in the spiral of the feminization of poverty. Moreover, there are clear indications in the Green Paper which threaten the future of child benefit. The government's basic dislike of child benefit was spelled out in the following passages.

Family credit will be an integral part of the take-home pay of the wage earner in low income families. It will put such families in a position where *they [sic] can see more clearly the level of income on which they can depend and on which they [sic] need to plan their lives* (vol. 1, p. 30, emphasis added).

The system of payments of [Child Benefit] usually to the mother is also well established and appreciated and, *although the result is that the value of the benefit as part of the general household income is often overlooked*, the Government do not wish to change it (vol. 2, p. 48, emphasis added).

These passages indicate a particular view of family life and of the power relationships therein. On the one hand, it is apparent that the Green Paper expresses a belief that income paid to a male breadwinner is synonymous with income for the family. It is presumed that a wife knows what her husband earns and that she and the children receive their fair or equal shares. Moreover, it presumes that wives have the opportunity to plan their lives on the basis of their husbands' earnings. On the other hand, it is presumed that money (child benefit) paid to the mother is invisible in the calculation of household income, presumably because it does not pass through the hands of the 'head of household'. There are a number of questions raised by this 'logic'. The first is why it should be presumed that men's income is visible to all family members while women's income is not. Such evidence as exists suggests that the opposite is more likely to prevail (Pahl 1980, 1982). The second is why the government was intent upon increasing the economic power of the husband in the family by directing more benefits through his wage packet, whilst reducing significantly the real value of child benefit paid to women.

The answer to this is complex but there are two main elements. The first is linked to the issue of privatization described above. It has been government policy to increase dependence upon individual, as opposed to collective, provision. As a part of this shift the so-called 'head of household', as the person most likely to have continuous contact with the labour market, becomes increasingly significant as a kind of gate-keeper to services and benefits for his wife, children and other dependants. It was anticipated that this arrangement would cut public expenditure as the individual entitlement of dependants would be highly contingent or even non-existent. In brief, the direction of state benefits to the husband is meant to increase the self-sufficiency of the family unit by reinforcing the power of the husband, while reducing costs to the Exchequer. The second element resides in the government's belief that paying benefits to low-paid breadwinners rather than their wives, would reduce the former's demand for wage rises. The Green Paper states,

The new scheme should offer significant advantages for employers in ensuring that employees perceive more clearly the total net remuneration they receive rather than earnings net of tax and national insurance alone (vol. 2, p. 49).

In this respect the government acknowledged the political and industrial strength of working-class men who can, through their unions, press for wage increases. They also acknowledged the powerlessness of women, especially those outside the labour market, who can exert far less pressure to increase their incomes if they are dependent upon their husbands, the universal child benefit and/or FIS.

While the economic position of women in the family would be

increasingly undermined by these proposals, the independence of young unemployed people between the ages of 16 and 26 years was also threatened. Based on the presumption that young people who are not in the labour market should be dependent upon their parents, the Green Paper proposed a different, lower level of income support for people of 25 or under (unless they are lone parents or have children). The single unemployed young person would find it extremely difficult to leave the family home, not only because of lack of money, but because of the lack of adequate housing provision for this group. The ideological grounding for this proposal is clear: as with the situation facing women, the proposals were designed to reduce public expenditure, while individual families would be made responsible for young unemployed adults.

While the Green Paper clearly documents an ideological position akin to previous laissez-faire ideology, it should be recognized that it is a version of this position which has the benefit of hindsight. In other words it has been influenced by Beveridge, the Webbs and Fabianism. There is no simple cycle of history with Victorian values merely repeating themselves *ad infinitum*, and no inevitability about the transformation of Victorian ideology into concrete policies in future. Yet there are important resonances of the Poor Law which are combined not only with the lessons of history but with the potential 'benefits' of new technology.

The Government believe that the outcome of this extensive review of social security will be a system of benefits which will reflect modern needs. Recourses will be better targeted, incentives will be improved and the scheme will be considerably easier to understand and administer. Together with the plans now moving ahead for computerising social security, the reforms in this Green Paper will produce a more efficient and effective system which will carry us forward into the next century (vol. 1, p. 48).

It seemed that we could look forward to a late twentieth-century, high technology Poor Law. Although the Green Paper was not translated into legislation at the time, it set out the New Right's programme for the 1980s and 1990s. Whether it can be implemented in the future will depend on the continuing debate between the ideologies we have discussed, and the social forces represented by them.

Bibliography

Abbott, E. and Bompas, K., 1943, *The Woman Citizen and Social Security*, Mrs Bompas.

Andreski, S. (ed.), 1971, *Herbert Spencer: Structure, Function and Evolution*, Michael Joseph.

Addison, P., 1977, *The Road to 1945: British Politics and the Second World War*, Quartet.

Anon, 1910, *Report of the Debate on the Poor Law Minority Report between G. Lansbury and H. Quelch* (Editor of *Justice*), Twentieth Century Pamphlet.

Bacon, R. and Eltis, W., 1976, *Britain's Economic Problem: Too Few Producers*, Macmillan.

Banks, O., 1981, *Faces of Feminism*, Oxford: Martin Robertson.

Barrett, M. and McIntosh, M., 1982, *The Anti Social Family*, NLB, Verso.

Beechey, V., 1979, 'On Patriarchy', *Feminist Review*, no. 3.

Bentham, J., 1789, *An Introduction to the Principles of Morals and Legislation*, in Mill, 1962.

Beveridge, W., 1942, *Social Insurance and Allied Services*, Cmnd 6404, HMSO.

Beveridge, W., 1943, *The Pillars of Security and Other Wartime Essays and Addresses*, George Allen and Unwin.

Beveridge, W., 1944, *Full Employment in a Free Society*, George Allen and Unwin.

Blunkett, D. and Green, G., 1983, *Building from the Bottom. The Sheffield Experience*, Fabian Tract 491, Fabian Society.

Bolger, S., Corrigan, P., Docking, J. and Frost, N., 1981, *Towards Socialist Welfare Work*, Macmillan.

Bosanquet, N. and Townsend, P., (eds) 1980, *Labour and Equality*, Heinemann.

Boyson, R., 1971, 'Farewell to paternalism' in Boyson, R. (ed.), 1971.

Boyson, R. (ed.), 1971, *Down with the Poor*, Churchill Press.

Brown, K. D. (ed.), 1974, *Essays in Anti-Labour History*, Macmillan.

Calder, A., 1971, *The People's War*, Panther.

Campaign for Legal and Financial Independence, 1975, *The Demand for Independence*.

Churchill, W. S., 1906, speech at St Andrew's Hall, Glasgow, 11 October 1906; reprinted in A. Bullock and M. Shock (eds), 1956, *The Liberal Tradition*, Oxford University Press.

Clarke, A., 1983, 'Prejudice, ignorance and panic! Popular politics in a land fit for scroungers' in Loney, Boswell and Clarke (eds).

Clarke, J. S., 1943, 'The staff problem', in Robson, (ed.).

Cole, G. D. H., 1917, *Self-government in Industry*, G. Bell and Sons Ltd., new edition with introduction by J. G. Corina, 1972, Hutchinson.

Cole, M., 1961, *The Story of Fabian Socialism*, Heinemann (page refs to paperback edition 1963).

Coote, A. and Campbell, B., 1982, *Sweet Freedom*, Picador.

Crosland, A., 1958, *The Future of Socialism*, Jonathan Cape.

Dangerfield, G., 1984, *The Strange Death of Liberal England*, Paladin.

Deacon, B., 1983, *Social Policy and Socialism. The Struggle for Socialist Relations of Welfare*, Pluto Press.

Deakin, N., 1983, 'Planning social priorities – locally', in Glennerster, H. (ed.), 1983a, pp. 212–21.

Deakin, N., 1984, 'Looking for a feasible socialism'. *New Society*, 67:1111:8 March, pp. 356–8.

Delphy, C., 1984, *Close to Home*, Hutchinson.

DHSS 1984, *Oral Hearing into the Review of Benefits for Children and Young People*, The Palantype Organisation.

DHSS 1985, *Reform of Social Security*, vols. 1 and 2, HMSO, Cmnd 9517, 9518.

Dilnot, A. W., Kay, J. A. and Morris, C. N., 1984, *Reform of Social Security*, Oxford: Clarendon.

Durham, M., 1985, 'Suffrage and after: Feminism in the early twentieth century' in Langan and Schwartz (eds).

Economist, 1895, 'Editorial', *The Economist*, 25 May.

Fleming, S., 1973, *The Family Allowance Under Attack*, Falling Wall Press.

Flynn, T., 1981, 'Local politics and local government', *Capital and Class*, 13, Spring.

Friend, A., and Metcalf, A., 1981, *Slump City*, Pluto Press.

George, V. and Wilding, P., 1976 and 1986, *Ideology and Social Welfare*, Routledge and Kegan Paul.

Gieve, K. *et al.*, 1974, 'The independence demand' in Allen, S. (ed.), *Conditions of Illusion*, Leeds, Feminist Books.

Glennerster, H. (ed.), 1983a, *The Future of the Welfare State: Remaking Social Policy*, Heinemann.

Glennerster, H., 1983b, 'The need for a reappraisal', in Glennerster (ed.), 1983a.

Gough, I., 1979, *The Political Economy of the Welfare State*, Macmillan.

Griffith, J., 1969, *Pages from Memory*, Dent.

Hadley, R. and Hatch, S., 1981, *Social Welfare and the Failure of the State*, George Allen and Unwin.

Hall, D., 1985, *The Cuts Machine*, Pluto.

Hall, S. and Schwartz, B., 1985, 'State and society 1880–1930', in Langan and Schwartz (eds).

Hay, J. R., 1975, *The Origins of the Liberal Welfare Reforms, 1906–14*, Macmillan.

Hayek, F., 1944, *The Road to Serfdom*, Routledge and Kegan Paul.

Hill, D. (ed.), 1977, *Tribune 40*, Quartet.

Hobhouse, L. T., 1964, *Liberalism*, Oxford University Press.

Hobson, J. A., 1896, 'The social philosophy of charity organisation', *The Contemporary Review*, 70.

Holyoake, G. J., 1879 'State socialism', *The Nineteenth Century*, June.

Jenkin, P., 1977, *Speech to Conservative Party Conference, 1977*.

Johnson, P., 1982, 'Family reunion', *The Observer*, 10 October.

Joseph, K., 1977, *Monetarism is not enough*, Centre for Policy Studies.

Kendall, W., 1969, *The Revolutionary Movement in Britain 1900–1921*, Weidenfeld and Nicholson.

Land, H., 1976, 'Women: supporters or supported' in Barker, D. L. and Allen, S. (eds), *Sexual Divisions in Society: Process and Change*, Tavistock.

Land, H., 1978, 'Sex-role stereotyping in the social security and income tax systems', in Chetwynd, J. and Hartnett, O. (eds), *The Sex Role System*, Routledge and Kegan Paul.

Land, H., 1983, 'Who still cares for the family? Recent developments in income maintenance, taxation and family law', in Lewis J. (ed.), *Women's Welfare, Women's Rights*, Croom Helm.

Land, H., 1983, 'Family fables', *New Socialist*, no. 11.

Langan, M. and Schwartz, B. (eds), 1985, *Crises in the British State 1880–1930*, Hutchinson.

Lansbury, G., 1928, *My Life*, Constable.

Lee, P. and Raban, C., 1983, 'Welfare and ideology', in Loney, Boswell and Clarke, (eds).

Le Grand, J., 1982, *The Strategy of Equality*, George Allen and Unwin.

Liddington, J. and Norris, J., 1984, *One Hand Tied Behind Us*, Virago.

Llewellyn Davies, M., 1978, *Maternity: Letters from Working Women*, Virago.

Loch, C. S., 1913, 'The spirit of enterprise. State aid and charity organisation', in Loch, C. S., 1923, *A Great Ideal and its Champion*, Allen and Unwin.

London Edinburgh Weekend Return Group, 1979, *In and Against the State. Discussion Notes for Socialists*, Publications Distribution Co-operative.

London Women's Liberation Campaign for Legal and Financial Independence and Rights of Women, 1979, 'Disaggregation now! Another battle for women's independence', *Feminist Review*, 2.

Loney, M., Boswell, D. and Clarke, J., (eds), 1983, *Social Policy and Social Welfare*, Open University Press.

Loney, M., 1986, *The Politics of Greed*, Pluto.

Macnicol, L., 1980, *The Movement for Family Allowances, 1918–45*, Heinemann.

McIntosh, M., 1981, 'Feminism and social policy', *Critical Social Policy*, 1(1).

Mackay, T., 1901, *The Public Relief of the Poor: Six Lectures*, John Murray.

Mallock, W. H., 1909, *A Critical Examination of Socialism*, John Murray.

Martin, A., 1911, 'The maternity benefit', *Common Cause*, 6 July, 11 (116).

Martin, A., 1913, *The Mothers and Social Reform*, National Union of Women's Suffrage Societies.

Martin, A., 1922, 'The father or the state', in *The Nineteenth Century and Other Reviews, 1910–1922*.

Meade, J. E., 1978, *The Structure and Reform of Direct Taxation*, Institute of Fiscal Studies.

Mill, J. S., 1962, *Utilitarianism*, Warnock, M. (ed.), Fontana.

Mishra, R., 1984, *The Welfare State in Crisis. Social Thought and Social Change*, Wheatsheaf.

Morris, W., 1893, *Communism*, Fabian Tract 113, in Briggs, A., 1962, *William Morris: Selected Writings and Designs*, Penguin.

The Nation, 1908, 'The State and unemployment', *The Nation*, no. 11, 14 March.

Offe, C., 1984, *Contradictions of the Welfare State*, Hutchinson.

O'Higgins, M., 1983, 'Issues of redistribution in state welfare spending', in Loney *et al.*

Orwell, G., 1968a, *Collected Essays, Journalism and Letters of George Orwell*, vol. 2, *My Country Right or Left. 1940–1943*, Secker and Warburg (page references to Penguin edition, 1970).

Orwell, G., 1968b, *Collected Essays, Journalism and Letters of George Orwell*, vol. 3, *As I Please 1943–1945*, Secker and Warburg (page references to Penguin edition, 1970).

Owen, D., 1981, *Face the Future*, Oxford University Press.

Pahl, J., 1980, 'Patterns of money management within marriage', *Journal of Social Policy*, **9** (3).

Pahl, J., 1983, 'The allocation of money and the structuring of inequality within marriage', *Sociological Review*, **31** (2).

Pankhurst, S., 1977, *The Suffragette Movement*, Virago.

Parker, H., 1982, *The Moral Hazard of Social Insurance*, Institute of Economic Affairs, Research Monograph, no. 37.

Pember Reeves, Mrs, 1979, *Round About a Pound a Week*, Virago (first published 1913, Bell and Sons, © 1953, Amber Blanco White).

Pethick Lawrence, F., 1911, 'Will the Insurance Bill be withdrawn?' *Votes for Women*, 15 September.

Rathbone, E., 1918, *A Proposal for the National Endowment of Motherhood*, Headley Bros.

Ritchie, D. G., 1891, *The Principles of State Interference*, S. Sonneschein and Co.

Robbins, L., 1947, *The Economic Problem of War and Peace*, Macmillan.

Robson, W. A. (ed.), 1943, *Social Security*, Allen and Unwin.

Rowbotham, S., 1973, *Hidden From History*, Pluto.

Rowbotham, S., Segal, L. and Wainwright, H., 1979, *Beyond the Fragments, Feminism and the Making of Socialism*, Merlin.

Royal Commission on the Poor Law and Relief of Distress, 1909, *Appendix to Vol. 3, Minutes of Evidence, 49th–71st days*, Cmnd 4755, HMSO.

Royden, A. Maude, 1918, *National Endowment of Motherhood*, no publisher.

Schwarz, B. and Langan, M. (eds), 1985, *Crises in the British State, 1880–1930*, Hutchinson.

Scott, H., 1984, *Working Your Way to the Bottom*, Pandora Books.

Scruton, R., 1983, 'Abolish council elections, too', *The Times*, 18 October.

Seabrook, J., 1984, *The Idea of Neighbourhood. What Socialist Politics should be about*, Pluto Press.

Seldon, A., 1977, *Charge*, Temple Smith.

Seldon, A., 1982, Preface to H. Parker, 1982.

Shaw, G. B., 1912, *The Common Sense of Municipal Trading*, Fabian Socialist Series no. 5, A. C. Fifield.

Socialist Party of Great Britain (undated), *Family Allowances – a Socialist Analysis*.

Spencer, H., 1868, *The Principles of Sociology, Vol. III*, Williams and Norgate.

Strachey, R., 1978, *The Cause*, Virago.

Sutton, D., 1985, 'Liberalism, state collectivism and the social relations of citizenship', in Langan and Schwartz (eds).

Thatcher, M., 1977, *Let our Children grow tall: selected speeches, 1975–1977*, Centre for Policy Studies.

The Women's Bulletin, 1943a, 'The economic status of the housewife', 6 September.

The Women's Bulletin, 1943b, 'Conference of the proposals in the Beveridge Report as they affect women', 6 November.

Townsend, P., 1984, *Why are the Many Poor?*, Fabian Society.

Tribune (1942), Editorial, 4 December

Walker, A., 1982, 'Why we need a social strategy', *Marxism Today*, September.

Walker, A., 1984, *Social Planning. A Strategy for Socialist Welfare*, Oxford, Basil Blackwell.

Webb, A., 1980, 'The personal social services', in Bosanquet, N., and Townsend, P. (eds).

Webb, S. and Webb, B., 1910, *English Poor Law Policy*, Longman (reprinted, 1963, Cass).

Index

Name index